New York Cooks

New York Cooks
100 Recipes from the City's Best Chefs

JOAN KRELLENSTEIN AND BARBARA WINKLER

sixth&spring books

233 Spring Street, New York, New York 10013

Managing Editor: Wendy Williams
Senior Editor: Michelle Bredeson
Art Director: Diane Lamphron
Associate Art Director: Sheena T. Paul
Copy Editor: Kristina Sigler
Vice President, Publisher: Trisha Malcolm
Production Manager: David Joinnides
Creative Director: Joe Vior
President: Art Joinnides

Library of Congress Control Number: 2008936329
ISBN-13: 978-1-933027-78-4
ISBN-10: 1-933027-78-9

Manufactured in China
3 5 7 9 10 8 6 4 2
First Edition

Information regarding chefs, restaurants and addresses were
correct at time of production. Neither the authors nor the
publisher are responsible for changes in location, situation
or status of any participants or places herein.

www.sixthandspringbooks.com

Contents

New York City

It's a restaurantgoer's Eden for both locals and visitors, with temptation on every corner and menus that promise paradise on a plate.

But even the most avid gourmet can't eat out every night, and out-of-towners may hit a Manhattan restaurant only once or twice in a lifetime. This means that the possibility of cooking up some great NYC restaurant meals at home would be a dream come true for anyone who loves food. So that's exactly what you'll find in this book—over 100 recipes from the city's top chefs, spectacular dishes that show off the tremendous creativity these pros have to offer. Along the way, the book also delivers a veritable freeze-frame of the ever-changing New York restaurant scene, as well as portraits of fascinating chefs.

You'll quickly learn that most of the chefs profiled here are obsessed with finding and serving the finest and freshest ingredients. As Marco Canora, the whiz behind Insieme, emphatically states, "Why make the effort to prepare a recipe if your produce is second-rate?" It's a mandate he encourages home cooks to follow.

Experimentation is another hallmark of these great chefs. While all have their signature styles, each is open to new ingredients and different cuisines. They take risks with their food and emphasize that amateurs should do the same. Carmen Quagliata of Union Square Cafe puts it this way: "It's the failures that lead to the successes." Indeed, the risks are what make the food on this little island so incredibly exciting. In fact, Jose Salgado of Nomad came to New York because, he says, "Here there are influences from everywhere," and he wanted to instill that magic into his own cooking.

Perhaps most enlightening of all, these chefs have fun with what they do and make the point that preparing a recipe is not a competition, but rather an opportunity to revel in the smells, the tastes, and the resulting alchemy. After all, if disaster strikes, you can always order pizza!

That said, these recipes go far beyond pizza (but definitely check out Anne Burrell's Taleggio, Speck and Egg Pizzetta on page 56). While some are complicated, they are well worth the effort. Others may have a familiar feel, but be assured there's something in every dish that takes it beyond the ordinary. There are a few exotic ingredients involved, and alternate options are given. Home cooks will find that even the most unusual items are available over the Internet or at specialty food stores.

Hopefully, most of the chefs featured will still be cooking at their restaurants at the time of publication, but in the volatile restaurant world, who knows? Some may have moved on to other restaurants (or to start their own), to travel the world in search of fresh ideas and methods, or to create great food with New York flair in another city.

One thing is certain: Wherever the chefs may be, their best recipes are right here, ready to inspire. ■

1

Depending on your perspective, New American may not be so new. For instance, if you grew up eating garden-ripe veggies, free-range chicken and dishes prepared with herbs, spices and techniques from around the globe, then this style of cooking is just everyday food. But if you, like many Americans and many New Yorkers, grew up with the processed, frozen and fast foods that came to dominance in this country's postwar years, then New American cuisine is a welcome change.

It may seem silly to even think it, but thank goodness for the 1970s! This was the decade that ushered in "California cuisine," a movement started by Berkeley's own Alice Waters and her restaurant Chez Panisse. Dishes featured fresh, seasonal ingredients and a type of cooking christened "fusion," which blended flavors and techniques from a variety of cultures. Over the next few decades, these two concepts grew stonger and, spurred on by a dose of national pride, resulted in a new cuisine marked by a sense of adventure and play. And nowhere are chefs more accomplished in this type of cooking than in New York, home to people from every corner of the globe. The names of the chefs in this chapter help tell the story: Lo, Anthony, Zakarian, Hara, Quagliata and Liu. Individually they create eclectic, exciting dishes that speak to today's tastes and draw on many traditions; together they represent some of the best New American cuisine that New York City has to offer.

New. American

Michael Anthony, Gramercy Tavern

August

Tony Liu, August

Geoffrey Zakarian

Geoffrey Zakarian, Town at the Chambers Hotel

Eric Hara, davidburke & donatella

Carmen Quagliata, Union Square Cafe

Carmen Quagliata

Anita Lo, Annisa

Michael Anthony
EXECUTIVE CHEF, GRAMERCY TAVERN

Farm to table

When *New York Times* critic Frank Bruni blessed Gramercy Tavern with a three-star review in June 2007, restaurantgoers breathed a sigh of relief. Not so long before, Bruni, along with other reviewers, had bemoaned the venerable icon's lackluster food and overall slip in quality. But once Mike Anthony took the reins, everything changed, and the restaurant has even garnered a coveted Michelin star. "It was a challenge," the recently anointed executive chef admits. "I walked into this beloved restaurant and I needed to respect its traditions. My mission wasn't to change it, just to make it fresher."

To that end, Anthony concentrated on sourcing the very best ingredients. He worked with local farmers to get the freshest produce, the most flavorful eggs, the choicest meat. A passionate locavore, Anthony is dedicated to knowing the story and the site behind his supplies. He even arranges for his staff to make field trips to farms in order to better understand the dishes they serve. Seeing where and how the animals live and the vegetables grow is just the beginning. "For me, cooking always starts with the ingredients. My goal is to take the food, cook it, put it on a plate and still have it retain its wonder. I want to maximize the ingredients to show off their inherent flavors, so I need top quality," he states.

So intent is he on seasonality that his menu, especially the Vegetable Tasting section, has become a snapshot of what's currently available at market. In early spring, for instance, you might find a carrot soup with spiced cashews, celery-and-lemon risotto with razor clams, and mushroom ravioli with wild mushrooms and aged balsamico. And when ramps appear, watch out! Anthony stretches their notoriously short season by grilling, sautéing, or pureeing the greens and even pickling the stems. Vegetables also play a significant role in the meat courses; bok choy and broccoli are prime ingredients in one of Anthony's favorite recipes, the rack of lamb, featured on page 14.

Anthony's farm-to-table ethos has also resulted in a new attitude toward Gramercy Tavern's meat dishes. He now buys whole carcasses and has his staff do the butchering. "This has been a learning curve for all of

GRAMERCY TAVERN
42 East 20th Street
New York, NY 10003
212-477-0777
www.gramercytavern.com

On the side...

What do you consider the most overrated ingredient?
Foie gras. A great meal doesn't have to lean on luxury ingredients.

The most underrated ingredient?
A potato.

What is your favorite comfort food?
Handmade pasta, carefully cooked.

What kitchen gadget is your must-have tool?
My Vita-Mix.

If you were not a chef, what would you be?
A journalist.

What was the last thing you ate?
Lentil stew with shallots that I ate standing up.

us, but the results are quite satisfying," says Anthony. Now the kitchen can take a side of grass-fed beef—all 85 pounds—slice up succulent filets, turn the shoulder into meatballs stuffed with fontina, braise the neck for a ragu, transform brisket into pastrami and use ground meat for smoked kielbasa. It's yet another important philosophy of the locavore to use every part of the animal whenever possible. "It pushes us to be more creative and generate multiple menu items," explains Anthony. "The only rule is 'Don't get in the way of the food.'"

Such a connection to the natural food cycle may seem like a flash to the past, but for this chef it's the future of cooking. And his diners are enjoying every last bite. ■

The recipes

Blackfish with Spaghetti Squash, Walnuts and Apples

SERVES 8

Blackfish, found in waters from Nova Scotia to South Carolina, is a lean, white-fleshed fish with a mild taste. Chef Anthony plays up its subtlety with a sherry sauce flecked with raw apples and toasted pumpkin seeds, then rests it on a tangle of honeyed spaghetti squash.

FOR THE SAUCE

2 cups manzanilla sherry
1 cup vegetable stock
1 teaspoon saffron
1 teaspoon mild curry
2 tablespoons shallots, peeled and minced
1 clove garlic, peeled and minced
Salt and pepper to taste
1 tablespoon lime juice
1 tablespoon butter
3 tablespoons pumpkin seeds, toasted
3 tablespoons apple, peeled, cored and minced

FOR THE SPAGHETTI SQUASH

1 spaghetti squash, cut in half lengthwise, seeds removed
Salt and pepper to taste
3 tablespoons olive oil, divided
3 tablespoons walnut pieces
1 teaspoon wildflower honey
1 teaspoon lemon juice

FOR THE BLACKFISH

8 (5-ounce) blackfish fillets, boneless and skinless (substitute bass or halibut if unavailable)
Salt and pepper to taste
2 tablespoons olive oil
1 clove garlic, peeled and smashed
1 sprig thyme

TO MAKE THE SAUCE

Place the first 6 ingredients in a saucepan.

Cook over medium heat until reduced by two-thirds.

Blend with a hand blender until smooth.

Season with salt and pepper to taste.

Add lime juice and butter and stir until butter is melted. Set aside until ready to serve.

TO MAKE THE SPAGHETTI SQUASH

Preheat oven to 375°F.

Season squash with salt, pepper and 2 tablespoons of olive oil.

Place squash, cut side down, on a baking sheet and roast in oven for 20–25 minutes or until flesh pulls away from skin (be careful not to overcook, as it is important for the squash to maintain its texture).

Using a fork, remove squash flesh from the skin and set aside.

On a baking sheet, toast walnut pieces in remaining tablespoon of olive oil.

When nuts turn light brown, remove from oven and place in a bowl. Drizzle with honey and toss to coat.

Add lemon juice to finish.

Fold walnuts into spaghetti squash and season with salt and pepper.

TO MAKE THE BLACKFISH

Season fish with salt and pepper on both sides. Heat olive oil in a large sauté pan with garlic and thyme.

Add fish and sauté, basting with olive oil, until slightly browned but still moist.

TO SERVE

Just before serving, warm the sauce and add the toasted pumpkin seeds and minced raw apple. Season again with salt and pepper to taste. Spoon spaghetti squash onto center of each plate. Place fish on top of squash. Spoon sauce on top of fish and also drizzle some around the edges of each plate. ■

Blackfish with Spaghetti Squash, Walnuts and Apples

The recipes

Rack of Lamb with Broccoli Puree, Cranberry Beans and Bok Choy

SERVES 8

Chef Anthony takes humble ingredients like broccoli and cranberry beans and magically converts them into sidekicks worthy of succulent roast lamb.

FOR THE SAUCE
10 pounds lamb bones (ask butcher for these)
½ cup diced carrots
½ cup diced celery
1 cup diced onion
½ cup tomato paste
1 sprig rosemary
1 teaspoon black peppercorns

FOR THE LAMB
2 racks lamb, bones removed
Salt and pepper to taste

FOR THE BROCCOLI PUREE
1 head broccoli
5 leaves basil
2 tablespoons brown butter
Salt and pepper to taste

FOR THE CRANBERRY BEANS
1 medium onion, peeled and quartered
1 carrot, peeled and cut into large chunks
1 leek, trimmed and cut into large chunks
5 cloves garlic, peeled
2 cups cranberry beans, shelled (fresh, if available)
Salt to taste

FOR THE BOK CHOY
1 tablespoon olive oil
1 clove garlic, peeled and smashed
1 pound baby bok choy
Salt and pepper to taste

TO MAKE THE SAUCE
Preheat oven to 450°F.

Place lamb bones in a roasting pan and cook until dark brown, approximately 2 hours. Remove from oven and transfer to a stockpot. Add carrots, celery and onion and sweat for 10 minutes.

Add tomato paste, stir to coat solids and add enough water to cover bones.

Bring to simmer over medium-low heat and cook for 2 hours. Strain and simmer until reduced to sauce consistency. Add rosemary and peppercorns and simmer 20 minutes longer. Reserve and keep warm.

TO MAKE THE LAMB
Preheat oven to 375°F.

Season lamb on all sides with salt and pepper. In a large, ovenproof skillet or Dutch oven, brown lamb on all sides.

Place pan in oven and roast lamb for 8 minutes. Remove from oven and let rest for 10 minutes.

TO MAKE THE BROCCOLI PUREE
Trim broccoli florets and discard stalks.

Prepare an ice-water bath. In a large pot of well-salted, boiling water, blanch broccoli (about 2 to 3 minutes). Drain broccoli and immediately plunge into ice water to preserve green color.

In a blender, combine broccoli tips, basil leaves and brown butter to achieve a smooth puree. Season with salt and pepper to taste, and reserve.

TO MAKE THE CRANBERRY BEANS
In a large saucepan, place onion, carrot, leek and garlic; cover with 4 quarts of water. Add cranberry beans and bring to a simmer. Simmer beans for 20 minutes or until tender, seasoning with salt after 15 minutes of cooking time. Drain beans and reserve.

TO MAKE THE BOK CHOY
In a sauté pan, heat oil and garlic. Add bok choy and sauté until just cooked through, about 3 minutes. Season with salt and pepper to taste. Reserve.

TO SERVE
Using a spoon, swish broccoli puree across center of each plate. Spoon cranberry beans and bok choy on top of puree.

Place two slices of lamb rack on top of vegetables, then lightly drizzle lamb sauce over meat. ▪

Tony Liu
EXECUTIVE CHEF, AUGUST

From surfer boy to top chef

The story goes like this: As a teenager in Honolulu, Tony Liu took a job as a dishwasher in a nearby restaurant so he could spend most of his days surfing. But life in the kitchen proved more and more alluring, and he spent less and less time at the beach. In fact, he enrolled in a local culinary school, and after working in some of Hawaii's top kitchens, came to New York and attended the CIA. "I always liked food, but never imagined I would build a career around it," states Liu, whose experience reads like a worldwide culinary tour.

He interned at Lespinasse, worked at Daniel and Tabla, cooked at a three-Michelin-star restaurant in Spain, and was a sous chef for Mario Batali at Babbo. French, Indian, Spanish, Italian, not to mention Hawaiian—quite a varied cooking background. But it's perfect for the innovative European fare that Liu serves up at August. "We have a very seasonal menu here based on regional classics from Europe. In the warmer months I go very Mediterranean, with a Provençal bouillabaisse perhaps or grilled shrimp with

Tony Liu
EXECUTIVE CHEF, AUGUST

green sauce. In winter I draw from northern and eastern Europe, with items like goulash, chicken paprikash [see page 17] or smoked whitefish," says Liu. "I like to be true to the original form of the dish, but do some improvising with local ingredients."

Obviously, the improvisation is working, because securing a table at this intimate Village hideaway can be tricky. And for good reason: The atmosphere, alluringly rustic with wide plank floors, distressed plaster walls and a cobblestone patio, is ideal for Liu's countrified dishes, many of which are prepared in a wood-burning brick oven. "This was the centerpiece of the restaurant and my biggest challenge," says Liu, who wasn't familiar with this type of cooking. "But now I love it. The wood imparts such a great flavor. I can braise meats, such as a pork shoulder, overnight at a slow heat, then jack it up during the day for something like an onion tart."

Because he doesn't like to repeat dishes, Liu is constantly coming up with new and exciting variations. "Even though we don't do Indian food, one of the best things I learned at Tabla was the magic of spices and the nuances they can create. I try to use this knowledge, playing with things like lavender and all kinds of peppers," he explains.

Unlike many chefs, Liu actually writes out recipes, figuring out the ingredients and techniques on paper before he goes to the stove. He might zero in on a

AUGUST
359 Bleecker Street
New York, NY 10014
212-929-4774
www.augustny.com

On the side...

What do you consider the most overrated ingredient?
Foie gras.

The most underrated ingredient?
A lemon—the skin, the pulp, the zest, even the pits.

What is your favorite comfort food?
Pasta…Italian or Asian noodles.

What kitchen gadget is your must-have tool?
A microplane. I use it for chocolate, spices, cheese, zest and more.

If you were not a chef, what would you be?
A marine biologist (I grew up near the ocean and miss it) or a landscaper (for the connection to nature).

What was the last thing you ate?
Bacon-wrapped hot dogs with a cheese sauce made by a Peruvian staffer at our restaurant.

particular seasonal item—rabbit, perhaps—then jot down the "go-withs," like carrots, peas and sweet wine, and from this concoct a final plan.

Yet when asked to name a favorite menu selection, Liu points to the simplest—blistered green peppers. "It's a variation on a dish I loved in Spain: just peppers, oil and salt. It's the perfect summer finger food, very sensual and very tasty," he says.

But then *sensual* and *tasty* could apply to all of Liu's dishes, no matter what country inspired them. ∎

The recipes

"I like to be true to the original form of the dish, but do some improvising with local ingredients."

Poussin Paprikash

SERVES 4

August has made a name for itself based on an atmosphere—and a menu to match—that's a little bit country, a little bit city. This paprika chicken with egg noodles evokes memories of Grandma's kitchen. The thing that's different about Chef Liu's version is that it takes less than 10 minutes to roast, thanks to his fan and high-heat technique.

FOR THE POUSSIN
4 (16- to 20-ounce) poussins (baby chickens)
Coarse sea salt to taste
8 garlic cloves, peeled
1 bunch fresh thyme, plus 5 sprigs
1 bunch fresh rosemary
8 ounces egg noodles
2 tablespoons vegetable oil

FOR THE SAUCE
¼ pound bacon
2 tablespoons vegetable oil
1 medium onion, peeled and cut into rings
6 tablespoons Hungarian paprika, sweet
2 tablespoons Hungarian paprika, hot
1 bay leaf
1½ cups chicken stock or chicken jus
6 ounces (about ¾ cup) crème fraîche
4 tablespoons chopped parsley
Salt and pepper to taste

TO MAKE THE POUSSIN

At least 2 hours in advance (the more time the better): Lightly salt the exteriors and cavities of the poussins. Divide the garlic, thyme and rosemary into four portions and stuff into the cavity of each poussin. (Reserve one sprig of rosemary for later use.)

Place poussins, uncovered, in the flow of a fan to thoroughly dry the skin. This produces a crisper skin. (The same procedure works for other poultry as well.)

Bring a large stockpot filled with water to a boil and season the water with salt. Once at a boil, cook the egg noodles until done and drain. Reserve.

Preheat oven to 500°F. Pat poussins dry and place in a roasting pan. Lightly oil them with 2 tablespoons oil and roast for 4 minutes. Then decrease the temperature to 300°F for approximately 5 minutes. The poussin is done when the cartilage on the drumette releases from the bone. (If necessary, cook a bit longer.) Remove from the oven and keep warm.

TO MAKE THE SAUCE

In a sauté pan on medium heat, add the bacon and 2 tablespoons oil. Render the bacon crispy, then remove it from the pan. Add the onion and caramelize over high heat until golden brown.

In a mixing bowl, combine the two paprikas together with a little water to form a slurry. Add the slurry to the caramelized onion and cook until the slurry resembles a paste.

Using string, tie the reserved sprig of rosemary, the 5 sprigs of thyme, and the bay leaf together. Add the chicken stock or jus and the herb bundle to the onion mixture and reduce by half. Add the egg noodles and crème fraîche to the pan. Once the crème fraîche is added, do not cook for more than 5 minutes. Season the sauce with chopped parsley and salt and pepper.

TO SERVE

Divide the noodles among 4 warm plates. Spoon half of the sauce over noodles. Cut the poussins in half along the breastbones and cut out and discard the backbones. Separate the legs from the breasts. Place the poussin parts on top of the noodles. Spoon the remaining sauce over the poussins and serve. ■

The recipes

Roasted Cod and Clam Estofado

SERVES 4

For this Spanish-influenced casserole, Chef Liu mixes clams with cod, chorizo with onion, dessert wine with white wine. Cocoa powder and pine nuts round out the ingredients for a savory meal-in-a-pot that's great fun to eat.

¼ cup yellow raisins

1 cup sweet dessert wine (sherry, white port)

½ teaspoon cayenne pepper

1 head cauliflower, broken into tiny florets

2 tablespoons pimentón (smoked Spanish paprika)

Salt to taste

Extra-virgin olive oil (as needed)

1 pound chorizo

2 pounds onion, roughly chopped

4 cloves garlic, roughly chopped

¼ teaspoon crushed red pepper flakes

2 tablespoons cocoa powder

1 tablespoon tomato paste

2 bunches kale, stems removed and washed

2 pounds littleneck clams, rinsed well

¼ cup clam juice

½ bottle white wine

1 pinch saffron

4 ounces day-old sourdough bread, cut into cubes and toasted

4 (6-ounce) cod fillets, skin on

¼ cup pine nuts, toasted

¼ bunch cilantro, chopped

¼ bunch curly parsley, chopped

Preheat oven to 450°F.

In a small saucepan combine the raisins, sweet wine and cayenne pepper. Add enough water to cover the raisins. Bring to a boil and simmer for 10 minutes; remove from the heat. Reserve for later use.

Place the cauliflower florets on a baking tray and dust with the pimentón and salt; drizzle with olive oil. Roast for approximately 10 minutes or until soft. Remove from the oven, cool to room temperature and reserve.

Peel skin off chorizo, roughly chop and place in a food processor to make a fine grind. Remove and place in a saucepan with extra-virgin olive oil to start rendering. Put the onions and garlic in the food processor and pulse to achieve a fine grind as well. Remove from the processing bowl and add to the cooked chorizo. Sweat out the onion mixture (sofrito) well. Add red pepper flakes, cocoa powder and the tomato paste to the sofrito and cook for another 5 minutes.

Add the cleaned kale to the sofrito and cook until soft.

Next, add the clams, clam juice, white wine and saffron.

Simmer until the clams open. Transfer mixture to a casserole and add the reserved raisins, bread and cauliflower.

Season and dry the cod fillets and sauté in a hot pan, skin side down. When a crispy skin is achieved, flip fillets over into the clam casserole so that the flesh is somewhat submerged in the broth. Finish cooking in the oven at 450°F, about 10 minutes longer.

TO SERVE

When fish is fully cooked, drizzle with olive oil and garnish casserole with pine nuts, cilantro and parsley. ■

August

Geoffrey Zakarian
CHEF AND OWNER, TOWN AT THE CHAMBERS HOTEL

The thinking man's chef

"I don't know anything about making pizza," states Geoffrey Zakarian, "so my next sabbatical is to Naples to learn the ins and outs of that art. I'm going with Sirio Maccioni [the esteemed owner of Le Cirque, where Zakarian got his training] and I can't wait." Did we hear right? After all, Zakarian is the acclaimed chef behind the ultra-chic Town restaurant, not to mention Country, Country Café and the newly opened Lamb's Club. The answer is a definite yes. This intrepid food-lover makes a ritual of going abroad annually to check out other cuisines and to work in other restaurants. "As a chef, you need to get out of your comfort level," he explains.

"You see, you meet, you work with different people and that has an effect on the way you think, and therefore, the way you cook."

And the way this guy cooks is quite revelatory. For the most part, he draws on history and memory. "Great dishes are anchored in history. It's amazing how the flavors that drive us now are the same ones that thrilled people centuries ago," says Zakarian, who pores through old cookbooks, especially those dating back to the 19th century. "If you're not motivated by the past, you just scramble onto the next trend and end up being all over the place."

He mentions a strawberry risotto he found in an antique tome. "It intrigued me, so I played with it, tweaked it and put in on the menu at Town." But that dish also illustrates something else. This chef likes to be whimsical; he tries to deliver surprises. "My formula is 80 percent reality, 20 percent fantasy," he proclaims, going on to explain, "I'm not one of those chefs who wants to reinvent the wheel, but I don't take any dish all that seriously. I want to throw in something unexpected."

That might mean mussels simmered in parsley chardonnay with kaffir lime and turmeric, quail baked over Marcona almonds, or wild striped bass roasted with a foie gras butter. These dishes are all rooted in the classics, but have the innovative twist that earned Town three stars from *The New York Times*. "I guess I'd describe my food as modern classic, but with French and Italian influences," says Zakarian, who goes against the mold by not changing his menus frequently. "We work so hard to make a dish worthy of serving that once it's on the menu, it usually stays on for a good time. I continue to finesse and bring the seasons in by adding a new item or two, like soft-shell

TOWN AT THE CHAMBERS HOTEL
15 West 56th Street
New York, NY 10019
212-582-4445
www.townrestaurant.com

On the side...

What do you consider the most overrated ingredient?
Tuna tartare. It's not so much overrated as overused.

The most underrated ingredient?
Acids, such as lemon and vinegar. They kick up a dish.

What is your favorite comfort food?
Red wine.

What kitchen gadget is your must-have tool?
The telephone.

If you were not a chef, what would you be?
A golfer or pianist. They're both done alone, and I like that idea.

What was the last thing you ate?
I sat at the bar at Raoul's and had two appetizers: an artichoke vinaigrette and steak tartare with frisée, along with a glass of Bordeaux. Fabulous!

crabs in summer or venison loin in winter."

Zakarian also feels passionately that "You can't please everybody all the time" and so is very comfortable with the fact that some dishes may not sell all that well. To him, it's important to include them because they keep the menu interesting and offer intriguing options for the adventurous diner. "Not everybody likes veal tongue, but it's on the menu at Town," he says, "and will probably remain for a while longer." Until he gets inspired by his next sabbatical, that is, or another vintage cookbook. ■

The recipes

"My formula is 80 percent reality, 20 percent fantasy."

Filet Mignon with Red-Wine Risotto

SERVES 4

It's not only the port and Syrah that give this risotto its full-bodied flavor. Chef Zakarian cooks it with bacon and brown chicken stock, which has a deeper flavor than ordinary stock. Although wonderful on its own—crowned with mascarpone cheese and porcini slices—it's out of this world with the three-pepper filet mignon.

FOR THE RISOTTO

3 thin slices of smoked bacon, finely minced
1 teaspoon minced fresh garlic
½ small white onion, finely minced
½ small celeriac, finely minced
1 cup port wine
2 cups red wine (preferably Syrah)
1 cup Vialone Nano or Carnaroli rice
3 cups brown chicken or mushroom stock, divided
2 tablespoons softened butter
1 tablespoon grated Parmesan cheese
1 tablespoon extra-virgin olive oil
Kosher salt and freshly ground black pepper to taste

FOR THE FILETS

1 tablespoon freshly ground black pepper
1 tablespoon coarse sea salt
1 teaspoon ground red Aleppo pepper
1 teaspoon ground Szechuan peppercorns
4 (6-ounce) portions organic or grain-fed filet mignon (note: bring to room temperature before cooking)
Olive oil for cooking filets
2 sprigs rosemary

FOR THE GARNISH

8 ounces Parmesan cheese, shaved paper-thin
4 tablespoons mascarpone cheese or crème fraîche
1 to 2 fresh porcini mushrooms, thinly sliced
1 sprig fresh thyme
Olive oil for drizzling

TO MAKE THE RISOTTO

In a medium-large saucepot over low heat, sweat the bacon, garlic, onion and celeriac until translucent and tender, about 5–10 minutes, by placing a lid over the pot.

Carefully add the port and red wine, bring to a simmer and reduce until dry. Add the rice, followed by one-third of the stock, and simmer until almost dry, stirring constantly.

Repeat this step of adding the remaining stock three more times until the rice is fully cooked and a creamy consistency is achieved. Finish by stirring in butter, Parmesan and olive oil; add salt and pepper to taste.

TO MAKE THE FILETS

Light a gas or charcoal grill to high heat or place stovetop grill pan over burners set to high heat.

Combine the ground pepper, sea salt, Aleppo pepper and Szechuan peppercorns in a mixing bowl.

Generously drizzle the filets with olive oil. Season on all four sides with the spice mixture.

Place rosemary sprigs on the grill, place filets on top and grill on high heat to desired doneness (about 3–5 minutes per side for medium rare). Allow to rest at least 4 or 5 minutes before serving.

TO SERVE

Divide the risotto into 4 warm serving bowls. Sprinkle on the shaved Parmesan, then top with the mascarpone, garnish with the sliced porcini mushrooms and a bit of the thyme, and finish with a drizzle of olive oil. Slice the warm filets and set them on top of the finished red-wine risotto. Serve immediately. ■

Filet Mignon with Red-Wine Risotto

The recipes

Atlantic Halibut Loin with Fennel and Blood-Orange Emulsion

SERVES 4

Chef Zakarian is known for his inspired combinations of ingredients, reaching into his own Armenian roots as well as pulling from other cuisines. In this innovative dish, he simmers marinated halibut in garlic and thyme, then jazzes it up with a vibrant blood-orange sauce and creamy fennel puree.

FOR THE FISH
4 (6-ounce) fillets of halibut
(preferably cut from the top fillet or loin)
Sea salt (about 1 tablespoon)
Freshly ground white pepper
1 tablespoon fennel seeds, coarsely ground
3 cups extra-virgin olive oil (for poaching)
1 head of garlic, split crosswise
2 sprigs thyme

FOR THE FENNEL PUREE
1 large head of fresh fennel, sliced into thin shavings
(reserve the green fronds for garnish)
1 teaspoon olive oil
½ cup cream
1½ teaspoons unsalted butter
Juice of ½ lemon
Salt and pepper to taste

FOR THE BLOOD-ORANGE EMULSION
½ cup blood-orange juice, frozen or fresh
(if not available, substitute regular orange juice)
2 fresh bay leaves
1¼ cups unsalted butter, diced
Kosher salt and white pepper to taste
Small pinch of sugar

FOR THE GARNISH
1 sprig fresh mint leaves, torn into shreds
1 tablespoon fresh dill, picked and washed
Handful raw fennel, shaved
Handful pitted, dried black olives, roughly chopped

TO MAKE THE FISH

Arrange the halibut fillets on a seasoning tray or cutting board and generously sprinkle with sea salt and fresh white pepper, then the ground fennel seeds. (This should be done at least 1 hour in advance.)

While the fish is marinating, prepare the fennel puree and the blood-orange emulsion.

Then, in a large saucepot over low heat, bring to simmer the extra-virgin olive oil, garlic and thyme.

Remove from heat, gently lower each fillet into the olive oil and let stand about 10 minutes, or until desired doneness.

Carefully remove from oil using a slotted spatula. Allow to drain for a minute before serving.

TO MAKE THE FENNEL PUREE

In a shallow pan over low heat, sweat the shaved fennel in 1 teaspoon olive oil by putting a lid on the pan. Cook until tender and translucent, about 5–10 minutes.

Next, add the cream and bring to a simmer over low heat, about 10–15 minutes.

Transfer to the bowl of a large blender and puree on high until smooth and creamy (if too thick, add a little water). Finish with the 1½ teaspoons butter, the lemon juice and salt and pepper to taste. Reserve and keep warm.

TO MAKE THE BLOOD-ORANGE EMULSION

In a small saucepot over low heat, bring the blood-orange juice to a simmer and reduce by about half of the original volume.

Next, add in the bay leaves and whisk in the 1¼ cups diced butter to create a beurre-blanc consistency. Season with kosher salt and white pepper to taste, then adjust with the pinch of sugar. Strain and reserve warm for serving.

TO SERVE

Divide the fennel puree evenly among 4 serving dishes, then top each with a portion of the poached halibut. Drizzle the blood-orange emulsion all around the dishes and garnish the emulsion with the mint leaves. Garnish the fish with dill sprigs, shaved raw fennel and some dried black olives. ◼

Town at the Chambers Hotel

The recipes

"I'm not one of those chefs who wants to reinvent the wheel, but I don't take any dish all that seriously. I want to throw in something unexpected."

Sea Scallop Cru

SERVES 4 AS AN APPETIZER

This is such a sophisticated appetizer, it's hard to believe that it's so simple to make. According to the chef, the most difficult part is slicing the scallops into thin medallions, so make certain you have a very sharp knife and take the time to cut carefully.

FOR THE DRESSING
1 tablespoon sherry vinegar
1 tablespoon honey
3/4 cup grapeseed oil
1 tablespoon peanut oil
Sea salt and freshly ground black pepper

FOR THE SCALLOPS
4 fresh, dry sea scallops, shucked and rinsed in cold, salted water (see note)
2 sprigs of fresh rosemary, finely minced
Sea salt
Freshly ground black pepper

TO MAKE THE DRESSING
(Can be done 24 hours in advance.)
Place the sherry vinegar and honey in a blender. Turn to high speed. Slowly drizzle in the grapeseed oil, then the peanut oil. Season with a little sea salt and pepper. Keep dressing refrigerated until ready to serve.

TO MAKE THE SCALLOPS
(Must be done just before serving.)
Quickly rinse the scallops in a bowl of very cold, salted water. Carefully pat dry each scallop.

On a clean, dry cutting board, place one scallop and carefully slice crosswise into 1/8-inch-thick slices. Repeat with each scallop.

TO SERVE
Arrange these scallop "medallions" on a serving plate or scallop shells, making sure to just slightly overlap each slice. Drizzle evenly with a little of the sherry/honey dressing, then scatter the minced rosemary evenly over the scallops. Finish by sprinkling each row of scallop "cru" with sea salt and a few grinds of fresh black pepper. ■

■ **NOTE** It is extremely important to use only "dry" or freshly shucked sea scallops for this preparation.

Eric Hara
EXECUTIVE CHEF, DAVIDBURKE & DONATELLA

Bring on the props

Syringes. Flower frogs. Little red wagons. Not usual materials for a chef, but for Eric Hara, they're almost as important as the fish, the poultry, the meat and the spices. "The challenge at davidburke & donatella is to present great food in a whimsical, unexpected way," explains this chef-artiste. "Although I focus on flavor first, I need to come up with some playful approaches that set us apart from other restaurants."

And that he does. A lovely shellfish soup, for instance, spiked with harisa, is coddled in a soup can emblazoned with a D&D label.

Chunks of spicy lobster are served on the spears of a flower frog. And what Hara calls a "foie gras noodle" is presented in a syringe. But make no mistake: All these bells and whistles take second place to the bold and gutsy American cuisine served up nightly at this chic, sophisticated East Side spot.

New American • Eric Hara 27

davidburke & donatella

Eric Hara
EXECUTIVE CHEF, DAVIDBURKE & DONATELLA

"Although my background is primarily in French cooking, I mix that up with other elements to take the classics to a more exciting, more modern level," says Hara. "I look at a dish and try to step it up with another technique or another ingredient—I might replace one protein with another, come up with a new combination of spices or use an entirely different cooking method."

The scallops benedict is a good example of what he's talking about, a riff on everyone's brunch favorite. Instead of the English muffin, Hara fries little cakes of shredded potato and shallot, then tops them with Spanish chorizo, lightly fried scallops and sunny-side-up quail eggs. Lobster foam stands in for the usual hollandaise sauce, and a drizzle of chorizo oil adds kick. Although the result is miles removed from the original, the concept is comfortably familiar.

According to Hara, home cooks can do similar things as long as they know some basic techniques and do their homework—meaning reading a recipe from start to finish and understanding all the steps. Then, says Hara, "Just do it. Fool around a little and don't be afraid to make mistakes. The only way to progress is to try again and again."

DAVIDBURKE TOWNHOUSE
(formerly davidburke & donatella)
133 East 61st Street
New York, NY 10065
212-813-2121
www.dbdrestaurant.com

On the side...

What do you consider the most overrated ingredient?
I like to use anything and everything, so nothing is overrated.

The most underrated ingredient?
Monkfish liver and shark fin.

What is your favorite comfort food?
Anything Chinese.

What kitchen gadget is your must-have tool?
A Vita-Prep. I couldn't cook without it.

If you were not a chef, what would you be?
A lawyer.

What was the last thing you ate?
Breaded chicken cutlets and potatoes that my wife made last night. Very different from the food at DB&D!

He should know. Hara is always experimenting; for him, it's the best part of the job. "I'm very lucky to be at a place where I am encouraged to have fun with the food, since I bore easily," he confesses. "I always say I have a severe case of ADD, but maybe that makes me a better chef."

We agree. This is a case where a restless spirit benefits from creating thoroughly exciting dishes. ■

The recipes

"Just do it. Fool around a little and don't be afraid to make mistakes. The only way to progress is to try again and again."

Crisp & Angry Lobster Cocktail

SERVES 4

Davidburke & donatella has a reputation for presenting provocative dishes with a whimsical touch. This spicy lobster cocktail, served on a flower frog and gussied up with fried basil leaves, always prompts smiles when it's brought to the table. More smiles ensue when each bite discloses a crunchy crust and underlying flavors of chile, lemon and sun-dried tomato.

2 (1½-pound) live lobsters
2 cups Wondra (or other "instant" flour)
¼ cup chili powder
2 tablespoons cayenne pepper
Sea salt to taste
1 large egg, beaten
¼ cup canola oil
1½ tablespoons minced garlic
1 tablespoon crushed red pepper flakes
½ cup fresh basil leaves
¼ cup chili oil
2 tablespoons sun-dried tomatoes, julienned
1 tablespoon lemon zest, julienned and cooked in simple syrup (see note)
½ cup lobster or chicken stock
2 tablespoons unsalted butter
Freshly squeezed lemon juice to taste (from zested lemon)
4 lemons, cut into eighths
Fresh basil leaves, deep-fried (for garnish)

Preheat oven to 475°F.

To prepare lobsters, place 1 lobster on a cutting board on its back and, holding it down firmly (with gloved hands), insert a knife where the tail and body meet. This will kill the lobster. Then, separate knuckles and claws from lobster with your hands (use knife if necessary). Split the lobster from head to tail with knife and separate tail from body with knife. Discard brain sac and any tomalley and roe. Repeat for second lobster.

Mix Wondra, chili powder, cayenne and salt on a plate; coat the lobster with beaten egg, then dredge the lobster pieces in flour mixture, shaking off excess; reserve.

In a large skillet set over medium-high heat, heat the canola oil. Add lobster pieces, cut side down; cook until they begin to color; turn with a spatula. When the other side starts to color, place in a roasting pan in oven; cook 7 to 8 minutes. Remove from oven; place lobster pieces on a platter and keep warm.

Set the skillet used to cook the lobsters over medium heat; add garlic, crushed red pepper flakes, basil and chili oil; cook 2 minutes. Add sun-dried tomatoes and lemon zest; cook 1 minute. Add stock; bring to a boil, then reduce heat to low; simmer 5 more minutes.

Add butter and swirl skillet until butter is incorporated; remove from heat. Stir in lemon juice to taste and reserve, keeping warm.

TO SERVE

Set round flower frogs (a small holder with spikes used for flower arrangements) on 4 large plates. Impale lemon eighths around perimeter of the frog; impale lobster pieces in the center of the frog (one claw, one half tail, one half body on each). Spoon sauce over lobster. Garnish with fried basil leaves. Repeat with 3 remaining frogs. ■

■ **NOTE** To make lemon-infused simple syrup: Bring ½ cup each water and sugar to a boil; simmer until sugar dissolves. Add lemon zest and simmer 3 to 4 minutes more. Remove lemon zest with slotted spoon; drain. Reserve.

davidburke & donatella

Bacon-Wrapped Muscovy Duck Breast

SERVES 1

This duck breast is something else—stuffed with lettuce, prawn and pistachio, then wrapped in bacon and seared. Chef Hara gets even more inventive by setting the slices atop a cool celery root puree.

FOR THE DUCK BREAST
1 Muscovy duck breast
3 tablespoons Bibb lettuce, cooked
1 prawn, cooked, sliced through middle
1 tablespoon pistachios, whole
5 slices applewood smoked bacon
Canola oil for sautéing

Preheat oven to 400°F.

Remove skin from duck. Butterfly the breast lengthwise. Place lettuce, prawn and pistachios over the duck breast. Lay out bacon lengthwise from 12 o'clock to 6 o'clock.

Place duck breast over bottom edges of bacon (at 6 o'clock) and roll up along with the bacon to 12 o'clock. Tie with butcher twine.

Pan-sear the roll in very hot canola oil until the bacon turns crisp. Remove from the pan and finish in the oven for 2 to 3 minutes for medium-rare, 4 minutes for medium.

FOR THE CELERY ROOT PUREE
1/2 cup celery, chopped
1/4 cup milk
1 shallot, chopped
1 teaspoon thyme leaves (preferably fresh)
1/4 cup water

Boil all of the above ingredients. Strain and puree until smooth.

FOR THE ROAST DUCK JUS
1 large onion, roughly chopped
1 small carrot, roughly chopped
2 celery stalks, roughly chopped
5 garlic cloves, chopped
2 cups red wine
2 duck bones, roasted
1 tablespoon fresh thyme leaves
Canola oil for sautéing

In a large skillet, sauté all vegetables and garlic until golden. Add the wine. Reduce by half. Add the bones, thyme and 3 cups water. Simmer and reduce until the liquid thickens, about 20–30 minutes. Remove from heat, strain out the solids; cover and keep warm or reheat before serving.

TO SERVE

Slice the duck into three pieces and place on top of celery root puree; spoon duck jus over the top. ▪

▪ **NOTE** Any remaining duck jus can be frozen or kept in the refrigerator for up to one week.

Carmen Quagliata
EXECUTIVE CHEF, UNION SQUARE CAFE

The pleasure principle

Ask Carmen Quagliata, executive chef of Union Square Cafe, why he became a chef, and the answer is as basic as can be. "I like to eat," he states, then shares a story about his early teens. "I was always jabbering about this meal or that to my friends because good food made me happy. They thought I was sort of weird and challenged me to cook for them one night. I was very nervous, but I did it—and everyone was impressed. In fact, word spread around to the girls at school and suddenly I became more popular."

Quagliata's story certainly gives credence to the old saying that the way to a person's heart is through the stomach.

However, it neglects to mention the pleasure the cook can get from the process. "My passion is creating meals that make people smile," he states, and he's brought that passion to positions at Tra Vigne in California and Felidia in NYC. The menu at Union Square Cafe also accomplishes that mission. Since he took over in 2007,

Quagliata's given the food more of an Italian twist, but he's kept the general style—inventive but approachable. "This restaurant is such an icon, I needed to be careful with any revisions, so I sneaked in little changes and introduced new dishes gradually." A ravioli of winter greens with crispy garlic and bread crumbs is one addition; ditto a duck confit with roasted potatoes and glazed cipollini. And the ever-popular filet mignon of tuna may now be accompanied by an artichoke puree and spinach olivada.

For Quagliata, the process of developing a recipe is very Zen-like. "I taste a new recipe in my mind first, then fool around with the actual ingredients with my sous chef, tasting and thinking very slowly," he explains. "We really take our time to calculate the new dimensions, the new textures. Then, at some point, everything comes together and we say, 'That's it.' I always get goose bumps. It's very emotional."

Even though he's developing recipes and managing the staff, Quagliata still gets a thrill from the actual cooking. "No matter what the title, a good chef is always a line cook," he says. "There's something about the last five minutes before you finish a dish that really gets the adrenaline going. You're part of a team with a shared goal, and plating that dish is a high. I wouldn't miss it for anything."

Personally, he prefers food that's "lusty, flavorful and not gimmicked up with too many ingredients."

UNION SQUARE CAFE
21 East 16th Street
New York, NY 10003
212-243-4020
www.unionsquarecafe.com

On the side...

What do you consider the most overrated ingredient?
Microgreens.

The most underrated ingredient?
Lemon juice. I walk around the kitchen with half a lemon in my hands to squirt on ingredients: The acid gives a nice balance to most foods.

What is your favorite comfort food?
My grandma's braciole. It's tender, moist, delicious and a nice connection to her.

What kitchen gadget is your must-have tool?
A juicer.

If you were not a chef, what would you be?
A doctor.

What was the last thing you ate?
Some beef carpaccio left over from the dinner service, rolled up with arugula, artichoke and Parmigiano.

Although Italy is in his soul—he grew up enjoying homemade breads and sausages from his mom and grandmothers (as well as tasty oil-cured olives from Sicilian relatives)—he loves Asian cooking. "There's a real pop to the flavors, a balance of acids and sugars that I like to apply to my dishes." In fact, Quagliata cooks Asian food a lot at home, and you can often find him eating at one of the city's many noodle bars.

For the rest of us, dinner at his place is just fine, thank you. ■

The recipes

Pan-Seared Sea Scallops with Sugar Snap Pea Salad

SERVES 4

With the greenmarket just steps away, Chef Quagliata can take his pick from beautiful local produce like the sugar snap peas, chanterelles and arugula he uses in this perky salad.
It's a sensational solo, but becomes even more appealing topped with the seared scallops.

1 tablespoon kosher salt
1 pound sugar snap peas
4 ounces pancetta, 1/16-inch thick, cut into 1-inch pieces
15 leaves fresh mint, about 2 tablespoons chopped (see instructions)
8 ounces chanterelle mushrooms
12 large sea scallops (size should be based on 10 scallops per pound, or U-10)
3 tablespoons vegetable oil
Salt and pepper to taste
1 tablespoon butter
2 tablespoons finely minced red onion (about 1/2 an onion)
1/8 cup lemon juice
1/8 cup champagne vinegar
1/2 cup extra-virgin olive oil, plus extra for garnish
2 teaspoons fleur de sel
1/2 teaspoon fresh ground black pepper
3 cups arugula (rocket), loosely packed

Bring 3 quarts of water to a boil with the kosher salt.

Trim both ends of the snap peas and add the peas to the water for 10 seconds, then drain in a colander. Immediately plunge peas into a bowl of ice water to stop the cooking and preserve the color. Remove the peas from the ice water after 2 minutes. Drain them well and pat dry with a towel. Julienne the peas by cutting them in a diagonal direction. Set the peas aside in the refrigerator.

Place the pancetta pieces in a 10-inch sauté pan over low heat with 1 tablespoon of water. Stir the pancetta gently with a wooden spoon to separate while it heats up. The water will eventually evaporate and the pancetta will start rendering out its fat (approximately 4 to 5 minutes). Turn the heat up to medium and cook, stirring and scraping the pan often until pancetta is completely rendered and crisp (another 4 to 5 minutes). Drain the pancetta in a colander. Reserve the fat for another dish and set the pancetta aside at room temperature.

Chop the mint by cutting the leaves into thin threads. Turn the pile of julienned mint and cut again as if you were dicing the mint. (This way the blade only touches the mint twice, minimizing the bruising of the herb.) Repeat two more times. This should get you the required 2 tablespoons of mint, but measure out and adjust if necessary. Set aside.

Wash and dry the chanterelles. Slice thinly and set aside.

To make scallops, heat the vegetable oil in a sauté pan over medium-high heat. Season scallops with salt and pepper on both sides. When the oil is wavy but not smoking, place the scallops in the pan away from the flame to avoid igniting the pan. Sear the scallops for 3 minutes on each side, or until a rich brown. Remove scallops from pan and set aside.

Remove the pan from the heat and discard the cooking oil. Add the chanterelles and the butter to pan and lower heat to medium. Stir and sauté with a wooden spoon, deglazing the pan by scraping up any of the browned scallop bits stuck to it. Continue to cook for 3 minutes until the chanterelles are tender. If they release a lot of water, cook them until the water evaporates. When the chanterelles are done, turn off the heat and leave them in the pan.

To mix the salad, place the finely minced red onion in a large mixing bowl. Add the lemon juice and vinegar to the onion; salt and pepper to taste. Add the olive oil and stir.

Add the peas, pancetta, the mint, chanterelles, fleur de sel and ground black pepper to the bowl with the vinaigrette. Mix the salad and taste. Adjust the seasoning if necessary. Lastly, gently toss in the arugula.

TO SERVE

Arrange 3 scallops on a plate equidistant from each other, leaving a little space in the center to pile up the pea salad. Drizzle a little high-quality extra-virgin olive oil over the scallops and serve. ■

Pan-Seared Sea Scallops with Sugar Snap Pea Salad

The recipes

"I taste a new recipe in my mind first, then fool around with the actual ingredients. At some point, everything comes together...I always get goose bumps. It's very emotional."

Cara Cara Orange and Bibb Salad with Mustard Vinaigrette and Manchego

SERVES 4–6

Union Square Cafe is a destination spot, a restaurant beloved by both locals and out-of-towners for its rustic but urbane food. Even the salads are spectacular; witness this medley of Bibb lettuce, oranges and cheese, doused with onion-laced vinaigrette.

FOR THE ONION MARMALADE
1 cup sugar
3 cups sliced cipollini onions
1½ cups white-wine vinegar

FOR THE MUSTARD VINAIGRETTE
¼ cup Dijon mustard
½ cup whole grain mustard
½ cup white-wine vinegar
1 ounce water
1¼ cups onion marmalade (see recipe)
1 cup extra-virgin olive oil, plus extra for finishing

FOR THE SALAD
3 Cara Cara oranges, sliced thin (about 20–24 slices) (see note)
2 heads Bibb lettuce (not the hydro Bibb), shredded into large bite-size pieces
4 ounces Manchego cheese, sliced into thin shavings
1 tablespoon minced fresh chives
Extra-virgin olive oil, to taste

TO MAKE THE MARMALADE
Combine the sugar, onions and vinegar. Cook slowly over low-medium heat until reduced to a dry but syrupy consistency.

TO MAKE THE VINAIGRETTE
Blend all ingredients in a blender, adding olive oil a little at a time. Process until consistency is smooth, but still thick.

TO MAKE THE SALAD
Arrange most of the sliced oranges on the bottom of a chilled plate or platter. Toss the Bibb with the desired amount of vinaigrette, adding the vinaigrette in small increments and tasting.

TO SERVE
Place the dressed Bibb lettuce on top of the oranges, then add another couple of orange slices on top of the lettuce. Top off the salad with the vinaigrette, a generous amount of cheese shavings, minced chives and a drizzle of extra-virgin olive oil. ▪

▪ **NOTE** Cara Cara oranges are a type of navel with deep pink interiors; if unavailable, substitute ordinary navel oranges.

Spaghettini Siciliana with Fresh Tomato, Anchovy, Chile and Lemon Zest

SERVES 4–6

Freshly made bread crumbs aren't the only ingredient that moves this pasta beyond the ordinary: Chef Quagliata emboldens the sauce with anchovies and lemon zest, and for a hit of heat, adds crushed red pepper flakes.

2½ quarts fresh summer tomatoes (about 6–8 large tomatoes)

2 teaspoons sea salt

6 slices Italian country bread like Pugliese or ciabatta (approximately 3/8-inch thick)

3 tablespoons, plus ½ cup extra-virgin olive oil

3 lemons

1 tablespoon kosher salt

4 tablespoons minced garlic

15 anchovy fillets

1½ teaspoons crushed red pepper flakes

1 pound spaghettini pasta (preferably Setaro or Rustichella d'Abruzzo brands)

3 tablespoons chopped Italian parsley

¼ cup high-quality extra-virgin olive oil, for finishing

Core the tomatoes and make an "X" with the tip of your paring knife on the bottom of each. Plunge the tomatoes in a pot of boiling water for 15 seconds. Remove and place in a bowl of ice water for 2 minutes to stop the cooking. Peel the tomatoes and cut in half around the equator. Squeeze the seeds into a small, fine-mesh sieve set over a bowl. Discard the seeds, but reserve the juice. Chop the tomatoes into ½-inch pieces, add the reserved juice, stir in the sea salt and set aside.

Preheat the oven to 275°F.

Tear the bread slices randomly into smaller pieces. Place the bread on a cookie sheet, toss with the 3 tablespoons olive oil. Toast until the bread is an even golden brown and crispy throughout, approximately 45–60 minutes. Place the toasted bread in a food processor and pulse until bread is just broken up into coarse, crispy, rather large crumbs. Store in an airtight container.

Zest the lemons using a traditional citrus zester or the small half-moon blades on a cheese grater. Do not use the spiked blades of a cheese grater or a microplane. Wrap and set aside.

Bring 6 quarts of water to a boil with 1 tablespoon of kosher salt for the pasta.

Meanwhile, in a large sauté pan over medium-high heat, heat the remaining ½ cup of olive oil. When the oil is wavy but not smoking, add the garlic, stirring often, until it just starts to become a light golden brown. Immediately add the anchovies and pepper flakes. Lower the heat and stir the anchovies with a wooden spoon to break them up and dissolve them into the oil (approximately 15 seconds). Immediately add the tomatoes and increase the heat to high. Reduce the tomatoes by half, cooking for 15 minutes, stirring often to prevent them from sticking to the bottom of pot. Shut the heat off when the sauce is reduced.

Drop the spaghettini in the boiling water. Cook to a toothsome doneness (4–7 minutes, depending on the brand). Drain the pasta, then add back to the pot. Pour the sauce over the pasta, making sure to scrape every bit out of the pan. If the pasta with sauce looks a little juicy that's OK; it will absorb some liquid as you finish prepping and serving.

Remove pasta from heat, add the parsley and lemon zest and gently but thoroughly incorporate; adjust seasoning if necessary.

TO SERVE

Place pasta on a flat platter. Sprinkle about 4 tablespoons of the bread crumbs evenly over the top and drizzle with a fine-quality extra-virgin olive oil. ■

■ **NOTE** This dish is a great way to use up very ripe tomatoes from the garden or from the farm stand, where you may get them at a discount if they're ready to burst.

Anita Lo
CHEF AND CO-OWNER, ANNISA

A woman of substance

Individualized attention is important to Chef Anita Lo. As she says of Annisa, "Every detail counts and makes people come back. I'm on the line most nights and cook for many regulars personally. Sometimes I make up things on the spot so they don't get tired of what's on the menu." This kind of perfectionism is probably one of the reasons Annisa has been blessed with a prized Michelin star, as well as an extremely loyal clientele. Lo has earned both with her willingness to put in 110 percent, again and again.

After studying French at New York's Columbia University, Lo attended the prestigious Ritz-Escoffier cooking school. She graduated first in her class with honors and honed her skills at Michelin-rated restaurants in Paris. But even with her four-star education, she still feels that cooking is an art, not a science. "Classical training is a luxury. You need some basics, but either you have it or you don't. You must have passion, a palate, organizational skills and speed."

Those four factors come in handy when Lo creates a new dish like her tuna with three mints or pan-roasted chicken with sherry, white truffle and pig's feet: "Sometimes what I make on the fly for a regular customer gets revised and put on the menu." But other times, seeing an ingredient in the market or getting a sample of something special from a purveyor is what gets Lo going. "I have a wide-ranging palate, from comfort food to the really high end. I'm interested in anything and everything culinary, including the new movements in science and food. I have an immersion circulator and would love to do more with that. There's really room for every kind of dish as long as it's well prepared."

And New York is the perfect place for Lo to practice her eclectic art. "I love New York. You find every culture here, and the setting is unbeatable." That's why she feels Annisa, with its simple, calming décor and wide-ranging menu, is a good fit. "Annisa is contemporary American but with a French base. It's very personal for me. People feel special when they're here, and the service, which is so important, is excellent." Part of what makes the service so good is

ANNISA
13 Barrow Street
New York, NY 10014
212-741-6699
www.annisarestaurant.com

On the side...

What do you consider the most overrated ingredient?
Fiddlehead ferns.

The most underrated ingredient?
Raclette cheese.

What is your favorite comfort food?
A Vietnamese sandwich.

What kitchen gadget is your must-have tool?
A little device that cuts off the top of an egg perfectly.

If you were not a chef, what would you be?
A travel writer.

What was the last thing you ate?
Hummus with a multigrain pita.

Lo's attitude that creating a true team is important to the whole dining experience. While staff meals are a tradition in the industry, Lo takes it one step further by planning and cooking unique dinners once a week. "Staff meals make for a strong organization. I cook something special every Friday—the food is much more casual but it's still enlivening."

Although Lo has a solid team in the restaurant, one thing she misses is the camaraderie of other female chefs. Not many women, she theorizes, want the lifestyle. "We lost a lot of women ten years ago. There are long hours with low pay—you really need to be obsessive. We lose a lot of women to kids."

Fortunately, Lo had an amazing role model: "My mother was a doctor who worked full time and then came home and cooked." And so Lo has never thought twice about the hard work the kitchen demands. ∎

The recipes

"I have a wide-ranging palate, from comfort food to the really high end. I'm interested in anything and everything culinary."

Chilled Tomato Soup with Wasabi, Shiso and Avocado

SERVES 4

Shiso, or perilla, is a leafy vegetable with a spicy flavor that comes in both red and green varieties. It can usually be found in Asian markets or well-stocked supermarkets, but even if you can't find it, don't skip this soup! The lively, fresh tomato base stands strong; wasabi and scallions bring it to its peak.

4 to 5 large, ripe beefsteak tomatoes, peeled and roughly chopped
Soy sauce, salt and pepper to taste
1 ripe California avocado
2 tablespoons scallion greens, finely sliced on a bias, plus 1 stalk scallion, green part only, julienned
3 leaves shiso, cut into small squares (optional)
1½ teaspoons lemon juice
1 tablespoon wasabi powder mixed with 2 tablespoons water

Place the tomatoes in a blender and process until smooth. Season to taste with soy, salt and pepper. This can be done a day in advance; allowing the mixture to sit overnight will improve its color.

Peel and seed the avocado and cut into small dice. Mix with scallion greens, shiso and lemon juice and season to taste with soy, salt and pepper.

TO SERVE

Divide the tomato mixture among 4 chilled bowls. Place a dollop of the avocado mixture in the center of each and top with a pinch of the julienned scallion. Ring with a few drops of the wasabi. ■

Pan-Roasted Breast of Chicken with Sunchokes and Meyer Lemon

SERVES 2

Annisa is known as one of the city's finest Asian-fusion restaurants, and this entrée proves why. Chef Lo's masterful recipe relies on easily accessible American ingredients, but mingles them in an unexpected way.

2 semi-boneless chicken breasts (preferably free-range), skin on, wing tips attached
Salt and pepper to taste
2 tablespoons vegetable oil
8 ounces sunchokes, peeled and sliced into ¼-inch thick rounds
2 medium Meyer lemons, juiced
3 tablespoons fruity extra-virgin olive oil
½ tablespoon butter
Zest of half a Meyer lemon, white pith removed and julienned (or grated)
1 pinch lemon thyme leaves (or regular thyme)

Heat a large sauté pan over high heat for 2 to 3 minutes. Season the chicken breasts with salt and pepper on both sides evenly. Add vegetable oil to pan and heat until smoking. Place the chicken in pan, skin side down. Reduce heat to medium-high and cook until golden brown and crispy, then turn to finish the cooking on the other side. Remove to a warm plate. Spoon excess oil from the pan and add the sunchokes, Meyer lemon juice and a little water (or chicken stock) to cover. Cook until sunchokes become slightly translucent yet retain some crisp texture, about 3 to 4 minutes. The juices should have reduced to about ½ cup. Add the olive oil, then whisk in the butter to emulsify. Add zest and season to taste with salt and pepper.

TO SERVE

Divide sunchokes and sauce between 2 warm plates. Sprinkle with thyme and place the chicken on top. ■

Pan-Roasted Breast of Chicken with Sunchokes and Meyer Lemon

Italian

With pizza and pasta places on almost every city block, it seems that Italian food has always been a part of New York. But the first Italian restaurants did not flourish until immigration from Italy picked up speed in the late 19th century. Starting from downtown's Little Italy, a neighborhood that remains strong and vibrant, this flavorful and aromatic cuisine spread to just about every corner of Manhattan, hitting all price points and satiating young and old from every background.

But with Italian food so widespread in New York, gourmands may wonder if the cooking has lost its authenticity, its flavor, indeed the very heart that made it so popular in the first place. Happily, the answer is a resounding "No!" The Italian repertoire has expanded from the well-known pasta, veal and fish dishes, eaten with gusto in many a trattoria, to encompass all of the country's culinary magic and to showcase little-known ingredients like farrotto and speck. Whether it's Abbocatto's northern-influenced menu, with a Friulian-style whole-roasted veal shank or Centro Vinoteca's guinea hen with truffles and chestnut puree, New York's Italian restaurants channel dishes from every region. And like the fashions spotlighted in Milan, today's Italian cooking combines a bit of the old with the very up-to-the-moment, as evidenced by Insieme's two-part menu— half featuring traditional recipes and half for contemporary creations.

So, to be sure, Italian cuisine is alive and well in the Big Apple.

Jim Botsacos, Abboccato

RECIPES

Patrick Nuti, Barolo Restaurant

RECIPES

Anne Burrell

Anne Burrell, Centro Vinoteca

RECIPES

Marco Canora, Insieme

RECIPES

Scott Conant, Scarpetta

RECIPES

Gemma

Chris D'Amico, Gemma

RECIPES

Jim Botsacos
CHEF AND PARTNER, ABBOCCATO

Feelin' the love

No one could say Jim Botsacos avoids going the extra mile. When this already established chef (at Molyvos, see page 170) was getting ready to open Abboccato in 2004, he flew to Italy and toured the countryside north of Rome to Friuli. This oft-overlooked region has both snowcapped mountains and Adriatic coastline, resulting in a cuisine all its own. Pasta, for instance, might be tossed in a rabbit ragu with roasted chestnuts; bass may be served with a walnut-fennel pesto. "I met with the people who make cheese, pasta, olive oil; one restaurant I visited closed its doors for the afternoon so I could sample more than 50 types of salumi," he recalls.

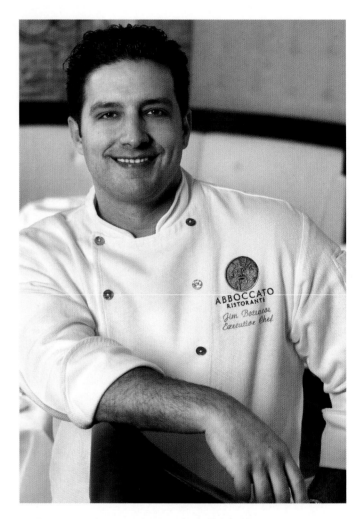

After listening, learning and tasting, Botsacos brought the local techniques and ingredients back home for his new restaurant. "But we began to incorporate some New York items, too, like creating house-cured shad roe, which we treat like dried mullet roe."

According to Botsacos, the most memorable thing about dining at Abboccato is that guests can enjoy real Friulian dishes and hospitality. It's not the Italian food most Americans know, but something else entirely, with influences from Austria and Eastern Europe and unexpected seasonings like wild herbs and poppy seeds. "At first, this worked against us, but now we have our following," Botsacos says. "The menu has evolved into a mix of the familiar and the out-of-the-ordinary, such as braised veal cheeks with a grace note of vanilla." But keeping the restaurant fresh is all about seasonality, he says. "The arrival of a new season and new ingredients is just 'Wow.' There's just nothing like a vine-ripe tomato. And the stuff that's coming in now—fava beans, ramps, morels...." His voice trails off as he speculates on the good things to come and all he can do with them.

Growing up in an Italian-American, Greek-American household in which relatives on both sides were chefs, cooking was definitely in Botsacos's blood. He remembers every Sunday as an eating marathon, with plates laden with specialties from both cuisines. "I still wake up on Sunday mornings and put out olives and cheese for my wife and kids to nibble on—there should always be something to eat," says Botsacos. "I always thought cooking was cool—and women love it. It's very romantic to be able to cook a meal for a

ABBOCCATO
136 West 55th Street
New York, NY 10019
212-265-4000
www.abboccato.com

On the side...

What do you consider the most overrated ingredient?
Salt.

The most underrated ingredient?
Greek oregano.

What is your favorite comfort food?
A big bowl of pasta.

What kitchen gadget is your must-have tool?
Tongs.

If you were not a chef, what profession would you be in?
Selling cars—it's a family business.

What was the last thing you ate?
Halibut with baby artichokes and fava beans.

woman at home instead of going out. And friends love it, too. I never felt like it was a chore."

But cooking is a chance to shine, admits Botsacos. "The best thing about being a chef is that feeling you get when you walk through the restaurant and see people enjoying what you created. It's almost like being on stage; in a sense you're performing. You need to interact with the guests and make them feel good." And you have to bring your passion and instinct to every dish. As he asks his cooks all the time, "Where's the love?"

At Abboccato, of course. ■

The recipes

Friulian-Style Whole-Roasted Veal Shanks

SERVES 6

The meat in this veal dish falls off the bone and the thick vegetable sauce is ready for the asking. For a more rustic version, serve the sauce unstrained as in the photo opposite.

FOR THE MARINADE
1 sprig rosemary, roughly chopped
3 leaves sage, roughly chopped
2 pieces thyme, roughly chopped
1/4 cup roughly chopped parsley
5 cloves garlic, sliced
Pinch salt
2 cups extra-virgin olive oil

FOR THE VEAL AND SAUCE
2 (2 1/2 pounds) whole veal shanks, trimmed
Salt and pepper to taste
3 tablespoons extra-virgin olive oil, divided
2 ounces pancetta, medium dice (about 1/4 cup)
2 cups Spanish onions, medium dice
2 cups celery, medium dice
2 cups carrots, medium dice
3 1/2 cups white wine
2 1/4 quarts (9 cups) light veal stock
1 head garlic, peeled and cut in half
2 sprigs rosemary

Combine all the marinade ingredients in a stainless steel bowl. Place shanks in a zippered plastic bag and pour marinade into the bag; seal. Place sealed bag on a baking sheet and refrigerate for at least 4 hours or overnight.

Preheat oven to 450°F. Remove shanks from bag, discarding all marinade. Season with salt and pepper.

Place an oven-to-stovetop roasting pan in the oven and heat for 10 minutes until hot. Remove pan from oven, add 2 tablespoons of oil and place the shanks in the pan, meat side down. Return the pan to the oven and sear for approximately 10 minutes, or until golden. Turn shanks to sear remaining side, approximately 10 more minutes. Remove the pan from the oven; take out the shanks and set them aside on a platter.

Place the pan on the stove over medium heat and add the remaining oil. Add pancetta and cook for 1 minute, then add the onions and a pinch of salt; cook about 5 minutes. Add celery and carrots and return the pan to the oven. Cook

15–20 minutes until the vegetables are lightly caramelized.

Remove the pan from the oven and set on the stove over medium heat. Add wine and deglaze the pan, scraping the bottom with a spoon to remove any browned bits. Cook until the liquid reduces; when pan is almost dry, add the stock and bring to a boil. Lower heat to a simmer and add the garlic and rosemary sprigs.

Return the shanks to the pan; cover with foil. (The liquid in pan should come between a quarter to halfway up the meat.) Return the pan to the oven; cook, basting every half-hour until tender, 3 1/2 to 4 hours.

Remove the pan from the oven. Set the shanks aside on a platter; cover to keep warm. Place the remaining contents of the roasting pan in a medium-sized saucepan over medium heat. Bring to a boil; lower to a simmer, skim off any impurities. Continue simmering until the liquid lightly coats the back of a spoon, about 5 to 6 minutes.

TO SERVE
Pass the vegetable sauce through a fine sieve and pour over the warm shanks. ▪

Escarole with Garlic, Oil and Chiles

SERVES 6

Cooking the escarole in water eliminates the bitterness, while the garlic, chiles and pancetta kick up the already intense flavor.

3 tablespoons extra-virgin olive oil, plus more to finish
4 cloves garlic, sliced
1 ounce pancetta, chopped (optional)
2 dried chiles
3 heads escarole, trimmed and washed
Salt and pepper to taste

In a large pot, heat the oil over medium heat, then add the garlic. When it begins to sizzle, add the pancetta and the chiles. Cook until fragrant, about 1 to 2 minutes, taking care not to burn the garlic.

Add the escarole; season with salt and pepper. Stir the greens to coat lightly with the garlic-pancetta mixture. Add about 1 cup of water, stir lightly, cover and cook until tender, stirring occasionally, about 10–12 minutes.

TO SERVE
Place in serving dish and finish with a drizzle of oil. ▪

Escarole with Garlic, Oil and Chiles

Friulian-Style Roasted Veal Shanks

The recipes

"The best thing about being a chef is that feeling you get when you walk through the restaurant and see people enjoying what you created."

Cacio e Pepe

SERVES 4–6

Chef Botsacos serves this peppery dish as its own course to highlight the extraordinary flavors he coaxes from the humble ingredients. He recommends a minimum of a gallon of water for cooking the pasta and likes to salt it liberally to mimic the sea. Don't skimp on the water—you'll need to use some of it to create the sauce.

Salt
1 pound imported spaghetti
1½ cups, plus 4 tablespoons reserved
pasta water, divided
2 tablespoons butter
2 tablespoons extra-virgin olive oil
3 teaspoons freshly ground black pepper,
plus more to taste (dry-roast peppercorns in pan,
then grind in a pepper mill)
1¼ cups Pecorino-Romano cheese, freshly grated
and firmly packed, plus more for serving
½ cup Parmigiano-Reggiano cheese, freshly grated
and firmly packed

Place a large, stainless-steel pot filled with water over medium-high heat; bring to a boil and season liberally with salt. Add the pasta to the boiling salted water and cook until just under al dente, according to the package directions.

Meanwhile, in another stainless-steel pot, over medium-high heat, place ½ cup plus 2 tablespoons cooking water from the pasta. Bring this water to a boil. Whisk in butter, cooking until slightly thickened, for approximately 30 seconds. Continue to whisk in olive oil and then add 1½ teaspoons of the black pepper to the butter mixture. Shut off the heat and reserve.

In a separate stainless-steel mixing bowl, combine the two cheeses and remaining black pepper. Remove 1 cup plus 2 tablespoons water from the pasta. Whisk in the water until a thick paste forms. Reserve.

When the pasta is cooked but still under al dente by a minute or so, strain it into a colander with a bowl underneath to catch the remaining pasta water. Remove the colander. (You do not want the pasta to sit in the water.)

Place the pasta in the pot containing the reserved butter and black pepper mixture. Return the pot to medium heat and coat the pasta well with the butter and black pepper mixture, cooking for approximately 30 seconds. Add the cheese mixture to the pasta and continue stirring, using long tongs, until cheese mixture coats the pasta and the sauce thickens, approximately 30 seconds. (If the sauce is too thick, add more of the reserved pasta water, 2 tablespoons at a time.) The pasta should be lightly coated with the cheese and black-pepper mixture.

TO SERVE

Divide the pasta evenly between 4–6 bowls and season with a light grating of Pecorino-Romano cheese and additional black pepper, if desired. ▪

Patrick Nuti
EXECUTIVE CHEF, BAROLO RESTAURANT

Everything old is new again

Like many a soon-to-be chef, Patrick Nuti grew up spending time in a professional kitchen—in his case, doing whatever odd jobs were assigned to him at his uncle's restaurant on the outskirts of Florence, Italy. According to Nuti, "Florence is mostly a tourist city and service is a big part of the economy. Naturally, many people are involved in restaurants and hotels." So for him this wasn't out of the ordinary; it was simply part of life.

Fast-forward through five years of culinary school as well as cooking gigs in Denmark and Japan. Nuti returned to his Italian roots, both literally and figuratively, when he took what turned out to be a career-boosting job in a Florentine restaurant. "Many American journalists went there when the lira was cheap," he explains, "so I not only got great press but met a lot of people who lived in New York." That made it much easier for Nuti to make the transition to the Big Apple, where he could present his traditional

Barolo

Patrick Nuti
EXECUTIVE CHEF, BAROLO RESTAURANT

dishes to a new audience. Enthuses Nuti, "New York is very forward in gastronomy—you are really exposed to everything here. It is not just the national cuisine plus French. Here you can see how a trend becomes a business and not something that disappears overnight. For example, today it's the ingredients that really make the dish, not just the technique of the chef. It's quite different from just a short time ago, when food was very manipulated and complex—such as a cup of foam that looks like cappuccino but tastes like shrimp. Now it's more about refining the old-fashioned basics."

Nuti does admit, though, that showcasing still exists, comparing some chefs to "fashion designers who make a dress for the runway that no woman would ever wear in real life. But that day is ending. The fact is chefs really have to *work* in the kitchen to maintain quality in a regular day-to-day environment."

For Nuti, one of the toughest aspects of that work was to lead the kitchen of a well-established restaurant—something that poses a challenge for any chef. "When I arrived here, Barolo had already been open for 20 years. It has a style of its own and a very popular menu." That menu includes such mainstays as roasted branzino and homemade ravioli stuffed with Granny Smith apples and served with a lamb ragu.

"The specials are really where I bring my own taste. I like to do very seasonal things, like risotto with roasted

BAROLO RESTAURANT
398 West Broadway
New York, NY 10012
212-226-1102
www.nybarolo.com

On the side...

What do you consider the most overrated ingredient?
Truffle oil.

The most underrated ingredient?
Grains, such as farro.

What is your favorite comfort food?
Pasta—any kind is good, but especially ravioli.

What kitchen gadget is your must-have tool?
A Teflon pan.

If you were not a chef, what would you be?
Something artistic, or maybe a philosopher.

What was the last thing you ate?
Greek salad.

peaches and sausage," Nuti says. "This morning, when I saw beautiful salami and figs, I knew I would use those to make something simple, but very complete in flavor and texture."

Turning seasonal ingredients into scrumptious dishes isn't the only trick up Nuti's sleeve. "Most food I cook is what I grew up with. It's not very showy and it's very time-consuming. I might take eight hours to make a stew of calves' feet, a traditional dish from five centuries ago. People don't know at first what it is, but when they taste it, they love it."

No surprise, when you consider that Nuti brings a heritage of old-world finesse to everything he makes. ▪

The recipes

Fried Rabbit Tempura with Mango and Cerignola Tapenade

SERVES 3

A favorite dish in the Italian countryside, these delicate and savory little snacks of fried rabbit are served with a sweet-tart garnish of mango and olives for a unique and flavorful appetizer.

FOR THE RABBIT

1 pound rabbit loin, cut in strips about 2 inches long
1 tablespoon fennel pollen
½ teaspoon salt
½ teaspoon pepper
4 tablespoons flour
1 (12-ounce) bottle beer (with malt)
Sparkling water (if needed to adjust density)
1 teaspoon fresh chopped rosemary
1 teaspoon fresh chopped sage
½ teaspoon salt
½ teaspoon pepper
Vegetable oil for deep-frying (about 3 inches high in a medium-sized saucepan)

FOR THE TAPENADE

1 mango, roughly chopped
10 large cerignola olives, pitted and roughly chopped
½ teaspoon curry
2 tablespoons date molasses
Endive leaves, for garnish

TO MAKE THE RABBIT

Rub the rabbit with the fennel pollen, salt and pepper and let sit, covered, in the refrigerator for 1 hour.
Prepare the batter by whisking together the flour and beer in a large bowl.

Slowly add sparkling water if needed to adjust the viscosity. The mixture should still be slightly liquid but thick enough to lightly coat the back of a spoon. (Trust your senses and play with the amount of water, because different flours can change the thickness of the batter.)

Add the chopped rosemary, sage, salt and pepper and mix thoroughly.

Heat the vegetable oil in a deep, medium-sized saucepot to around 300°F.

Coat each rabbit strip in the batter. With tongs, carefully place strips in hot oil for about 3 minutes until golden-bronze and crispy. Note: If the batter falls off in the oil, thicken it with more flour.

Remove rabbit strips to paper towels to drain.

TO MAKE THE TAPENADE

Mix mango and olives with the curry. Add molasses to coat thoroughly. Set aside.

TO SERVE

Spoon tapenade onto endive leaves and surround with rabbit pieces. ■

Rice Balls with Prosciutto and Melon

SERVES 6

In Italy, *arancini* are usually made from leftover risotto, kicked up with cheese and then served as a snack or hors d'oeuvres. Chef Nuti's version is summery and distinctive, thanks to the addition of cantaloupe and fried prosciutto.

4 medium shallots, finely chopped
5 tablespoons olive oil, divided
1 pound Italian rice (short-grain, such as Arborio)
½ cup white wine, at room temperature
1 medium cantaloupe, cleaned and pureed in a food processor
8 cups chicken stock
10 ounces prosciutto, diced (about 1¼ cups)
Salt and pepper to taste
1 tablespoon butter
2 tablespoons grated Parmesan cheese
2 cups all-purpose flour
3 eggs
2 cups bread crumbs
Vegetable oil for deep-frying (about 3 inches high in a medium-sized saucepan)

■ Barolo Restaurant

In a large sauté pan over low heat, sauté shallots in 4 tablespoons olive oil until softened.

Add rice and cook, stirring constantly until translucent, about 5–7 minutes. Add white wine and stir until evaporated. Add cantaloupe puree and enough chicken stock to just cover the rice. Cook, stirring constantly, until the liquid is almost completely absorbed.

Continue adding chicken stock by ¼ cupfuls, cooking and stirring after each addition until rice is soft with a creamy texture.

Meanwhile, in medium skillet over high heat, sauté the prosciutto in the remaining olive oil until crispy. Remove to paper towels to drain.

When the risotto is nearly finished, stir in the prosciutto and season with salt and pepper. Remove the risotto from heat, stir in butter and Parmesan and spread on a large baking sheet. Let cool for 15 minutes.

As the rice is cooling, place flour in a large, shallow plate.

Whisk eggs together in a large pie plate or shallow bowl. Place bread crumbs in a third shallow plate. With a large spoon, make 1-inch balls of the cooled risotto. Roll each ball in flour, then egg, then bread crumbs.

Bring a medium saucepan of vegetable oil to between 300–350°F over constant heat.

Carefully place the rice balls in the hot oil and, working in batches if necessary, fry until golden-bronze in color. Remove to paper towels to drain.

TO SERVE
Immediately place on a platter or individual small plates, figuring 4 to 5 arancini per person. ▓

Anne Burrell
CHEF, CENTRO VINOTECA

Girl on the go

People first got to know Anne Burrell as Mario Batali's spiky-haired sous chef on television's *Iron Chef*, but now she has her own program *(Secrets of a Restaurant Chef)* as well as her own restaurant, Centro Vinoteca. "Who knew?" she laughs, referring to the fact that she didn't envision cooking as a career until she was 23. "I was stuck in a job I hated and decided I was too young to be so miserable. I had an epiphany, realized I wanted to cook and enrolled in the CIA." More courses in Italy, followed by jobs in Umbria and Tuscany, corroborated her feeling that she had made the right decision.

It also instilled in her a passion for fresh ingredients and olive oil. In fact, Burrell reveres any cuisine, like Italian, that puts an emphasis on olive oil. "It allows food to be what it is and doesn't mess with the flavors," she enthuses.

And flavor—bold, aggressive, hearty—is something Burrell is recognized for. Her dishes combine the simple and rustic with a little something extra. For instance, she adds chiles to a pasta with shellfish for a dose of heat, simmers monkfish in a broth laced with saffron, fries wedges of cauliflower in a Parmesan crust. Some not-so-familiar ingredients like farrotto and fennel pollen are staples in her restaurant pantry, as are a wealth of cured meats, such as speck and guanciale, that she may put on a pizzetta (see page 56) or toss with a sauce. Other scintillating accompaniments come in the form of black truffle butter and chestnuts, which she serves alongside roasted guinea hen thighs (see page 58). Not at all timid when it comes to creating a recipe or trying new ingredients, Burrell encourages home cooks to do the same. "I've developed a theory that food is like a dog; it smells fear. If you're nervous about cooking, the food reacts." Like many other pros, she also stresses first reading any recipe through and through. "I know this isn't the fun part, but once you're familiar with the instructions, you can concentrate on the larger picture and you will be more confident about making changes," she states.

Coming from someone who taught for three years at the Institute of Culinary Education, this is advice well worth considering. Indeed, Burrell credits teaching with honing both her cooking and organizational skills. "In order to explain things to my students, I needed to internalize the entire process of cooking," she says. "I had to know exactly why A led to B, why one thing worked and another didn't."

Such skills are certainly needed at her restaurant,

CENTRO VINOTECA
74 Seventh Avenue South
New York, NY 10014
212-367-7470
www.centrovinoteca.com

On the side...

What do you consider the most overrated ingredient?
Foie gras.

The most underrated ingredient?
Eggs. You can use them in all kinds of dishes, from pasta to dessert to in between.

What is your favorite comfort food?
I have so many! But a turkey sandwich with lettuce, tomato and mayo and chips is always on my list.

What kitchen gadget is your must-have tool?
A wooden spoon, or a food mill.

If you were not a chef, what would you be?
Nothing. I'd be dead if I weren't doing this. It is my passion, my everything.

What was the last thing you ate?
A big plate of broccoli rabe with beans and fagiolini, dressed with olive oil, garlic and hot pepper flakes.

which serves breakfast, lunch and dinner, not to mention a wide selection of *piccolini,* or small plates, such as eggplant cakes with ricotta or truffled deviled eggs. As for the TV show, it's another challenge, but one Burrell is very happy about. "Long before Food Network approached me, I was fascinated at the way TV had made food a superstar. It turned cooking into entertainment and got people involved in everything from what cuts of meat to buy to how to stir risotto," she states. "People are so smart about food now—and that forces me to do a better job as a chef." ■

The recipes

Burrell reveres any cuisine ... that puts an emphasis on olive oil. "It allows food to be what it is and doesn't mess with the flavors."

Taleggio, Speck and Egg Pizzetta

SERVES 4

Centro Vinoteca specializes in small plates, and not surprisingly, the individual pizzettas are some of the most popular. This one is quite a departure from the usual tomato-cheese-and-something-else topping; it offers salty slices of speck (a type of cured ham), taleggio and a scrambled egg.

1 pain ordinaire (recipe follows) or purchased pizza dough (enough for 4 individual pizzas)
Extra-virgin olive oil to brush dough
1/4 pound speck or prosciutto, sliced thin
1/2 pound taleggio cheese, orange rind removed
4 eggs, lightly beaten
2 tablespoons Parmesan cheese, grated
Salt
Crushed red pepper flakes (optional)

TO MAKE THE PAIN ORDINAIRE
1/2 cup warm water
1 1/2 teaspoons dry yeast
1/2 teaspoon sugar
1 1/3 cups flour
1/2 teaspoon salt
1 1/2 teaspoons extra-virgin olive oil, plus more to coat bowl

Combine the warm water, yeast and sugar and let sit for 5–10 minutes. The mixture should look a little bubbly and smell very yeasty.

Combine the flour and salt. Make a hole in the center of the flour and add the yeast-and-water mixture along with the olive oil. Stir to combine. When the dough becomes a homogeneous mixture, adjust the consistency with flour or water if necessary.

Knead the dough for 5–10 minutes or until it is very smooth and elastic. Put the dough in a bowl coated with olive oil and cover with plastic. Put it in a warm place for about an hour. The dough should double in size.

After the dough has risen, punch it down and portion it into desired size. A golf-ball size is good for an individual pizzetta. Roll the dough into desired shape (I like an imperfect, rustic shape). If using the dough right away, grill now. If saving it for later, wrap the portions individually in plastic wrap.

Preheat, brush and oil the grill or grill pan.

Lay the dough on the grill until it starts to bubble and is able to hold its shape. Turn it over and grill it on the other side. It may be necessary to flip the dough back and forth so it will be crunchy but not burned.

TO ASSEMBLE THE PIZZETTAS
Preheat the oven to 375°F.

Brush the grilled dough with olive oil. Lay the speck on the dough and dot with pieces of taleggio. (Just break off marble-sized pieces of taleggio and scatter them over the speck.) Carefully pour beaten egg in 4 equal parts onto each dough and sprinkle with Parmesan.

Bake the pizzettas in the preheated oven for 3–5 minutes or until the eggs are set.

TO SERVE
Present piping hot; sprinkle with crushed red pepper flakes, if using. ▪

Taleggio, Speck and Egg Pizzetta

The recipes

"I've developed a theory that food is like a dog; it smells fear. If you're nervous about cooking, the food reacts."

Guinea Hen with Black Truffles, Chestnut-Potato Puree and Fagiolini

SERVES 4

Rustic chic is an excellent way to describe this entrée—roasted guinea hen gussied up with truffle butter. Even the sides take on a sophisticated spin: elegant haricots verts, and Yukon Gold potatoes cooked with chestnuts and heavy cream.

FOR THE GUINEA HEN
2 sticks butter (room temperature)
1 can black truffle peelings
Salt to taste
8 guinea hen thighs
(substitute chicken thighs if not available)
Extra-virgin olive oil for coating pan
1/2 cup dry white wine
1 1/2 cups chicken stock
1/2 pound haricots verts (fagiolini), stem ends removed, blanched and cooled

FOR THE PUREE
1 bag frozen, peeled chestnuts
Salt to taste
1/2 pound Yukon Gold potatoes, peeled and quartered
1/2–1 cup heavy cream, heated
1/4 cup (1/2 stick) cold butter, cut into pieces

TO MAKE THE GUINEA HEN
Preheat oven to 375°F.

In a food processor, puree the butter and truffle peelings and season with salt.

Season each piece of guinea hen with salt.

Coat a large sauté pan with olive oil and bring to a high heat. Place the thighs skin side down in the hot sauté pan and cook until the skin is very golden brown. Don't crowd the pan; you may have to do this in batches. Once the skin is a lovely color and crispy, remove the thighs from the sauté pan and reserve them on a baking sheet.

Remove the excess oil from the sauté pan and add the white wine, scraping to deglaze the pan. Once the wine has reduced almost all the way, add the chicken stock and reduce by half. Season with salt and reserve.

Using your fingers, make a pocket between the skin and the meat of the thigh. Fill each pocket with the prepared truffle butter.

Place the prepared thighs in the preheated oven and roast for 8–10 minutes or until the meat is cooked through.

Add the fagiolini to the sauté pan with reduced stock and wine. Bring to a high heat to warm up the beans. If the liquid reduces too much, add water to the pan.

TO MAKE THE PUREE
Place the chestnuts in a large saucepot and fill with water. Season generously with salt and bring the pot to a boil. Add the potatoes and continue to boil until the potatoes are fork-tender, about 20–25 minutes.

Drain the cooked potato-chestnut mixture and return to the pot. Add the hot cream and cold butter and stir vigorously until combined. Check the seasoning; add salt if needed. If the mixture is a little stiff, add more cream and butter until it reaches the desired consistency. Place it in a serving bowl and cover with foil; keep it in a warm place until ready to use.

Place a scoop of the chestnut-potato mixture in the center of each plate and arrange the fagiolini on the puree. Lean 1 or 2 guinea hen thighs on the puree and fagiolini and spoon the reduced wine-stock mixture over the poultry. ▦

Shrimp and Herb Farrotto with Meyer Lemon Zest

SERVES 4–6

With this dish, Chef Burrell goes risotto one better—instead of rice, she uses farro, a dark, firm Italian grain with a heartier flavor than rice. A bounty of fresh herbs and rock shrimp, along with wine, butter and stock, turn everything into a creamy sensation that's very satisfying.

Extra-virgin olive oil
1 medium or two small onions, chopped
(about 1½ cups)
Kosher salt to taste
2 cups farro
2 cups dry white wine
6–8 cups hot chicken or vegetable stock
½- to ¾-pound rock shrimp, rinsed and picked
through for shells
2 tablespoons butter
¼ cup grated Parmesan cheese
1 cup chopped herbs (a mixture of parsley, oregano,
marjoram, mint and chives is best, but use
whatever is available)
Zest of 2 Meyer lemons

Coat a large saucepan with extra-virgin olive oil. Add the onions and season generously with kosher salt.

Bring the pot to a medium-high heat. Cook the onions, stirring frequently until they are very soft and aromatic but have no color.

Add the farro and stir to coat with the olive oil. Cook the farro for 2 to 3 minutes to toast, stirring frequently.

Add wine to cover the surface of the farro and stir until it has been completely absorbed. Add enough hot chicken stock to the pot to cover the surface of the farro and stir until it has been completely absorbed. Repeat this process two more times. Check for seasoning; you will probably need to add salt.

During the third addition of stock, add the shrimp. When the stock has absorbed into the farro and the farro is cooked but still al dente, remove the pot from the heat. Add the butter and cheese, whisking into the farro. Add the herbs and lemon zest. The farro should be very aromatic and slightly creamy.

TO SERVE
Ladle into 4–6 small bowls and serve immediately. ▦

Marco Canora
CHEF AND CO-OWNER, INSIEME

A self-made man

He oversees the kitchen at three Manhattan hot spots—Hearth, the Michelin-starred Insieme, and his wine bar Terroir—but this innovative chef never went to culinary school. Instead, Marco Canora learned his trade at his mother's stove and in the kitchens of highly acclaimed restaurants, such as Cibrèo in Florence, Italy. "Taking classes, even with the best teachers, will never beat an apprenticeship. Standing beside a gifted chef, watching him season and sear and work his magic, doing the grunt work along with everything else, is the best way to learn about cooking," he says.

Now he's the one that aspiring chefs want to stand beside—and no wonder. After he opened Hearth, his homey East Village restaurant, in 2002, critics applauded his predominantly Italian menu, referring to the food as "bursting with flavor." Patrons agreed, going back again and again to dine on monkfish osso buco, saffron risotto with calamari, and roasted mushrooms so delicious that requests for seconds have become a given.

At this point Canora could certainly have rested on his laurels, but this ever-striving chef wanted, as he puts it, "to flex my culinary muscles." He launched Insieme, a sophisticated Midtown restaurant, in 2007 to even greater acclaim. "My concept was to offer something old and something new, so the menu is divided in two, with traditional Italian dishes on one side, contemporary on the other. It proves both worlds can coexist," he explains. Diners wishing for cutting-edge cuisine might order the decidedly modern saffron farfalle with shrimp, mussels, mint and Pecorino, while the more traditional-minded can feast on Canora's much-praised lasagna verde—all seven layers' worth.

As at Hearth and his wine bar, Canora's dishes build on his own heritage. "This is the food I know, what I grew up with; dishes based on vegetables from the garden, pasta made by hand," he says, referring to his Tuscan mother's cooking. "There's a soulfulness to Italian cuisine that comes through in the finished dish. It's cooking from the heart, with a lot of love and a depth of flavor that stems from the ingredients themselves." Canora's Braised Rabbit (see page 62) is a testament to this concept—its slow-cooked meat is

INSIEME
777 Seventh Avenue,
at the Michelangelo Hotel
New York, NY 10019
212-582-1310
www.restaurantinsieme.com

On the side...

What do you consider the most overrated ingredient?
Summer truffles.

The most underrated ingredient?
Cauliflower. It's delicious and very versatile.

What is your favorite comfort food?
Pasta with a Bolognese sauce.

What kitchen gadget is your must-have tool?
The food mill.

If you were not a chef, what would you be?
An architect or a furniture designer. Both are similar to being a chef in that you follow something through from beginning to end.

What was the last thing you ate?
Chicken livers. I was making up a batch of paté at the restaurant and just dug in.

rich with the flavors of rosemary, olives and wine.

Indeed, it's ingredients that turn Canora on as a chef. He haunts the greenmarket and admits to being "driven by the seasons. For me, the greatest satisfaction is picking up beets or fennel still gritty with dirt, figuring out what works with them, and composing a meal," he states. "My ultimate goal is to let the ingredients express themselves, to coax out the purest flavor."

At Insieme, it seems Canora has achieved his goal. ■

The recipes

"There's a soulfulness to Italian cuisine…. It's cooking from the heart, with a lot of love and a depth of flavor that stems from the ingredients themselves."

Braised Rabbit with Rosemary and Black Olives

SERVES 4

At Insieme, Chef Canora unites old-world Italian with new-world flourishes. This robust dish is earthy and aromatic with briny niçoise olives acting as a saucy complement to the tender, slow-cooked rabbit. If rabbit isn't to your liking, the chef suggests substituting chicken pieces.

1 small red onion, peeled and coarsely chopped
2 ribs celery, trimmed and coarsely chopped
1 small carrot, peeled and coarsely chopped
About 6 tablespoons extra-virgin olive oil
1 rabbit (about 3 pounds), cut into 8 pieces (see note)
Kosher salt and freshly ground black pepper to taste
1½ tablespoons tomato paste
4 canned tomatoes
½ cup niçoise olives
¾ cup dry red wine
1 large sprig rosemary
About 1 cup chicken stock, preferably brown

Preheat oven to 350°F.

Combine the onion, celery and carrot in a food processor and pulse until finely chopped. Alternatively, mince the vegetables by hand, then reserve.

Heat the oil over medium-high heat in a large, high-sided ovenproof pan (cast iron works well) or Dutch oven.

Season the rabbit pieces on both sides with salt and pepper. Working in batches if necessary to avoid crowding the pan, brown the rabbit, about 5 minutes per side. Remove the rabbit from the pan and reserve.

Reduce the heat to medium. If the pan looks dry, add a little more oil. Add the finely chopped vegetables. Season with a little salt and pepper, and cook, stirring constantly at the beginning, then a little less often as the vegetables soften and brown slightly, about 10 minutes.

Stir in the tomato paste. Make sure the paste is well distributed and the vegetables are well covered. Cook, stirring frequently, for 5 minutes.

Using your hands, break the tomatoes into the pot. Raise the heat to medium-high and cook until the tomato juices concentrate and evaporate, about 5 minutes.

Add the olives and wine and simmer until the pan is almost dry, just a few minutes. Return the rabbit to the pan. Break the rosemary sprig into smaller pieces and add them to the pan.

Add enough stock to surround, but not cover the rabbit: It should come about two-thirds up the sides of each piece.

Bring the stock to a simmer on top of the stove, then cover the pan and braise in the oven for 20 minutes. Baste the rabbit with the stock, then recover and braise for 20 minutes more. Baste again, then braise, uncovered, basting every 10 minutes until the rabbit is tender, about 20 minutes more.

TO SERVE

Present immediately, serving in an ovenproof dish so diners can help themselves, or cool, then refrigerate or freeze. ▨

▨ **NOTE** You can substitute 3 pounds of chicken pieces, but you may need to adjust the braising time. Since you check the pot every 20 minutes, this shouldn't be a problem.

Braised Rabbit with Rosemary and Black Olives

The recipes

"For me, the greatest satisfaction is picking up beets or fennel still gritty with dirt, figuring out what works with them, and composing a meal."

Stuffed Cabbage in Easter Broth

SERVES 4

In Italy, Easter is a joyous day celebrated with much eating, drinking and rejoicing. Home cooks spend hours preparing special feasts, and a popular starter is Easter broth, *brodetto Pasquale*, a meaty, herb-infused stock. Chef Canora gives the traditional recipe his own twist and uses his broth to float cabbage leaves filled with a sublime mixture of veal sweetbreads, ricotta and Parmesan.

FOR THE BROTH
1 chicken, cut up
2 pounds beef shank
2 turkey legs
2 bay leaves
1 tablespoon black peppercorns
2 carrots, peeled and chopped
1 stalk celery, chopped
2 onions, peeled and chopped
6 whole peeled tomatoes with their juices

FOR THE STUFFED CABBAGE
¼ cup lemon juice
1-pound piece sweetbread
2 tablespoons canola oil
Kosher salt and freshly ground black pepper
2 tablespoons butter
⅔ cup ricotta cheese, drained overnight
½ pound finely ground veal
½ cup freshly grated Parmesan cheese
1 egg
¼ teaspoon nutmeg
4 large outer leaves Savoy cabbage

FOR THE GARNISH
1 cup peas
1 cup diced carrot
¼ cup pastina
Kosher salt and pepper to taste

TO MAKE THE BROTH

Combine all of the broth ingredients in a very large pot. Add water to cover and bring to a simmer over medium heat. Gently simmer, skimming frequently, until the broth is flavorful, about 4 hours.

Strain the broth, skim the fat once again, and reduce by one-third. Reserve.

TO MAKE THE STUFFED CABBAGE

To start the stuffing, combine lemon juice with 3 quarts of water and bring to a boil. Plunge the sweetbread into the boiling water, then drain and refresh in ice water. Cool completely, then clean the sweetbread, removing as much skin and membrane as possible.

In a medium skillet over high, heat canola oil. Salt and pepper the sweetbread and add it to the pan. Cook until firm and golden, about 3 minutes per side. Reduce the heat and add butter. Baste the sweetbread with the melting butter, cooking for about 2 minutes more. Remove the sweetbread from the pan and reserve.

In a large bowl, combine the drained ricotta, ground veal, Parmesan, egg, salt, pepper to taste and nutmeg and mix vigorously with your hands until the stuffing is smooth.

Bring a large pot of salted water to boil. Blanch the cabbage leaves in the water, then refresh in ice water. Remove the center vein from the leaves, cutting each in two. Reassemble each leaf by overlapping the two halves to form a large disc. Divide the veal mixture between the cabbage leaves.
Cut the sweetbread in 4 pieces and place a piece in the center of each leaf. Roll the leaves around the filling, folding in the ends (like a burrito). Wrap each cabbage roll in plastic wrap. Tightly twist the ends so the filling will not escape during steaming.

Steam cabbage rolls, still wrapped, in the top of a double boiler for 10 minutes. Unwrap each roll and cut into thirds.

TO MAKE THE GARNISH
Shortly before serving, first blanch the peas, then the carrots, then the pastina in boiling salted water, then reserve. Heat the broth, adjusting the seasoning with salt and pepper.

TO SERVE
Ladle broth into shallow bowls. Arrange three pieces of cabbage roll in each bowl; garnish with carrots, peas and pastina. ◾

Chicken Liver Crostini

MAKES ABOUT 40 APPETIZERS
Everyone has a favorite chicken liver appetizer, but this one is particularly tasty, with a salty kick from the anchovy and capers. A bit of cognac doesn't hurt either, adding yet another layer of flavor.

1 pound chicken livers
2 teaspoons butter
4 tablespoons extra-virgin olive oil, divided
2 cups finely chopped onions
Kosher salt and pepper to taste
2 sprigs sage
1 sprig rosemary
1 anchovy fillet, minced
1 tablespoon capers
¼ cup cognac or other deglazing liquid
(see note)
1 to 2 baguettes, sliced, toasted and seasoned
with salt and pepper

Clean the livers, removing any veins, sinew and fat. Lay on paper towels to dry.

Heat the butter and 1 tablespoon of the oil in a large skillet over medium-high heat. Add the onion. Season with salt and pepper and add the sage and rosemary. Cook, stirring occasionally until the onions start to soften and color, about 5 minutes. Add minced anchovy and capers, reduce the heat slightly and continue cooking until the onions are soft and caramelized, about 10 minutes more. Transfer the onion mixture to a bowl and wipe out the pan with paper towels.

Pat livers dry with a towel. Heat the skillet over high heat. Add the remaining 3 tablespoons of oil. Season the livers with salt and pepper and place them in the pan.

Cook the livers without disturbing them until they get nicely browned, about 2 minutes, then flip them over. Cook for 1 minute more, then add onions. Mix to distribute the onions evenly. Carefully add the cognac (it will flame) and cook until the flames burn out and the skillet is more or less dry, about 30 seconds.

Allow the liver-onion mixture to cool for 15 minutes. Remove and discard the herbs, then chop the livers finely or pulse the mixture in a food processor. Taste and adjust the seasoning, if necessary, with salt and pepper.

TO SERVE
Serve at room temperature on toasted baguettes. The chicken liver mixture will keep in the refrigerator for about a week. ◾

◾ **NOTE** Instead of cognac, you can use brandy, white or red wine, sherry or marsala. Or, if you want to avoid flaming the livers, Chef Canora suggests deglazing with sherry vinegar.

Scott Conant
CHEF AND OWNER, SCARPETTA

The perfect match

When Chef Scott Conant left his posts at Midtown hot spots Alto and L'Impero in the spring of 2007, diners, critics and fellow chefs were shocked. After all, Conant had gathered many accolades, including three stars from *The New York Times* and a *Food & Wine* Best New Chef award for his work at L'Impero. But Conant had a yen to start his own company. "I was very pleased with the food at the restaurants, but I wanted a different environment to grow and expand." And a year later, he's achieved his goal with Scarpetta, located in the Meatpacking District, and now firmly on the map with its own three-star *New York Times* review.

Explaining what might be considered a uniquely New York phenomenon, he laughs, "Downtowners just wouldn't come uptown, where my other restaurants were. But people from uptown and midtown will go downtown, so we felt it was important to be in a place that appeals to both ends and doesn't alienate anyone."

And that desire to please all comers is evident in his

airy and elegant new place and its trimmed-down menu. Conant elaborates on what's happening: "We want diners to take a little piece of bread at the end of the meal and use it to get every last bit from the plate. That's what *scarpetta* is—the little heel of bread used for that. It's what you do when the food is really delicious." Of the menu, he admits, "It's food that people have seen before, but it resonates with them. It's a bit more rustic than what I've done previously. I'm focusing on taking away ingredients from a dish to focus the flavors on a specific element." And his signature dishes, like fritto misto with fried herbs or creamy polenta with a fricassee of mushrooms (see page 70), are getting rave reviews.

He continues. "I've done *alta cucina* [the high-end, aristocratic Italian] and now I'm taking *cucina rustica* [the rustic style] and giving it a hint of refinement. For example, I might take something quite simple, like a macaroni, but toss it with porcini, fava beans and Pecorino to dress it up, then garnish it with long-cut—instead of chopped—chives to elevate the dish."

This seems to come easily to Conant. "I'm very fortunate in that I can visualize taste sensations in my mind," he says. "I taste something and then try to envision the perfect match. With a goat cheese, for instance, there may be a grassy note. I can take that element and push it to the next level by combining it

SCARPETTA
355 West 14th Street
New York, NY 10011
212-691-0555
www.scarpettanyc.com

On the side...

What do you consider the most overrated ingredient?
Anything can be new in the right hands.

The most underrated ingredient?
Everything has a place.

What is your favorite comfort food?
Skippy reduced-fat extra-crunchy peanut butter.

What kitchen gadget is your must-have tool?
Big spoons—the 1.5-ounce kind— I have dozens of them all over the kitchen.

If you were not a chef, what profession would you be in?
I'd be in marketing.

What was the last thing you ate?
A double espresso.

with the flavor of a green tomato and mustard so the flavors are definitely singular but still harmonious."

While the food at Scarpetta has people clamoring for reservations, what also keeps the tables filled is the attitude. Insists Conant, "The most important thing is the approach to the guest. I never want the 'You're lucky to even be here' vibe. We hope that immediately upon walking in the door, people sense warmth and a real gratitude for their presence."

At Scarpetta, courtesy of Conant's food, diners have a lot to be grateful for, too. ■

Agnolotti dal Plin

The recipes

"I've done alta cucina [the high-end, aristocratic Italian] and now I'm taking cucina rustica [the rustic style] and giving it a hint of refinement."

Agnolotti dal Plin

SERVES 10

Agnolotti dal plin, or "pinched priest's hats," is a typical pasta of Italy's Piedmont region. Usually filled with meat or cheese, Conant's delightful little purses contain both. He first boils, then quickly sautés them with vegetables and tops the dish with a light and cheesy froth.

FOR THE FILLING AND PLIN
½ pound boneless chicken thigh or leg meat
½ pound pork stew meat
5 shallots, sliced
8 cups brown chicken stock
1 cup milk
¾ pound fontina cheese, cut into small cubes
Salt and pepper to taste
Fresh pasta sheets, cut into 1-inch squares
(about 180 total)

FOR THE PARMIGIANO FROTH
2 cups white chicken stock
4 ounces Parmesan cheese rind
2 tablespoons butter
½ cup grated Parmesan cheese
2 teaspoons truffle oil

FOR THE GARNISH AND PLATING
Salt (for pasta water)
Oil for sautéing
Honshimeji mushrooms
Baby carrots
1 tablespoon butter
2 tablespoons pasta water
Preserved truffles
Parmesan cheese, freshly grated
Chives, chopped

TO MAKE THE FILLING AND PLIN
Cut poultry and pork into 2-inch cubes and sear in a hot pan until brown in color. Add shallots, cover with brown chicken stock and bring to a boil.

Lower the heat and simmer until meat is thoroughly cooked.

Strain the meat from the stock and set it aside.

Over a double boiler, heat the milk and slowly add fontina cubes, stirring constantly with a whisk to make sure there are no lumps. The fondue is finished once the cheese has melted into the milk.

In a food processor, puree the meat mixture; combine with the fontina fondue and season to taste with salt and pepper.

Fill each pasta square with approximately 1 thimble-sized portion of the meat and cheese fondue; seal at the top so that the pasta square resembles a small purse.

Cook pasta in well-salted water and reserve the cooking water. Coat a sauté pan lightly with olive oil, add mushrooms and carrots and sauté until soft; add butter and pasta water to pan; cook, stirring until butter is melted. Add the cooked plin and preserved truffles and toss to coat; sprinkle with Parmesan cheese and chives.

TO MAKE PARMIGIANO FROTH
Bring the white chicken stock to a boil, then add the Parmesan rind and simmer for 15 minutes. Add butter, grated Parmesan and truffle oil; set aside. Remove and discard the rind.

TO SERVE
Transfer the plin to individual plates—about 18 per serving. To garnish, use a hand blender to whip the Parmigiano froth to a foamy consistency; add a dollop to each serving. ■

The recipes

"I taste something and then try to envision the perfect match."

Creamy Polenta with a Fricassee of Mushrooms

SERVES 4

This rustic dish can be served as a hearty appetizer or as a main dish with a soup or salad. The polenta, though simple, does require attention and a long simmer on the stove.

FOR THE POLENTA

2 cups heavy cream

2 cups milk

1½ teaspoons kosher salt

2/3 cup cornmeal, preferably coarse-ground

1 tablespoon unsalted butter

2 tablespoons Grana Padano or Parmigiano-Reggiano cheese, freshly grated

1 tablespoon fresh chives, chopped (optional)

FOR THE MUSHROOM FRICASSEE

¼ cup olive oil

2 medium shallots, thinly sliced

½ pound (approximately 2 cups) mixed domestic and wild mushrooms, sliced

½ cup chicken reduction (homemade or purchased), diluted with water until a little thicker than chicken stock

1 tablespoon fresh chives, snipped

½ teaspoon white truffle oil

TO MAKE THE POLENTA

In a heavy-bottomed saucepan, combine the cream and milk over medium-high heat just until small bubbles begin to appear on the surface. Add the salt and whisk the cream and milk until quite frothy.

Add the cornmeal and continue to whisk the mixture as it comes to a boil. Continue whisking for an additional 3 minutes. Reduce the heat to very low, cover the pan and cook, stirring every 5 minutes or so, until the cornmeal is completely cooked and quite tender, about 1 hour and 45 minutes. Be patient. Even if the polenta has thickened and seems good after an hour, longer cooking will make it even better. As the polenta cooks, a skin will form on the bottom and sides of the pan (if you are not using a nonstick pan), which is proper and which gives the polenta a slightly toasty flavor.

TO MAKE THE MUSHROOM FRICASSEE

In a large sauté pan, heat the oil over medium heat. Add the shallots and cook, stirring, until they just begin to color on their edges. Add the mushrooms and cook until the liquid is released.

Add the chicken reduction and bring to a boil. Lower the heat to a bubbling simmer and cook until the liquid is reduced by half. (You can prepare the mushrooms ahead up to this point; reheat them over medium-high heat just before serving.)

Toss the mushrooms with the chives and drizzle a little of the truffle oil over the mushrooms. Cook for just a few seconds, no more, because the flavor and aroma of the truffle oil dissipate quickly.

TO SERVE

Stir butter, cheese and chives into the polenta. The polenta should pour from the spoon as you serve it and will thicken as it cools. (If necessary, you can thin the polenta with a little milk just before serving.)

Portion polenta out into warm bowls. Spoon mushrooms and some of the cooking juices over each serving of polenta. ■

Chris D'Amico
CHEF, GEMMA

The downtown juggler

Anyone who knows anything about the food-service business knows that being a chef and running a kitchen is a grueling job. But Chris D'Amico is a veritable juggler. "Unlike most restaurants, which serve lunch and dinner or even just dinner, Gemma is open for breakfast, too, because it's in the Bowery Hotel. We're also responsible for room service. So the kitchen actually operates twenty-four hours a day, seven days a week," explains D'Amico. He's quick, however, to give credit where it's due. "For something of this scale to work, it really is a team effort. I have to depend a lot on the sous chefs."

But not only is D'Amico running the restaurant and room service; he's got a third iron in the fire. "We also do the food for special events—there is no separate banquet staff. Last week, for example, we

Chris D'Amico
CHEF, GEMMA

prepared a sit-down dinner for 360 people, and the restaurant was open, too."

Regardless of the situation, D'Amico insists that dishes focus on one or two superior ingredients so that individual flavors stand out rather than blend. "Because we have so much going on, it's very important that we get high-quality product to work with. For example, we may do Italian-style sashimi for starters—raw dishes such as wild bass with capers or snapper with olive oil and a similar olive. For dishes like these, the ingredients are the stars, so they need to be truly great."

While the restaurant serves a wide range of updated and traditional Italian flavors, D'Amico confesses to a love for the classics. "The roast chicken is my favorite thing on the menu—we get raves about it. I'm told those chickens have a really great life, growing up on an Amish farm. It's really the best organic chicken I've had. The skin so crispy!" And he's willing to introduce new things. "Special-event menus are Gemma-style, but people may ask for something totally different, and of course we try to accommodate them. We've been asked for American-style items like little hamburger hors d'oeuvres, and Asian-influenced dishes."

GEMMA
335 Bowery
New York, NY 10003
212-505-9100
www.theboweryhotel.com

On the side...

What do you consider the most overrated ingredient?
Panini.

The most underrated ingredient?
Sea urchin.

What is your favorite comfort food?
Chicken soup.

What kitchen gadget is your must-have tool?
A Hobart dough mixer.

If you were not a chef, what would you be?
A fireman.

What was the last thing you ate?
Spaghetti and meatballs!

As all confident chefs will admit, though, a large part of the experience at a restaurant has nothing to do with the food. Says D'Amico, "Even as a chef, I have to say one of the best things about Gemma is the service. If the service is bad, the experience is bad, no matter how good the food tastes. People want to eat something great, but the environment, and how they feel in it, is very important—that's the make or break of a restaurant."

Luckily for Gemma diners, both the food and the service happen to be outstanding. ■

Gemma

The recipes

"People want to eat something great, but the environment, and how they feel in it, is very important—that's the make or break of a restaurant."

Braised Oxtails

SERVES 6

To make things a bit easier, Chef D'Amico suggests asking your butcher to cut the oxtails into chunks. They make a terrifically hearty winter dish that warms you twice—while they're cooking and while you're eating.

3 pounds oxtails
Salt to taste
4 ounces pancetta
3 cloves garlic
2 bunches parsley, divided
3 carrots
1 Spanish onion
3 tablespoons extra-virgin olive oil
1 cup white wine, divided
Freshly ground black pepper to taste
4 tablespoons tomato paste
6 celery stalks
1 tablespoon crushed red pepper flakes
1/4 teaspoon cinnamon

Rinse the oxtail pieces under running water. Bring 6 cups of salted water to a rolling boil and drop the chunks of oxtail into the water. Simmer for 10 minutes. With a slotted spoon, remove the oxtails from the water and drain thoroughly. Reserve 2 cups of oxtail broth.

Cut the pancetta into thin strips. Mince garlic and half of the parsley. Chop the carrots and onion. Put them into a mixing bowl with the minced parsley and garlic.

In a Dutch oven, heat the extra-virgin olive oil on medium high. Add pancetta and sauté until golden brown, about 2 to 3 minutes. Gradually add the oxtails and brown thoroughly on all sides.

Add the prepared vegetables and sauté. Moisten with 1/2 cup of white wine and simmer, uncovered, until the liquid has reduced by half. Add remaining wine and season with salt and pepper.

Dissolve the tomato paste in the remaining broth and pour the reserved broth over the meat.

Cover the Dutch oven and cook on low heat for at least 2 1/2 hours.

After 2 hours, trim and clean the celery. Set aside the tender greens and the tops of the stalks for later use. Slice the celery and add to the Dutch oven. Simmer for 15 minutes or more.

Rinse the celery greens and the remaining parsley, and mince. As soon as the meat is done, season the gravy with salt, pepper, red pepper flakes and cinnamon.

TO SERVE

Portion the meat into 6 warm bowls and sprinkle with celery greens and parsley. ▪

Spinach Dumplings

SERVES 4–5

A few very basic ingredients combine to form pretty extraordinary dumplings, tender in texture and complex in flavor.

8 pounds white bread, crust removed
½ cup milk
1 pound fresh spinach
Salt to taste
2 eggs
5 tablespoons all-purpose flour
Freshly ground black pepper to taste
Nutmeg
3 tablespoons butter
8–10 sage leaves
1 cup grated Parmesan cheese
(preferably Parmigiano Reggiano)

Dice the bread. Drizzle the bread with milk and mix thoroughly. Cover and set aside for at least 2 hours to allow the bread to absorb the milk. Wash the spinach leaves. Bring salted water to a boil. Blanch the spinach for 2 minutes.

Prepare an ice-water bath. Remove the spinach and drop it into the ice water. Drain thoroughly and set aside to cool off. When the spinach is cold, squeeze the remaining moisture out of it and chop it as finely as possible. Mix and knead together the chopped spinach, soaked bread, eggs and flour. Season with salt, pepper and nutmeg. In a pot, bring salted water to a rolling boil. With two tablespoons, form a test dumpling.

Depending on the dumpling's consistency, either add more flour or milk to make it hold together. When the dough is at the proper consistency, form the dumplings and simmer them in water for 5 minutes. Drain the dumplings with a slotted spoon and place them on preheated plates. Melt the butter with the sage leaves, allowing the butter to soak up the flavor of the sage.

TO SERVE
Spoon the sage butter over the dumplings, sprinkle with the Parmesan and serve in small bowls. ■

Barley Soup

SERVES 4

Speck, a juniper-flavored variety of prosciutto, lends a surprisingly different taste to this soup. However, if it is difficult to come by, regular prosciutto also works well.

2 thick slices speck
2 small fresh leeks
3 stalks celery
1 carrot
2 Idaho potatoes
1 onion
3 cloves garlic
3 tablespoons extra-virgin olive oil, divided
1 cup barley
1 bay leaf
8 cups beef broth
Salt and freshly ground black pepper
1 bunch parsley

Cut the speck into thin strips.

Thoroughly clean the leeks and celery and slice thinly. Slice the carrots and dice the potatoes. Mince the onions and garlic.

In a large pot, sauté the speck in 2 tablespoons of extra-virgin olive oil.

Add the vegetables and remaining olive oil and sauté for 5 minutes. Add the barley, bay leaf and broth. Bring everything to a boil.

Reduce the heat and let simmer for 45 minutes. Remove the bay leaf and season with salt and pepper.

TO SERVE
Chop the parsley. Ladle soup into individual bowls, sprinkle with parsley and serve. ■

3

Perhaps only in Manhattan could one combine the words *urban* and *country* without any sense of irony. This may be because, amid the pressures of city life, many New Yorkers crave a simpler existence—at least once a week—without giving up big-city perks. Happily, in the New York restaurant world, simple doesn't mean ordinary. It means food that's homey and soul-satisfying, loaded with flavor but not overdone; it's familiar ingredients served up in new ways.

Urban Country

The demand for such cooking has inspired the launch of many restaurants of late, most of them located in the East and West Villages, Tribeca and SoHo. Melissa O'Donnell and John Schaefer are just two of the chefs who manage urban country spots: O'Donnell fosters a neighborly mood with Salt's communal tables, while Schaefer welcomes diners to a farmhouse-inspired room at Irving Mill, located just off Gramercy Park. Both rely on the freshest seasonal products and offer wonderfully homey menus. Equally tempting—and exciting—menus can be found at other downtown spots. Kenny Callaghan's Blue Smoke makes Smothered Grilled Pork Chops that will put the country in just about any city kid. For something a bit more more citified, there's Joey Campanaro's Duck Breast— oh so chic, but still quite comfy. Neil Ferguson's brilliant lamb combo and Mikey Price's short ribs are both rustic, but each has a touch of luxe. So, in this day and age, there's really no need to leave the city for a little R&R. Just sample any of these chefs' creations. Or kick off your shoes and try their recipes.

John Schaefer,
Irving Mill

RECIPES

Roasted Cod with Brussels Sprouts, Carrots, Apple Butter and Cider Vinaigrette PAGE 80

Butternut Squash and Blue Cheese Salad with Chicory and Grain Mustard Vinaigrette PAGE 82

Ricotta Dumplings PAGE 82

John Schaefer

Neil Ferguson,
Allen & Delancey

RECIPES

Shaved Hamachi with Pink Grapefruit Beads, Pickled Fennel and Mint PAGE 85

Lamb Chops Persillade, Braised Middlenecks and Potato Puree PAGE 86

Mikey Price,
Market Table

RECIPES

Braised Short Ribs with Mashed Yukon Gold Potatoes and Roasted Brussels Sprouts PAGE 91

Blood Orange and Red Onion Salad PAGE 91

Joey Campanaro,
The Little Owl

RECIPES

Gravy Meatball Sliders PAGE 94

Roasted Char with Olive Crostini and Cucumber Slaw PAGE 96

Duck Breast with Arugula and Almond Salad with Parmesan and Truffle Oil PAGE 96

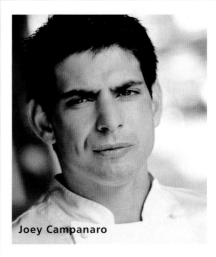
Joey Campanaro

Kenny Callaghan,
Blue Smoke

RECIPES

Deviled Eggs PAGE 99

Herb-Marinated Hanger Steak PAGE 99

Smothered Grilled Pork Chops PAGE 101

Salt

Melissa O'Donnell,
Salt

RECIPES

Chicken Liver Mousse with Sweet and Sour Shallots PAGE 104

Cream of Cauliflower Soup with Mushroom Fricassee and Truffle Essence PAGE 106

Slow-Roasted Eggplant with Beet Tartare and Blue Cheese Fondue PAGE 107

John Schaefer
CHEF, IRVING MILL

Good vibrations

One of the first things you notice about Irving Mill is that it seems so comfortable, so welcoming; there's a nice feeling here. No surprise, considering that John Schaefer's major mission was to create "a place with a good vibe, where people could get good food at a good price point; a restaurant that didn't need to be saved for a special occasion." To that end, Irving Mill offers a large, beamed dining room with an interesting array of vintage prints and paintings and a cozy "no reservations" taproom with a long, curved zinc bar.

As for the food, Schaefer drew from his background as chef at Gramercy Tavern. "I haven't changed my cooking style from my days over there," he asserts, "but now I don't use luxury ingredients like foie gras; I've said good-bye to the bells and whistles." And so the menu emphasizes such rustic plates as rabbit with shallots, olives and garlic sausage, and a roasted baby chicken accompanied by artichokes, wilted chicory and a tomato vinaigrette.

Like many chefs, Schaefer is hooked on seasonality, and his formula for prime-time dishes is one home cooks can easily borrow. He relies on tried-and-true recipes, but rejiggers them by changing what he calls "the garnishes." For instance, roasted monkfish might be served with onions, peppers and bacon during early spring, but come summer, he pairs it with a corn succotash and roasted tomatoes. Autumn gets a whole new turn with cabbage and apples and in winter months he might frame the fish with root vegetables and a pea puree. Similarly, an autumn-themed roasted cod gets the treatment through root vegetables, cider vinaigrette and spicy apple butter (see page 80). Even a favorite like his famous ricotta dumplings (see page 82) teams up with different partners for the changing seasons, from rutabaga to pears to sugar snap peas and speck.

Schaefer, who grew up in New Jersey "eating pretty well, with a working mom who managed to put together a real good Sunday meal," points to early restaurant forays into Manhattan as his foodie trigger. "I'd hit Chinatown and Little Italy and other places and get really inspired," he explains. So much so that he enrolled in the CIA, and then followed up with several jobs before joining Tom Colicchio at Gramercy Tavern.

And Schaefer still gets inspired by other restaurants. "I'm not so turned on by four-star establishments; I prefer more low-key places with more toned-down food, but there's always something to pick up on." His other catalyst is the greenmarket: "It's all there, just waiting to be turned into something wonderful.

IRVING MILL
116 East 16th Street
New York, NY 10003
212-254-1600
www.irvingmill.com

On the side...

What do you consider the most overrated ingredient?
Mesclun greens. It's not the product it once was; now you're better off buying individual greens and layering them.

The most underrated ingredient?
Salt, sugar and olive oil.

What is your favorite comfort food?
A wedge of iceburg lettuce with blue cheese.

What kitchen gadget is your must-have tool?
A good serving spoon for plating.

If you were not a chef, what would you be?
Something hands-on, like a furniture refinisher.

What was the last thing you ate?
A charcuterie plate at the restaurant, followed by vanilla ice cream with rhubarb and strawberries.

Especially in the summer, when the market is in full stride with heirloom tomatoes, all kinds of fresh herbs and loads of lettuces and greens."

But what Schaefer likes most of all about being a chef is interacting with people, both staff and guests. "Sure, it's about the food," he agrees, "but seeing someone start off as a busser and grow into a line cook is enormously rewarding. And seeing guests come back again and again so that you get to greet them on a first-name basis makes my job special."

It's this kind of caring that makes his restaurant so special, too. ■

The recipes

> "It's all there [at the greenmarket], just waiting
> to be turned into something wonderful."

Roasted Cod with Brussels Sprouts, Carrots, Apple Butter and Cider Vinaigrette

SERVES 4

The homespun ambience of Irving Mill is reflected in the food, which could be called "updated rustic." That update shows up in Chef Schaefer's cod, a dish he animates with a fruity cider vinaigrette and a spicy apple butter.

FOR THE APPLE BUTTER
2 Granny Smith apples, peeled and cut into wedges
1 star anise
1 cinnamon stick
½ cup apple juice

FOR THE VEGETABLES
Cooking oil
2 cups Brussels sprouts, cleaned and halved
1 cup carrots, peeled and cut into uniform
2-inch pieces
1 cup pearl onions, peeled
Salt and pepper to taste

FOR THE CIDER VINAIGRETTE
1 cup apple cider
2 tablespoons cider vinegar
½ cup olive oil
Salt and pepper to taste

FOR THE COD
4 (4–6 ounce) cod fillets
Salt and pepper to taste
Cooking oil
4 sprigs fresh thyme
Melted butter for basting

TO MAKE THE APPLE BUTTER
Place all ingredients in a small saucepan and cook until apples are tender. Remove star anise and cinnamon stick. Puree mixture in a blender. The "butter" will resemble apple sauce. Set aside.

TO MAKE THE VEGETABLES
Preheat oven to 350°F.

In a large, ovenproof sauté pan coated with oil, place all the vegetables. Season with salt and pepper and cook over medium-high heat until lightly browned. Place pan in the oven and roast until tender, about 25–30 minutes. Remove vegetables from the pan and let cool.

TO MAKE THE CIDER VINAIGRETTE
Bring apple cider to a boil in a small saucepan, lower heat and simmer until reduced to ¼ cup. Remove from heat. Mix 2 tablespoons of the cider reduction with the cider vinegar. Add the olive oil. Season to taste and add more reduction if needed.

TO MAKE THE COD
Preheat oven to 400°F.

Season the cod fillets and place in a sauté pan with cooking oil. When fish is lightly golden, place in the oven for 8–10 minutes. Baste with fresh thyme and melted butter mixture.

TO SERVE
Place the roasted vegetables on the side of the dish with a scoop of apple butter beside them. Place cod next to the vegetables and drizzle the cider vinaigrette over the cod and the vegetables. ■

Roasted Cod with Brussels Sprouts, Carrots, Apple Butter and Cider Vinaigrette

The recipes

Butternut Squash and Blue Cheese Salad with Chicory and Grain Mustard Vinaigrette

SERVES 4

Warm butternut squash and tangy blue cheese may not be the usual suspects for a salad, but in Chef Schaefer's hands they make delicious sense. He sets them beside a helping of mustard-dressed greens, sprinkles on toasted squash seeds and adds a drizzle of balsamic vinegar for a salad that's delightfully different.

1 butternut squash, peeled
1 head of chicory
Small bunch fresh chives
1 egg yolk
5 ounces olive oil
2 tablespoons red-wine vinegar
2 tablespoons Dijon mustard
2 tablespoons grain mustard
Salt and pepper to taste
6 ounces American blue cheese, such as Maytag, cut into small pieces
1 tablespoon balsamic vinegar

Preheat oven to 400°F.

Cut the squash into wedges, reserving the seeds. On a baking sheet, roast squash until tender, about 30–35 minutes. Toast the seeds in a skillet over medium heat until golden brown. Tear the chicory into small pieces, using only the yellow leaves. Cut the chives into 1-inch lengths.

Blend the egg yolk, olive oil, red-wine vinegar and the two mustards until mixture becomes thick, like a mayonnaise. Season to taste.

TO SERVE

Assemble by coating the chicory with the mayonnaise dressing, then add the pieces of cheese and warm butternut squash. Season and top with the chives and toasted squash seeds. Drizzle with balsamic vinegar. ▪

Ricotta Dumplings

SERVES 4

Yes, it's offbeat, but Chef Schaefer's combination of airy ricotta dumplings and the underappreciated rutabaga tastes wonderful. Crispy bacon and fresh sage mellow the vegetable's flavor and meld nicely with the cheesy egg dumplings.

1 cup ricotta cheese
1 egg
Salt and pepper to taste
1/8 teaspoon nutmeg
1/2 cup grated Parmesan cheese, plus 2 tablespoons
3/4 cup all-purpose flour, plus more for dusting
2 tablespoons butter
1 medium rutabaga, peeled and cut into 1/4-inch wedges, then blanched
4 slices of bacon, cut into squares and cooked until crisp
4 fresh sage leaves, cut into small pieces

Drain any liquid from the ricotta. Mix in the egg, stirring thoroughly. Add salt and pepper to taste. Add the nutmeg and 1/2 cup grated Parmesan. Add the flour and mix to combine. Chill in the refrigerator for at least 2 hours.

After the required chilling time, remove the ricotta batter from the refrigerator. Bring a pot of salted water to a boil. Form the ricotta batter into tablespoon-sized balls, then roll the balls in the extra flour. Drop the balls into the boiling water.

As the dumplings boil, melt butter in a large pan and heat until lightly browned. Add the blanched rutabaga.

When the dumplings rise to the top of the pot, drain and place into the pan of butter and rutabagas. Add the bacon, sage and remaining Parmesan; adjust seasoning and heat for about 1 minute.

TO SERVE

Ladle dumplings into separate dishes or serve alongside an entrée, topping with the rutabaga-bacon mixture. ▪

Neil Ferguson
EXECUTIVE CHEF, ALLEN & DELANCEY

Homey, not haute, cuisine

So what's a British chef who worked at Michelin-starred restaurants in England and France doing at a Lower East Side bistro? "I'm on a high," laughs Neil Ferguson, executive chef and culinary director of Allen & Delancey. "No more starchy white linen, no more haute cuisine, no more pomp and circumstance—just really good, flavorful food that fits the neighborhood." And indeed it does. Far away from the likes of L'Arpège in Paris and Gordon Ramsay in London, Ferguson studied his new locale extensively before stirring any pots.

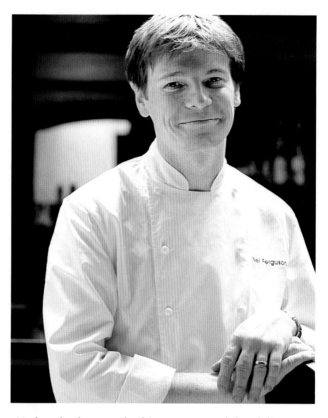

He brushed up on the history, scouted the delis, shopped the Essex Street Market and ate at many of the nearby dives. "I needed to get a feel for the neighborhood so I could develop a food-appropriate menu. I wanted dishes that were hearty but refined and that reflected the local tastes," he explains. He even did a tasting tour of top U.S. restaurants to broaden his knowledge and expand his palate. "Remember, I'm from 'over there,'" he reminds us.

Neil Ferguson
EXECUTIVE CHEF, ALLEN & DELANCEY

During his research project he was surprised and impressed by the helpfulness of the American food community. "In Europe, chefs are much more secretive. They're very protective of their recipes and their suppliers. Here people were willing to share their sources and give me advice. It was so refreshing and so very helpful," he states.

His homework has resulted in a place with a Michelin star and an atmosphere that's warm and nostalgic. The brick-walled rooms are studded with artwork and beveled mirrors reflect the glow of dozens of candles. Guests sit at polished wood tables enjoying posh but homey dishes like caramelized bone marrow gussied up with caviar and a puree of shallots, a duo of lamb consisting of both a chop and braised middlenecks over a velvety potato puree (see page 86) or seared sea scallops with celery root cream and candied grapes. Ferguson's cabbage, beef and onion entrée, inspired by the original immigrants that settled the area, has become an unexpected hit, as has the hamachi recipe he shares on page 85. This one is hardly traditional, but Ferguson chose it as a sophisticated change of pace. Yet, as with any new restaurant, getting it right wasn't easy.

"When I create a dish, I usually start with an ingredient and work from there, flanking the central flavor with others. Next, I think about colors and textures and fats to create a marriage of ingredients, and once that's in my

ALLEN & DELANCEY
115 Allen Street
New York, NY 10002
212-253-5400
www.allenanddelancey.net

On the side...

What do you consider the most overrated ingredient?
Yuzu.

The most underrated ingredient?
Mustard.

What is your favorite comfort food?
Braised oxtails.

What kitchen gadget is your must-have tool?
A microplane. It's just so useful.

If you were not a chef, what profession would you be in?
Something to do with nature… marine biology, perhaps, or working to preserve the Galápagos.

What was the last thing you ate?
A breakfast of eggs, strawberry yogurt and vanilla. It's my way to start the day.

head, I 'road-test' the recipe with other people on the staff. Then it's back to the drawing board to get the right mouth feel and the right flavor. Usually after five or six attempts, it's ready to serve," he explains.

Five or six attempts? That's what it takes, says Ferguson, to make sure the dish will be perfect every time. "It keeps us on our toes, but the great thing about being a chef is the instant gratification. You find the ingredients, you cook them up and you get a reaction. I like that." he says.

We do, too. ■

The recipes

"In Europe, chefs are much more secretive... Here people were willing to share their secrets and give me advice."

Shaved Hamachi with Pink Grapefruit Beads, Pickled Fennel and Mint

SERVES 4

With its exposed brick walls and vintage artwork, Allen & Delancey creates such a comforting cocoon, one is sometimes surprised by the sophistication of the food. This sliced hamachi is definitely über-chic, studded with rings of fennel and shallot and bejeweled with grapefruit.

FOR THE PICKLED SHALLOTS AND FENNEL
1½ cups white-wine vinegar
¾ cup water
½ cup sugar
½ cup white wine
1 spice bag containing 1 star anise, 10 coriander seeds, 2 green cardamom pods, 4 black peppercorns
4 small shallots
4 baby fennel bulbs

FOR THE GRAPEFRUIT VINAGRETTE
2 teaspoons mirin
10 teaspoons olive oil (something clean and crisp, not too peppery)
Salt and pepper to taste
1 lime
4 teaspoons fleur de sel
1-ounce piece gingerroot
1 ruby-red grapefruit

FOR THE HAMACHI
1 pound cleaned hamachi fillet
4 sprigs of mint

TO MAKE THE PICKLED SHALLOTS AND FENNEL
This needs to be done a day in advance, so plan accordingly.

Make the pickling liquid by bringing the vinegar, water, sugar and white wine to a simmer with the spice bag in the liquid. Cool to room temperature and remove spice bag. Thinly slice the shallots into rings, discarding the tiny central ones; place in a pan and cover with half the pickling liquid.

Thinly slice the fennel, ideally with a mandoline, place in another pan and cover with the remaining pickling liquid. Bring both pans to a boil and remove from heat. Allow both the shallots and the fennel to marinate for 24 hours, covered, in refrigerator.

TO MAKE THE GRAPEFRUIT VINAIGRETTE
Make a simple vinaigrette by whisking the mirin and olive oil together; season to taste with salt and pepper. Set aside. Using a fine microplane, grate the lime zest directly into the fleur de sel, then rub thoroughly between your fingers to make lime salt. Refrigerate until needed.

Peel the gingerroot, then grate finely with the microplane until it appears almost pureed. Set aside.

Using a serrated knife, remove the skin and pith of the grapefruit, then remove the sections of flesh from the membrane. Place the grapefruit sections in a stainless-steel pan, adding juice squeezed from the core. Heat rapidly, then quickly transfer to a small bowl and cover with a double layer of plastic wrap. Shake the bowl carefully but vigorously—the sections will naturally break down into "beads." Place the bowl in a container of ice water to stop the cooking process and retain the color. Set aside.

TO SERVE
Chill 4 plates. Thinly slice the hamachi against the grain and carefully lay in circles on each plate. Season lightly and evenly with lime salt. Drain shallot rings and fennel on paper towels and liberally place over the hamachi.

Take the mint sprigs and carefully tear them into little pieces; dot these over the hamachi.

Finally, complete the dressing: In a small bowl, mix thoroughly 4 teaspoons of grapefruit beads, the grated gingerroot, and 4 tablespoons of vinaigrette. Spoon evenly over each dish. Serve immediately. ■

The recipes

"When I create a dish, I usually start with an ingredient and work from there, flanking the central flavor with others. Next, I think about colors and textures...[and then we] 'road-test.'"

Lamb Chops Persillade, Braised Middlenecks and Potato Puree

SERVES 4

Critics have praised Chef Ferguson for taking homey dishes and making them luxurious. This lamb entrée shows the reason for their raves. A meaty chop coated with a mustardy persillade is seared and paired with falling-off-the-bone middlenecks fragrant with cumin, coriander and white peppercorns.

FOR THE PERSILLADE
4 ounces fresh bread, semi-diced (about 3 or 4 slices)
1 cup flat-leaf parsley leaves, plus more for serving
4 tablespoons rosemary
4 tablespoons thyme
2 tablespoons Dijon mustard
2 tablespoons melted butter
Salt and pepper to taste

FOR THE POTATO PUREE
1 pound fingerling potatoes
½ cup (1 stick) butter, diced
½ cup milk
Salt and pepper to taste

FOR THE BRAISED MIDDLENECKS
2 ounces olive oil, plus extra for caramelizing
2 whole lamb middlenecks, on bone (if not available, substitute lamb shanks or lamb shoulder, boned and tied)
2 carrots, diced
1 fennel bulb, diced
2 celery stalks, diced
1 onion, diced
2 garlic cloves, minced
1 sprig thyme
1 sprig rosemary
2 bay leaves
20 fennel seeds
Pinch celery seed
12 cumin seeds
12 coriander seeds
12 white peppercorns
1 tablespoon tomato paste
6 fresh ripe tomatoes
1 bottle white wine
Salt and pepper to taste
Chopped parsley for garnish

FOR THE LAMB CHOPS
1 ounce olive oil
1 lamb rack (preferably Colorado lamb), cut into separate chops
Salt and pepper to taste
Trace butter

TO MAKE THE PERSILLADE
In workbowl of a food processor, pulse the semi-diced bread to a fine crumb. Add the parsley, rosemary and thyme and continue to blend until the crumbs turn green. Add mustard and melted butter and blend until all is combined. Season to taste. Reserve at room temperature.

TO MAKE THE POTATO PUREE
Wash potatoes thoroughly, then place them in a pan and cover with water. Bring to a simmer and cook until soft but slightly firm. While still warm, peel the skins off and pass the potato flesh through a ricer or food mill. Transfer to a clean pan, add butter and cut with a spatula until absorbed into the pureed potato. The potatoes may appear greasy at this point, but don't worry. Boil the milk and add it a little at a time, gently working it into the mix. This will bring the mixture back together. Season to taste. Reserve, keeping warm.

TO MAKE THE MIDDLENECKS
Preheat oven to 350°F.

In a deep, large ovenproof pan, heat olive oil. Add meat and cook just long enough to turn very brown. Remove meat from pan and reserve. In the same pan, add a little fresh oil and caramelize the diced carrots, fennel, celery and onion over low heat until completely golden. Add garlic, herbs, spices and tomato paste and cook for another minute or so, until blended. Add tomatoes and white wine and continue to cook until the mixture reduces to a syrup. Return meat to the pan, cover with water and bring to a boil, seasoning the liquid with salt and pepper once it is hot. Place a lid on the pan and place it in the oven until the meat is tender and comes off the bone easily, about 3 to 3½ hours.

Cool down until meat can be handled, then remove from the bone.

Strain off the cooking liquid into a saucepan and over low heat, slowly reduce, skimming off impurities until a sauce consistency is achieved. Adjust seasoning and reserve.

TO MAKE THE LAMB CHOPS
Heat olive oil in a pan. Season lamb chops and sear on all sides until golden brown, adding a bit of butter for the last minute. Cook to desired doneness, then reserve on a rack.

■ Allen & Delancey

TO SERVE
Warm the middleneck meat in some of the braising liquid until glazed.

Gently warm the potato puree over low heat.

Spread a generous amount of persillade on the lamb chops and flash-cook in a hot oven (450°F) for 2 to 3 minutes to heat the meat and warm the crust.

Warm the sauce from the middlenecks and finish off with some chopped parsley.

Spoon a bit of potato puree on each plate, then top with middleneck meat and one chop. Glaze with sauce. ■

Mikey Price
EXECUTIVE CHEF AND CO-OWNER, MARKET TABLE

What's mine is yours

As much corner grocery as restaurant, Market Table seems to belong on a country byway rather than a street in Manhattan. Right up front are floor-to-ceiling shelves stocked with olive oils, maple syrup and other condiments; fresh-baked goods sit on a counter; a glassed-in case displays meat from one of the finest butchers around. Just beyond is the open kitchen, where it's not unusual to spot a patron getting a quick lesson in searing. "I wanted to make the ingredients I use available to everyone," explains Chef and Co-owner Mikey Price.

"I wanted a place that connected with the community, where people could come in to buy a loaf of bread or get advice on a cut of meat. They don't need to sit down and order dinner."

Well, this former farm boy got exactly what he wanted. Market Table is casual, with a mom-and-pop quality that's utterly captivating. The menu is limited—seven appetizers, seven entrées—and as every dish is based on seasonality, selections change frequently. "I believe in good food done well and would rather concentrate on a small menu than spread my efforts on a larger selection," says Price. "For me, the emphasis is on simplicity: fabulous ingredients, great seasoning."

In autumn you might relax in the wood-beamed dining room and order an appetizer of tender gnocchi floating in a hearty broth with short ribs and escarole, or feast on the pan-roasted chicken in a hazelnut brown butter. Or you could try Price's fave: the skate. "That was a tricky one," he laughs, describing how he first served the skate with just a salad of cucumbers, grapes and almonds. "It didn't go over too well, so I decided I needed a sauce to make the dish more cohesive. I tried pureeing the salad ingredients, but that was too watery; I added red onion but it was still a mess; finally, to thicken things up, I soaked white bread in milk and mixed that in. It worked!"

Price describes his food as "definitely American but with some Mediterranean touches." Maybe that's because he grew up on a farm on the Chesapeake Bay, and keeping close to his roots is what makes his dishes sing. "We had cows, pigs, chickens; we grew corn and soybeans. I always knew where the food on the table came from, and we never ate frozen food," he states. Add to that the fact that his grandfather was a butcher and his grandmother a dietitian, and you can see why he has such a deep connection with food. From the age of 4 or 5 he could be found in the

MARKET TABLE
54 Carmine Street
New York, NY 10014
212-255-2100
www.markettablenyc.com

On the side...

What do you consider the most overrated ingredient?
Portobello mushrooms. They're just used too much.

The most underrated ingredient?
Old Bay seasoning. It has such a distinctive flavor; we use it in our calamari flour and sprinkle it on steak.

What is your favorite comfort food?
Chili with cornbread.

What kitchen gadget is your must-have tool?
A knife or tongs.

If you were not a chef, what would you be?
A teacher. I get such enjoyment teaching my staff.

What was the last thing you ate?
A salad with croutons, Parmesan and hot sopressata, and a cherry blintz for dessert.

kitchen; by 8 he was trusted with "making rice and baking apples"; by the time he was a teenager he was cooking entire meals. On a course that seems almost predetermined, he enrolled in the CIA and went on to various restaurant jobs, including a much-praised sojourn as chef at the seafood-only Mermaid Inn. But after four years, Price yearned for something else. He teamed up with The Little Owl's Joey Campanaro to collaborate on Market Table, and in so doing, finds himself comfortably at home again. ■

Blood Orange and Red Onion Salad

The recipes

Braised Short Ribs with Mashed Yukon Gold Potatoes and Roasted Brussels Sprouts

SERVES 4

These wine-soaked short ribs are typical of the straightforward but satisfying dishes Chef Price prepares in his open kitchen.

2 pounds beef short ribs, 2-inch cut
Salt and pepper to taste
Vegetable oil for searing
1 carrot, roughly chopped
1 onion, roughly chopped
1 stalk celery, roughly chopped
2 cloves garlic
2 sprigs thyme
2 cups red wine
2 cups beef stock
1 pound large or baby Brussels sprouts
4 large or 6 medium Yukon Gold potatoes
3 tablespoons butter, divided
½ cup milk

Preheat oven to 300°F.

If possible, cut the ribs into 4 equal-size portions for easier serving. Season with salt and pepper and sear in oil in a medium-sized braising pan over high heat. Once the short ribs are a deep brown color, remove from the pan and reserve. Add the carrot, onion and celery along with garlic and thyme to the braising pan and cook over medium heat until caramelized, about 10–15 minutes. Deglaze with red wine and add beef stock.

Place short ribs in braising liquid and put lid on pan or cover with aluminum foil if no lid is available. Place in oven for about 1½ hours. Meat is done when almost falling off the bone.

While meat is cooking, clean Brussels sprouts by clipping the stem portion to remove any discolored outer leaves. Place Brussels sprouts in a medium pot of boiling salted water and cook over high heat until fork-tender. Remove from water and place in a cold bath to stop the cooking process. Once cold, drain and reserve.

Peel and roughly chop potatoes. Place in a medium-sized pot, cover with cold water, season with salt and pepper and cook over medium heat until tender. Drain potatoes, add 2 tablespoons butter, ½ cup milk, and mash with a fork. Season with salt and pepper.

Take reserved Brussels sprouts and sauté in a skillet with the remaining 1 tablespoon butter, salt and pepper.

TO SERVE

Place short ribs on a plate and surround with the Brussels sprouts and potatoes. Strain braising liquid and pour over meat. (If too thin, reduce in saucepan over medium heat.) ▨

Blood Orange and Red Onion Salad

SERVES 4

Pretty-as-a-picture is a phrase that aptly describes this lively salad with brightly hued orange rounds, jewel-like pomegranate seeds and sprightly sprigs of basil.

4 blood oranges (if unavailable, use Valencia)
1 red onion
¼ cup rice-wine vinegar
Salt and freshly ground black pepper to taste
1 pomegranate
2 sprigs of fresh basil, stems removed
1 tablespoon extra-virgin olive oil
1 tablespoon sea salt (preferably Maldon)
Cracked pepper to taste

Peel blood oranges with a knife and cut into rounds to create cross-cuts of the segments. Shave red onion as thin as possible with a Japanese mandoline or a very sharp knife. Marinate onion shavings in rice-wine vinegar for about 20 minutes and season with salt and black pepper.

Cut pomegranate in half (around the equator). Hold half of the pomegranate in your hand and smack the skin side with a metal spoon, releasing the seeds into a bowl.

TO SERVE

Arrange blood oranges on a plate with the pickled onions, basil leaves and pomegranate seeds, reserving any extra blood-orange juice. Whisk juice with olive oil to create a quick vinaigrette. Drizzle over oranges and sprinkle with sea salt and cracked pepper. ▨

Joey Campanaro
CHEF AND CO-OWNER, THE LITTLE OWL

The place for taste

When a chef says he's inspired by Mexican food because "you can pick it up and eat it in your hands," you know this is a guy who cooks from the heart. No chitchat about spices. No mention of exotic produce. What's the story here?

The story is the phenomenal success of Joey Campanaro's gravy meatball sliders (see page 94) and his restaurant, The Little Owl. When the tiny eatery (only 10 tables) opened in 2006, newspapers, magazines, blogs and even TV shows heralded his version of the sloppy joe—a messy but mouthwatering trio of garlic and Pecorino buns filled with moist little meatballs in a garlicky tomato sauce.

"The sliders sum up the mood of the restaurant, which is comfortable, relaxed and homey," says Campanaro. "Diners don't need to worry about etiquette; they can just kick back and relax."

Already acclaimed for his cooking at The Harrison and Pace, Campanaro creates wonderfully lusty food. Think gnocchi with oxtails, lamb shanks in a fontina fondue and a dish referred to simply as "the pork chop." But what a chop it is—big and juicy, marinated in fennel and garlic, laced with curry and cayenne, and grilled to perfection. Even when he uses luxe ingredients like oysters or duck breast, the result is food that comforts the soul.

That may be due in part to Campanaro's childhood. He grew up in Philadelphia, where food was the heart of the home, nurtured by meals from his Italian grandma. (In fact, her recipe inspired the sliders.) After taking a job as a dishwasher on the Jersey Shore, he became hooked on the warm fraternity of the restaurant kitchen. "I liked the work ethic; everyone had something to do, and there was always something to be done" he explains. "Now I'm in the leadership role, but I'm still using my hands and seeing something through from start to finish."

Which can be a real challenge in a kitchen as small as the one at The Little Owl—only 7 feet by 10. "We had no room for a pastry chef, so I needed to learn how to make pastry," says Campanaro, laughing at the memory. "It turned out to be a blessing in disguise, because now our sweets really complement our savories." And the desserts are as down-home as the entrées—a fruit tart with mascarpone gelato or raspberry beignets or chocolate cake.

He goes on to explain how the logistics of turning out a dish govern his creativity. "Cooking in a restaurant is so different from cooking at home. You

THE LITTLE OWL
90 Bedford Street
New York, NY 10014
212-741-4695
www.thelittleowlnyc.com

On the side...

What do you consider the most overrated ingredient?
I don't think any ingredient is overrated, but some, like salt, can be misused. You always need to keep a balance.

The most underrated ingredient?
Curry.

What is your favorite comfort food?
Macaroni and cheese.

What kitchen gadget is your must-have tool?
The hand sink. I do a lot of mixing and working with my hands, so I need to wash up a lot.

If you were not a chef, what would you be?
An architect.

What was the last thing you ate?
Monkfish for dinner at Market Table.

need to think in multiples, so technique is extremely important, as is organization," he states. "And, of course, you need to consider the wow factor." This may mean an unexpected side, such as glazed butterbeans doused with Parmesan, or an innovative presentation like wrapping oysters in lettuce leaves to produce yet another finger food.

But for Campanaro it all boils down to this: "I wanted a place that delivered quality, value and fun, where people didn't have to drop a lot of money for a memorable experience."

And he has it in The Little Owl. ■

The recipes

"The sliders sum up the mood of the restaurant, which is comfortable, relaxed and homey."

Gravy Meatball Sliders

SERVES 12 AS AN APPETIZER

From the day The Little Owl opened, these sliders were a hit, garnering praise from *The New York Times*, *New York* magazine and other publications and blogs. Make them with the recipe here and find out for yourself what all the fuss is all about.

1 pound ground beef
1 pound ground pork
1 pound ground veal
3/4 cup freshly grated Pecorino-Romano cheese, plus 1/4 cup for garnish
1 cup panko (Japanese bread crumbs)
3 large eggs
1 bunch fresh parsley, chopped and divided
Salt and pepper to taste
3 cups vegetable oil for frying meatballs
2 to 3 tablespoons olive oil
1 Spanish onion, chopped
1/4 cup chopped fresh garlic
1 bunch fresh basil
1 tablespoon fennel seed
1 #10 can (96 ounces) whole peeled tomatoes
1 bunch arugula, well washed and dried

Mix the ground meats with the cheese, the panko, 2 cups cold water, the eggs, three-fourths of the chopped parsley, and salt and pepper to taste.

Form the mixture into 36 golf-ball-size meatballs. In a large, shallow saucepot or cast-iron skillet, heat the vegetable oil.

When hot, add the meatballs and cook until browned all over. With a slotted spoon, remove the meatballs and set aside.

Discard the vegetable oil but leave the browned bits of meat in the pan and heat the olive oil. Add the onion, the garlic, the basil, and fennel seed. Cook for 5–8 minutes until slightly brown.

Add the can of tomatoes and half a can of water. Cook the sauce over medium heat for 30 minutes; pass the sauce through a food mill and return to the pan. Add the meatballs to the sauce and cook for an additional 30 minutes.

TO SERVE

Either buy or make 36 small garlic buns. Cut buns in half and toast, cut sides up, in oven. Top the meatballs with the remaining Pecorino and remaining parsley. Place a few arugula leaves on the bottom half of bun, place the meatball on top with a bit of sauce; add the top of bun, using a skewer or toothpick to hold it in place. Repeat until all buns are assembled; serve 3 per portion. ◼

Gravy Meatball Sliders

The recipes

Roasted Char with Olive Crostini and Cucumber Slaw

SERVES 12 AS AN APPETIZER
This dish turns simple seared fish into a memorable mélange of flavors.

FOR THE FISH
12 (2-ounce pieces) boned Arctic char (or Spanish mackerel or bluefish, skin removed)
Sea salt (Maldon is a good choice)
Freshly ground pepper
½ cup extra-virgin olive oil plus extra for searing and for olives

FOR THE SLAW
2 hothouse cucumbers
½ red onion, sliced thin
1 tablespoon chopped fresh basil
Salt and freshly ground pepper to taste
1 tablespoon Dijon mustard
½ cup extra-virgin olive oil
Juice from 1 lemon
¼ cup cherry tomatoes, cut in halves
1 head frisée

FOR THE CROSTINI
Extra-virgin olive oil
¼ cup pitted kalamata olives
1 baguette

TO MAKE THE FISH
Season fish with sea salt and pepper and drizzle skin side with olive oil. In a large skillet over high heat, sear the fish, skin side down, keeping burner on high to retain heat. Turn fish and quickly sear on the other side, adding more oil if necessary. Remove and reserve at room temperature.

TO MAKE THE SLAW
Julienne the cucumbers and mix them with red onion and basil.

Season with salt and pepper.

Mix the mustard, the olive oil and lemon juice. Add to the cucumber mixture and reserve.

TO MAKE THE CROSTINI
Preheat oven to 400°F.

Chop the olives and mix with a little olive oil to bind.

Cut the bread into thin slices, top with the olives and toast in oven for 15 minutes.

TO SERVE
Mix tomatoes and pieces of frisée with the cucumber slaw and place in the center of the plate. Top the salad with the seared fish. Serve with olive crostini on the side. ■

Duck Breast with Arugula and Almond Salad with Parmesan and Truffle Oil

SERVES 4
A satisfying lunch or first course, perhaps as a prelude to pasta.

1 shallot, minced
1 tablespoon sherry vinegar
¼ cup extra-virgin olive oil
1 teaspoon truffle oil
1 teaspoon Dijon mustard
1 (6 ounce) Long Island duck breast
Salt and pepper to taste
¼ cup sliced almonds
1 bunch arugula, cleaned
1 tablespoon grated Parmesan cheese

First make a vinaigrette by whisking together the shallot, vinegar, olive oil, truffle oil and mustard. Reserve.

Season the duck with salt and pepper and place in a cold pan over medium heat, skin side down. Cook until the fat is separated from the meat and the skin is golden brown and crispy. This will take approximately 6–8 minutes. Then turn the breast over and turn off the heat. Keep in the pan for about 3 minutes. Remove the duck breast and allow to rest. Discard fat or save for later use.

In a small skillet, toast the almonds over low heat until uniformly browned. Note: Watch them carefully, stirring or shaking the pan often so they do not burn!

In large bowl, place arugula, almonds and Parmesan and toss with the vinaigrette.

TO SERVE
Place the salad in the center of 4 plates. Slice the duck thin and place on top of salad. ■

Kenny Callaghan
EXECUTIVE CHEF AND PITMASTER, BLUE SMOKE

Smokin' hot

One would think that the mastermind behind Manhattan's premier barbecue restaurant would hail from one of America's great barbecue capitals—Texas, maybe, or the Carolinas. But one would be wrong. Kenny Callaghan, executive chef and pitmaster of Blue Smoke, is a Jersey boy. "I needed to do a lot of homework for this job," he admits. Indeed, his experience at the Helmsley, the Russian Tea Room and Union Square Cafe had nothing to do with dry rubs and the art of smoking. But stoked by the challenge of something different, he hit the road, traveling throughout the South and entrenching himself in all things barbecue.

"The trip was fascinating, but not too good for the belly," laughs Callaghan, referring to the amount of food he "needed" to eat. Along the way he learned the finer points of the culture and the regional differences. Kansas City barbecue, for instance, is famous for ribs and relies on a sweet and tangy tomato-based sauce, while the Carolinas swear by a concoction of vinegar and peppers and specialize in pulled pork. Texas, on the other hand, is all about beef, notably beef brisket.

Kenny Callaghan
EXECUTIVE CHEF AND
PITMASTER, BLUE SMOKE

The more Callaghan learned, the more his restaurant concept kept changing. "I wanted to bring a little of my former experience here, so the menu and the service is more sophisticated than a typical barbecue joint. I also wanted to offer something for everyone: We serve a number of different regional dishes, some homestyle favorites like fried chicken and pork chops, a variety of fish and wonderful fresh greens and vegetables from the greenmarket."

The biggest surprise for Callaghan in cooking barbecue was "the fact that you can't redo." What he means is that most barbecue takes hours, even days to make. First, the meat (think big, big cuts) must be thawed; then it needs to be butchered, then the dry rub is applied. Finally, it gets put into the pit, where it takes anywhere from 7 to 18 hours to smoke. "So if something gets overcooked, you can't just grab another piece of meat and put it on the sauté pan. It's a much more complicated and expensive process than people imagine," explains Callaghan.

So what advice does this BBQ pro have for the home griller? First, choose a charcoal grill over a gas one: "The flavor is far superior." Second, remember that smoke is supposed to enhance the flavor of the meat, not overpower it, so use the wood judiciously. Callaghan likes applewood and cherry chips for ribs and prefers hickory, oak or mesquite for thicker cuts, such as

BLUE SMOKE
116 East 27th Street
New York, NY 10016
212-447-7733
www.bluesmoke.com

On the side...

What do you consider the most overrated ingredient?
Sweeteners. Many dishes don't need such a high content of sugar or other sweet ingredients.

The most underrated ingredient?
Pepper. Black, white, mixed, Aleppo... any of them.

What is your favorite comfort food?
Pizza.

What kitchen gadget is your must-have tool?
The grill—of course!

If you were not a chef, what would you be?
A guitarist in a rock band.

What was the last thing you ate?
Pizza! I made it for my family: mozzarella and tomato for the kids, fontina, white truffle oil and grilled mushrooms for my wife. I had both!

prime rib, beef brisket or pork shoulder. Third, feel free to experiment with different rubs, but remember that the best are a little spicy, a little sweet and include something acidic, such as lemon, for balance.

And, finally, always have some great sides on hand. Some obvious good choices are cole slaw, baked beans, collard greens and cornbread, but two of Callaghan's biggest sellers are his famous deviled egg appetizer (opposite) and his mac and cheese side dish.

"Go figure!" he says. ■

The recipes

Deviled Eggs

SERVES 5–6 AS AN APPETIZER

The deviled eggs at Blue Smoke are always a treat. Two mustards and curry powder give them real snap, and Chef Callaghan's toasted almond garnish brings unexpected crunch.

10 eggs
Salt to taste
7 tablespoons mayonnaise
1 teaspoon of champagne vinegar
1/2 teaspoon of Coleman's dry mustard
2 teaspoons Dijon mustard
1/4 teaspoon cayenne pepper
Freshly ground pepper to taste
1/4 teaspoon curry powder
Watercress and toasted almonds (for garnish)

Place eggs in a 4-quart pot of cold salted water. Bring to a boil over high heat, then lower heat and simmer the eggs for exactly 9 minutes.

Remove eggs from water and run under cold water to cool.

Gently crack the shells of the hard-boiled eggs and peel under cool running water.

Cut a small sliver off each end of each egg, so that they sit flat on a plate.

Cut the eggs in half widthwise, making sure to leave the same amount of egg white on either side of the knife.

Remove the yolks and set aside.

The egg whites should now look like equal-size "cups."

Place egg yolks in a food processor and blend until smooth.

Mix in mayonnaise, vinegar, the two mustards, cayenne, salt and pepper and curry powder.

Place egg-yolk mixture into a pastry bag with a star tip.

Pipe mixture into egg-white cups so they resemble rosettes.

Refrigerate immediately.

TO SERVE
Serve chilled on a large platter with sprigs of watercress and toasted almonds as a garnish. ▪

Herb-Marinated Hanger Steak

SERVES 4

As proof that sometimes the simplest preparation can be the smartest—Callahan grills these steaks, marinated with garlic and a trio of herbs. Although the steaks need to sit in their fragrant bath at least overnight, the total effort on your part takes less than 10 minutes.

4 (6–8 ounce) pieces hanger steak, trimmed
4 large sprigs fresh rosemary
4 sprigs fresh thyme
4 sprigs fresh sage
4 cloves garlic
1 cup olive oil
Kosher salt and freshly ground black pepper to taste

Place trimmed hanger steaks in a bowl.

Place all the herbs in the bowl with the steaks. With the side of a knife, lightly crush garlic cloves; add to bowl. Add olive oil. Mix all ingredients together to coat steaks evenly. Allow to marinate for 12–36 hours, mixing occasionally. Remove steaks from marinade and allow most of the oil to drip away.

Season steaks liberally with kosher salt and black pepper to taste.

On a hot grill, cook steaks for 3 to 4 minutes per side, turning occasionally.

TO SERVE
Remove the steaks from grill, allowing the meat to cool for at least 5 minutes before slicing. Slice steak thinly against the grain and serve. ▪

Smothered Grilled Pork Chops

The recipes

"[With barbecue,] if something gets overcooked, you can't just grab another piece of meat and put it on the sauté pan. It's a much more complicated and expensive process than people imagine."

Smothered Grilled Pork Chops

SERVES 2

In addition to the authentic pit-barbecued ribs that Blue Smoke is noted for, Chef Callaghan offers other down-home classics. These grilled pork chops, slathered with a roasted pepper-onion sauce, are sure to satisfy the country soul in you.

2 large red bell peppers
2 tablespoons plus 2 teaspoons vegetable oil
1 large Spanish onion, peeled and thinly sliced
1 tablespoon all-purpose flour
2 tablespoons capers
2 tablespoons apple-cider vinegar
¼ cup white wine
1 cup chicken broth or veal stock
Kosher salt and freshly ground black pepper to taste
1 tablespoon fresh parsley, chopped
2 (10-ounce) center-cut, bone-in pork chops

Preheat grill to medium-high heat.

Spear each pepper with a kitchen fork or skewer and hold over an open flame until charred. Place the charred peppers in a paper bag until they are cool enough to handle. (This step completes the cooking of the peppers and facilitates removing the skin.) Rub off the skins (never run them under water, which washes away the flavorful oils) and discard the seeds. Cut peppers into long, thin strips and reserve.

Place a medium-sized, heavy-bottom skillet over medium heat and add 2 tablespoons of the vegetable oil. Add sliced onion and cook, stirring frequently, until onion is soft and lightly brown, about 15 minutes. Stir in the flour and cook an additional 2 minutes, stirring constantly. Stir in reserved peppers and the capers.

Add vinegar and white wine and reduce until almost dry. Add chicken or veal stock and bring to a simmer.

Reduce until the sauce thickens and coats the back of a spoon. Adjust seasoning with salt and pepper. Stir in the parsley and remove from the heat.

Lightly brush pork chops with remaining 2 teaspoons vegetable oil and season with salt and pepper.

Place pork chops on hot grill and cook for 6 to 7 minutes per side. As the pork chops are finishing on the grill, return sauce to the heat and bring to a simmer.

TO SERVE

Transfer the pork chops to a heated platter and, using a large spoon, smother them with the onion-pepper sauce and serve immediately. ▪

Melissa O'Donnell
CHEF AND OWNER, SALT

The happy chef

Salt features long, communal tables and an open kitchen. It offers a menu that allows patrons to select their own sides or choose pairings the chef has arranged. It has a small, capable staff that delights in pleasing its customers. What does all this tell you about the chef-owner, Melissa O'Donnell? Well, she definitely aims to please. Right off the bat she'll tell you, "My food's not about me. Food is a medium that allows people to connect. I like seeing people happy—that's one of the reasons I have an open kitchen."

O'Donnell has long been on a mission to make people happy.

In her twenties, she took a job at Covenant House, helping homeless youth. But the salary was not enough to live on, so she supplemented it with tips from waiting tables. Those tables became more and more important in her life, and she decided she wanted to cook for others. (It didn't hurt that her boyfriend at the time wanted to marry a female chef.)

The idea of good things happening around good food was always in O'Donnell's mind. Once she's drawn people into her intimate space, she keeps them coming back by giving them memorable flavors based on the freshest ingredients and lots of choice. "At Salt, we change the menu more than four times a year, as new ingredients come in to the purveyors. I'm constantly in touch with them, because everything depends on the weather," she explains.

"I try to put out the best ingredients possible. We use only organic meats and fish, and our customers really respond to that. I cook the way I do so I can showcase products at their peak. I don't want to wow anyone by changing something into something else. A really good carrot is truly great—it doesn't need to be anything else."

As a nearly lifelong resident of New York, O'Donnell loves the city but acknowledges that its hectic pace can come with a high price tag: a stressful, rushed lifestyle that leaves little time for making new friends and enjoying family. "I want to provide an environment where people can come together," she states. "In New York, there are fewer and fewer places where we can get that neighborhood feel. At Salt, the customers contribute to the environment. On a weeknight, there are two cooks, two waiters and me. It's very intimate

> SALT
> 58 MacDougal Street
> New York, NY 10012
> 212-674-4968
> www.saltnyc.com

On the side...

What do you consider the most overrated ingredient?
Foam. I'm sick of foam on everything.

The most underrated ingredient?
Bluefish. It's one of the best fish, but no one ever puts it on the menu. If it came from New Zealand and cost $20 per pound, everyone would want it.

What is your favorite comfort food?
Hot dogs.

What kitchen gadget is your must-have tool?
A fish spatula. I'm not really into gadgets, but since I cook a lot of fish, it's really helpful. I also like the hand blender.

If you were not a chef, what would you be?
I'd be a cooking teacher.

What was the last thing you ate?
A steak sandwich at Salt.

and very different from a big corporate restaurant."

And different, too, is her attitude about cooking. "I think men and women approach cooking very differently. I'm not convinced cooking is an art. My job is to make what's good better, to enhance but not to change. I'm a minimalist, a strong believer that less is more. I was once asked if I was passionate about food, and I didn't really know how to answer. I thought about it and realized that even though I tried to quit a few times and do something else, I was always pulled back in. I'm just happiest in the kitchen." ■

The recipes

Chicken Liver Mousse with Sweet and Sour Shallots

SERVES 6–8

Chef O'Donnell notes that this very versatile appetizer recipe is great for entertaining—whether or not you make the sweet and sour shallots: "You can present the mousse with the sweet and sour shallots on the side, or spread it on the toast points and top with the shallots. If you don't have time, top the mousse with a marmalade or chutney of some sort. At the restaurant we make a fig, balsamic and almond compote that goes well."

FOR THE CHICKEN LIVER MOUSSE
1 pound chicken livers
Salt and pepper to taste
2 tablespoons cooking oil (preferably a canola/olive oil blend)
2 shallots, diced
1/4 cup chopped fresh thyme
10 tablespoons unsalted butter, COLD and cut into small cubes, divided
1 teaspoon ground nutmeg
1/4 cup brandy
Salt and pepper to taste

FOR THE SWEET AND SOUR SHALLOTS
1/2 cup butter
10 shallots, peeled and sliced thinly
1/3 cup sherry or balsamic vinegar
1/2 cup honey
2 tablespoons chopped thyme
1/3 cup dried cherries

ON THE SIDE
Toast points, crostini or small loaf of bread

TO MAKE THE CHICKEN LIVERS

Drain and wash the chicken livers. Pat dry. Season the livers with salt and pepper. Place a sauté pan over high heat until very hot, then add oil. Bring the oil up to the smoking point. Add the chicken livers, turning to get color on all sides. Add the shallots, thyme and 2 tablespoons of butter to the pan. Cook for a short time until butter melts, shallots and thyme are slightly soft, and chicken livers are medium-rare. Do not overcook the chicken livers, as the flavor and appearance are much nicer when they are pink inside.

While the chicken liver mixture is hot (this is very important!) place it in a food processor workbowl with the nutmeg and blend until smooth. While the processor is still running, add the brandy. Add 5 1/2 tablespoons butter cubes very slowly in small batches. (You are emulsifying the mixture to give it the mousse texture, so it is important that the butter is cold and gets blended slowly.) Taste to check flavor. If you want a subtler, creamier texture, rerun the processor and add the remaining 2 1/2 tablespoons butter cubes. Salt and pepper to taste. Pass the mixture through a fine-mesh strainer. Place in a ramekin and refrigerate until set (about 2 hours). You can also line a timbale or terrine mold with plastic wrap, fill with the mousse, refrigerate, and then unmold for a different presentation.

TO MAKE THE SHALLOTS

Melt butter in a sauté pan over medium heat and add shallots. Cook slowly until they are soft and start to brown. Add vinegar and reduce until almost dry. Add honey and thyme and simmer. The honey will bubble up, so leave room in the pan for it to do so. Cook until the honey thickens and has a chance to caramelize a little and develop a nutty flavor (about 15–20 minutes). Add cherries in the last 5 minutes of cooking; remove from heat and cool.

TO SERVE

Present the chicken liver mousse with the cooled sweet and sour shallots on the side, along with toast points or crostini. Chef O'Donnell prefers toasted challah or brioche for an elegant mood, or toasted stirato or even rye for a more rustic country feel. ∎

Salt

The recipes

"My food's not about me. Food is a medium that allows people to connect. I like seeing people happy—that's one of the reasons I have an open kitchen."

Cream of Cauliflower Soup with Mushroom Fricassee and Truffle Essence

SERVES 4

Chef O'Donnell is known for creating a warm, communal atmosphere that features seasonal ingredients. Of this recipe, she says, "We use a mixture of cremini, portobello and shitake mushrooms at the restaurant, but you could make it with just the shitake or the portobellos. I don't think the creminis can stand on their own."

FOR THE SOUP
1 head of cauliflower, chopped into very small pieces
3 shallots, chopped
3 tablespoons fresh thyme, chopped
½ cup unsalted butter
2–3 cups chicken stock
1 cup heavy cream
1 tablespoon ground nutmeg
Salt and pepper to taste

FOR THE MUSHROOM FRICASSEE
1 cup mixed mushrooms (preferably portobello, cremini and shitake), diced
Cooking oil (preferably a canola/olive oil blend)
¼ cup chicken stock
1 tablespoon butter
1 shallot, diced
1 tablespoon fresh thyme, chopped
Salt and pepper to taste
Truffle oil for garnish

TO MAKE THE SOUP
In a nonreactive pot, sweat cauliflower, shallots and thyme by cooking, covered, in the butter over very low heat until moisture is released and all are soft. Do not brown. Add chicken stock to cover the cauliflower and simmer for 20 minutes or until cauliflower is very soft. Place in a blender and process until smooth. Add cream and nutmeg and blend. Add salt and pepper to taste.

TO MAKE THE MUSHROOM FRICASSEE
Clean mushrooms. For portobello and creminis, remove stems and dice into ½-inch cubes. Remove stems from the shitakes and discard; leave caps whole.

Place a nonreactive pan on the stove over high heat and let it become very hot. Lightly coat with cooking oil and heat until smoking. Add mushrooms and sauté quickly until oil is absorbed and mushrooms get color on all sides. (Make sure not to overcrowd the pan or the mushrooms will steam and not brown.) Add chicken stock and reduce until the pan is almost dry and the mushrooms are soft. Add butter, shallot and thyme and simmer for 3–5 minutes. Add salt and pepper to taste. Remove from pan.

TO SERVE
Divide soup into 4 bowls. Top with mushrooms spooned into the center of the soup. Drizzle generously with truffle oil. ■

Slow-Roasted Eggplant with Beet Tartare and Blue Cheese Fondue

SERVES 4

Most of the components of this recipe can be made in advance. In fact, the beet tartare improves with one day in the refrigerator. If you have to reheat the fondue, add a little milk or heavy cream to keep it from burning. However, the eggplant is best made just before serving.

FOR THE EGGPLANT
1 eggplant
Salt, pepper and olive oil for drizzling

FOR THE BEET TARTARE
1 pound beets
Extra-virgin olive oil for roasting beets,
plus 1/2 cup for processing
1 shallot, sliced
2 tablespoons chopped cornichons
4 tablespoons capers
1 tablespoon prepared Dijon mustard
4 tablespoons sherry vinegar
Salt and pepper to taste
2 tablespoons chopped Italian parsley (optional)

FOR THE FONDUE
1 cup heavy cream
1 stalk of rosemary
3 1/2 ounces blue cheese
2 ounces cream cheese
Salt and pepper to taste

FOR THE TOPPING
1 cup mesclun greens
1 1/2 teaspoons olive oil
1 teaspoon sherry vinegar
Salt and pepper to taste

TO MAKE THE EGGPLANT
Preheat oven to 350°F. Cut eggplant horizontally into 1-inch rounds. Lightly oil a baking sheet. Place eggplant on the baking sheet and season with salt and pepper on both sides. Allow the eggplant to sit for 15 minutes so that the salt can draw out the bitterness. Sprinkle the top of the eggplant rounds with olive oil, cover with parchment paper and then aluminum foil and place in oven. Cook for 30 minutes or until the eggplant is cooked through to the center.

TO MAKE THE BEET TARTARE
Preheat oven to 500°F. Wash beets and coat with olive oil; wrap in aluminum foil. Place on a sheet pan and roast in the oven until a knife can be easily inserted into the center of the beets. Remove from oven and allow to cool slightly. Peel the beets by rubbing them with a dishtowel while they are still warm. Cut roughly to fit into the bowl of a food processor. Add shallot, cornichons, capers and mustard to the bowl with the beets and process until smooth. While running the processor, pour in sherry vinegar and then the remaining olive oil in a slow stream to emulsify the ingredients and smooth the texture of the tartare. Add salt and pepper to taste. If desired, stir in some chopped parsley by hand.

TO MAKE THE FONDUE
Place cream and rosemary in a nonreactive pot and bring to a simmer on the stovetop over low heat. Watch carefully so that as the cream comes up to a boil, it does not overflow. With a whisk, slowly stir in the blue cheese and cream cheese by adding about a tablespoon at a time. At this point, you may turn the burner down to very low, as you are not trying to cook anything, but rather just melt the cheeses into the cream. When cheese is incorporated, add salt and pepper to taste and remove the rosemary stalk.

TO SERVE
Toss the mesclun greens in olive oil and sherry vinegar; add salt and pepper to taste. On each plate, place about 1/4 cup of the warm (not hot) blue cheese fondue. On top of that place one large slice of eggplant. On top of that spoon about 1/4 cup of beet tartare. Artfully top with tossed mesclun greens and serve. ■

4 French

Throughout the seventies, eighties and even mid-nineties, the New York hot spots were high-end French establishments such as Lutèce, La Caravelle and La Côte Basque. Best-selling authors set scenes in their dining rooms; newspapers cited the people they served; the very monied and the very powerful maintained regular tables. These venues and the chefs who presided in their kitchens had great clout and great status. Multilayered dishes, complicated sauces and luxurious preparations were the order of the day, even for home cooks who zealously labored to re-create Julia Child's recipes.

As times and tastes changed, however, many fine French venues closed their doors. People made their way to more casual spots where prices weren't as steep and where dinner didn't take four hours. Yet the craving for French food remained and these days popular bistros and brasseries are tucked away in all corners of Manhattan. Some are endearingly classic, but many have taken on a brand-new guise. Consider Landmarc, a contemporary Tribeca eatery that fuses Italian and American flavors with traditional French favorites in a friendly, come-as-you-are style. For those who want something a bit more upscale, there's Terrance Brennan's Picholine, a bastion of sophisticated French cooking with vibrant new introductions such as Roquefort parfait.

Respect for French cuisine continues to run deep in the city. Many chefs interviewed for this book praise French technique, and cooks everywhere are still entranced by the idea of turning out the perfect soufflé. So actually, this is a very good time for Francophiles because there is so much choice, from sidewalk cafés and brasseries to old-world charmers like Café des Artistes, where you can find an authentic pot-au-feu alongside a crispy skate wing almondine. Vive la France!

Terrance Brennan, Artisanal

RECIPES

Wild King Salmon with Horseradish Crust, Cucumbers, Crème Fraîche and Salmon Caviar PAGE 112

White Gazpacho PAGE 114

Marc Murphy

Marc Murphy, Landmarc

RECIPES

Orecchiette alla Norcina PAGE 118

Mussels Marinière PAGE 118

Grilled Pork Chops with Caramelized Apples and Onions PAGE 118

Cyril Renaud

Cyril Renaud, Fleur De Sel

RECIPES

Butternut Squash Soup with Coconut Foam and Sautéed Scallops PAGE 122

Halibut with Glazed Endive and Pecan-Bacon Balsamic Reduction PAGE 123

George Lang, Café des Artistes

RECIPES

Pot-au-Feu PAGE 126

Bourride with Aioli PAGE 128

Marco Moreira, Tocqueville

RECIPES

Brandade-Crusted Cod with Olive Vinaigrette PAGE 131

Oven-Roasted Quail PAGE 132

Café des Artistes

Terrance Brennan, Picholine

RECIPES

Diver Scallops with Cauliflower and Blood Orange Grenobloise PAGE 137

Wild Mushroom and Duck Risotto PAGE 139

Terrance Brennan
CHEF AND OWNER, ARTISANAL FROMAGERIE & BISTRO

More than cheese

Terrance Brennan is a true Francophile with a lust for cheese. As he says, "Living and working in France, I developed a passion for cheese." When Brennan opened his fine-dining French restaurant Picholine (see page 134), he wanted to incorporate that obsession. "First, I did a cheese cart at the restaurant. Then, a selection of eight cheeses turned into ten, then twelve, and sixteen, and finally it just became too much—it was too time-consuming." But the concept of combining his love for cheese with classic French dishes remained at the back of his mind.

"Originally I wanted a cheese shop and a restaurant, but when I saw the beautiful space that became Artisanal in 2001, I just didn't want to chop it up. Putting a retail area in front wasn't going to work, so we ended up with the restaurant." Luckily, there is a counter near the bar where patrons can get goods to go, but the heart is the main dining room.

As Brennan says, "It's a very solid bistro—all about execution and correct cooking. You are transported to Paris when you walk in the door. It really is fun, with great food. People walk out talking about what a good time they had." Yes, it's a cheese-lover's paradise, with fondues to die for and a decadent Stilton parfait with contrasting textures of cheese, port gelée and crunchy walnuts. But the steak frites, slow-cooked lamb shank, Friday's bouillabaisse, and the baked salmon draw their own crowds, too.

Brennan's enthusiasm for the bistro style is clearly shared by patrons; the enjoyment is evident from the moment the door opens. As he explains, "The noise level is just right—there's a definite buzz, but you can hear what's being said at your table. It's exciting and the food is reasonably priced for New York. You could come in a few times a month." He muses, "Maybe it's because of the wines—there are 160 by the glass—and it's not a typical bar."

He's equally enthusiastic about his job as a chef. "The best thing about being a chef is giving pleasure to people and making things enjoyable. It's different every day. You're only as good as your last meal, so you have to stay focused." In addition to pleasing customers, Brennan revels in the process of developing new dishes. "I enjoy coming up with new menus. I keep lists of things that are available in each season

> ARTISANAL FROMAGERIE & BISTRO
> 2 Park Avenue
> New York, NY 10016
> 212-725-8585
> www.artisanalbistro.com

On the side...

What do you consider the most overated ingredient?
White truffle oil—it's full of chemicals and should not be used.

The most underrated ingredient?
Vegetables in general.

What kitchen gadget is your must-have tool?
A thermal circulator.

What is your favorite comfort food?
Thin-crust pizza cooked in a wood-burning oven.

If you were not a chef, what would you be?
A Broadway singer or an opera singer.

What was the last thing you ate?
Yogurt with dried fruit and nuts.

and I go back to them to work up some dishes and then taste everything," he explains. "I also go online to see what's happening around the world—and think about how different ingredients and different textures can be combined. New ideas come, and I tinker a lot before anything goes on the menu."

And as for cooking at home, Brennan counsels, "The home cook should keep it smart and simple. Think about how many pots and pans you'll be using, especially when you're entertaining. Do as much as you can ahead of time. In winter think about slow-cooked dishes that don't need constant attention, and in nice weather think about grilled things and just one or two simple hors d'oeuvres, like charcuterie or very high-quality cheese and olives." Just like at Artisanal. ∎

The recipes

Wild King Salmon with Horseradish Crust, Cucumbers, Crème Fraîche and Salmon Caviar

SERVES 4

Firm and mellow salmon can be easily paired with bold flavors. Here Chef Brennan creates a zesty crust for the fish fillets, then tops that with a creamy cucumber sauce and adds a final crown of caviar for a dish that's layered with amazing texture and taste.

FOR THE CUCUMBERS
1 (18-ounce) English cucumber
1/2 teaspoon salt plus extra to taste
4 tablespoons crème fraîche

FOR THE HORSERADISH CRUST
2 cups packed small bread cubes, crusts removed
1 tablespoon prepared mustard
2 tablespoons freshly grated horseradish
2 tablespoons smoked salmon, minced
2 1/2 tablespoons butter, softened
Salt and pepper to taste

FOR THE SALMON
4 (6–7 ounce) wild king salmon fillets, center cut, skin removed
Salt and pepper to taste
2 tablespoons oil
4 tablespoons salmon caviar

TO MAKE THE CUCUMBERS

Peel cucumber. Slice cucumber into 1/8-inch slices on a mandoline. Place in colander and toss with 1/2 teaspoon salt. Set aside for 1 hour to drain water from cucumbers. In an 8-inch sauté pan over medium low heat, add drained cucumbers and crème fraîche and toss to coat. Cook for 5 minutes until crème fraîche reduces and thickens. Add additional salt to taste. Set aside.

TO MAKE THE CRUST

Place bread cubes, mustard, grated horseradish, smoked salmon and soft butter in the bowl of a standing mixer fitted with a paddle attachment. Mix until mixture is well blended. Season with salt and pepper. Divide mixture into 4 rectangles, each 1/4-inch thick, 1 3/4-inch wide and 4-inches long. Set aside.

TO MAKE THE SALMON

Preheat broiler. Season salmon with salt and pepper. Place a 12-inch sauté pan over medium heat, add oil and heat. Add salmon fillets and cook for 2 minutes on each side. Salmon will be rare. Remove fillets from heat and let rest for 5 minutes. Using a spatula, place formed horseradish crust on top of each fillet. Place under broiler for 5 minutes until golden brown.

TO SERVE

Place each salmon fillet on a plate and spoon a dollop of caviar on top. Place cucumbers next to the fillet. Serve immediately. ▪

Wild King Salmon with Horseradish Crust, Cucumbers, Crème Fraîche and Salmon Caviar

The recipes

White Gazpacho

SERVES 6

This unusual soup makes an elegant first course on a summer evening or a refreshing lunch on a blazing hot day. For a heartier meal, Chef Brennan suggests garnishing the soup with chilled poached shellfish, such as bay scallops, shrimp or lobster.

2 cups plus 3 tablespoons peeled, thinly sliced almonds
1 cup seedless green grapes
3/4 cup cucumber juice, extracted from peeled cucumbers in a juicer or purchased from a juice bar
1/4 cup verjus (see note)
1 cup fruity extra-virgin olive oil
2 tablespoons plus 2 teaspoons sherry vinegar
2 small cloves garlic, peeled
1 cup small, crustless white-bread cubes
(from 1 1/2 ounces, or 3 slices bread)
1 tablespoon salt
1/2 teaspoon cayenne pepper
1 tablespoon red pepper, finely diced (optional)
1 tablespoon peeled, seedless cucumber, finely diced (optional)
1 tablespoon red onion finely diced, (optional)
1 tablespoon celery, finely diced (optional)
Red Gazpacho Granité (recipe follows)
30 cilantro leaves

Prepare the following in batches: Place 2 cups of the almonds, the grapes, cucumber juice, verjus, oil, vinegar and garlic into a blender. Pour in 3 cups of water and blend until uniformly smooth, approximately 4 minutes. Add the bread and process for 1 more minute. Taste, season with the salt and cayenne, taste again, and add more salt if necessary. Cover, and refrigerate for at least 3 hours or up to 24 hours. If it appears too thick after refrigeration, whisk in some cold water to thin it:

When ready to serve, put the remaining 3 tablespoons almonds in an 8-inch sauté pan and toast over medium heat, shaking constantly, until fragrant, 1 to 2 minutes. Transfer to a small bowl and let cool to room temperature.

If using all or some of the optional vegetables, combine them in a small bowl and stir gently but thoroughly. (This is your garnish.)

RED GAZPACHO GRANITÉ

1 pound fresh beefsteak tomatoes, cored and passed through a food mill (about 1 1/2 cups milled tomatoes)
2 tablespoons cucumber juice, extracted from peeled cucumbers in a juicer or purchased from a juice bar
1 tablespoon red-pepper juice, extracted in a juicer or purchased in a juice bar
2 teaspoons celery juice, extracted in a juicer or purchased in a juice bar
1 tablespoon sherry vinegar
1 teaspoon finely chopped garlic
Kosher salt
Pinch cayenne pepper, or more to taste

Put all ingredients except the salt and cayenne in a mixing bowl and stir together. Season with salt and a pinch of cayenne, or more for a spicier granité. Pour the mixture into a 9- x 9-inch freezerproof dish and put in the freezer. Freeze for at least 2 hours or until frozen, scraping the mixture with a fork every half-hour to break it into crystals.

The granité can be covered and frozen for up to 1 week. When ready to serve, scoop out portions with an ice-cream scoop.

TO SERVE

Divide the gazpacho among 6 shallow soup bowls. Place one 1/4-cup scoop of granité in the center of each bowl, sprinkle the vegetable garnish over each serving and arrange 5 cilantro leaves decoratively on top. ■

■ **NOTE** Verjus is the pressed juice of unripened grapes and has a gentler flavor than vinegar. It is available at gourmet shops, but if you can't find it, substitute 2 tablespoons sherry vinegar.

Artisinal Fromagerie & Bistro

Marc Murphy
EXECUTIVE CHEF AND OWNER, LANDMARC

The comfort zone

For someone who only wanted "a neighborhood restaurant where people could drop by for good, simple food," Marc Murphy has certainly come a long way. His Tribeca eatery, Landmarc, was a hit from the day it opened its doors in April 2004. So much so, in fact, that a larger version now sits in the famed Time Warner Center. And somewhere in between those two launches, Murphy also christened Ditch Plains, a casual fish and oyster bar where most of his staff hangs out.

But these endeavors aren't all that surprising, considering this is a guy who grew up in Italy and France, surrounded by good food and wine.

"I always loved eating, and when it came time to decide what I wanted to do with the rest of my life, I signed up for a three-month cooking course and was hooked," laughs Murphy. So, it seems, are patrons of his restaurants. Unlike many current menus, 70 percent of Landmarc's selections remain the same year-round, with only occasional changes. (For instance, in spring Murphy switches winter's braised lamb shank to a grilled lamb chop with a watercress salad on top.) "I want customers to be able to come back and order what they loved the time before," he explains. "There's a comfort level to that." Dishes are listed with straightforward descriptions, and standbys like steaks and mussels can be ordered with the customer's preferred sauce. "Diners should be able to 'see' what they'll be getting before it's on the plate. If a waiter needs to explain what the dish is, I don't serve it," Murphy states. This concept seems to be working, since "best-sellers are all over the place. There's no one dish—or even two or three—that sells that much better than others."

Murphy describes his food at Landmarc as "French bistro with Italian influences," which is why his 'plat du jour' is always pasta, while mozzarella and ricotta fritters share space on the appetizer array with foie gras terrine and French onion soup. "I keep things pretty classic," admits Murphy. "I don't go that far afield in my cooking; I don't jump on the new fad ingredient. I want the menu to be normal."

Where he does experiment is with the specials—and he really listens to the feedback. "My waitstaff keeps me informed about what people are saying. They're the diplomats who filter the info and give it back to me." So no matter how many plates went out, if

> *LANDMARC*
> *179 West Broadway*
> *New York, NY 10013*
> *212-343-3883*
> *www.anvilny.com*

On the side...

What do you consider the most overrated ingredient?
That foam stuff.

The most underrated ingredient?
Salt and pepper, of course. Or, the pig—all parts.

What is your favorite comfort food?
Pasta carbonara.

What kitchen gadget is your must-have tool?
Tongs.

If you were not a chef, what would you be?
An architect.

What was the last thing you ate?
A new cod dish at Landmarc, with white beans, chorizo, anchovies, sautéed spinach and a parsley pesto.

sweetbreads and kidneys didn't get a good reaction, you won't find it at the restaurant again.

Another thing you won't find are bland flavors. Murphy is a huge fan of salt and pepper and admits that he urges his staff to use more, more, more. "Adding the seasoning to the finished dish just doesn't do it," he says. "You need to put it on before you cook, whether you're boiling pasta or grilling meat." To prove his point, he encourages home cooks to cut a steak in half, season one half the way they normally would and put twice as much on the second section. Murphy swears the second half will taste much better. If it's anything like the food at Landmarc, he's right. ∎

The recipes

Orecchiette alla Norcina

SERVES 6–8

At Landmarc, a different pasta is served every day and one wishes they were all available all the time. This orecchiette is especially fantastic.

1 pound orecchiette pasta
Salt to taste
2 pounds Italian sausage (without fennel seeds)
3 tablespoons olive oil
3 cloves garlic, sliced thin
1 quart heavy cream
1½ tablespoons chopped fresh rosemary
1 cup freshly grated Parmesan cheese
Pepper to taste

Bring a large pot of salted water to a boil. Add pasta and cook until al dente. Strain and reserve; keep warm. Remove casings from sausage and crumble into small pieces. Heat the oil in a large sauté pan over medium heat. Add the sausage and brown lightly. Add the garlic and brown lightly. Add the cream and cook for about 3–5 minutes. Add pasta, rosemary and Parmesan. Season to taste with salt and pepper.

TO SERVE

Place pasta in small bowls and serve with Parmesan. ▧

Mussels Marinière

SERVES 4

Mussels take well to many preparations. This classic version always hits the spot and requires only minutes to make.

2 tablespoons olive oil
1 large shallot, peeled and sliced
2 garlic cloves, minced
2 pounds mussels, scrubbed and debearded
1½ cups dry white wine
Salt and ground black pepper to taste
6 tablespoons (¾ stick) unsalted butter, cubed
½ bunch chopped parsley
½ pint grape tomatoes

Heat oil in a large sauté pan over medium-high heat. Add shallots and garlic and cook until they begin to brown. Add the mussels and the wine and season with salt and ground black pepper. Cook until the mussels all open, around 4 minutes and remove with a slotted spoon to a large bowl.

(Discard any unopened mussels.) Reduce the heat to medium and add the butter, swirling around to emulsify. Toss in the parsley and the grape tomatoes and cook until just heated through. Season to taste with more salt and pepper.

TO SERVE

Pour sauce over mussels and garnish with more parsley, if desired. Serve with crusty bread or French fries. ▧

Grilled Pork Chops with Caramelized Apples and Onions

SERVES 4

Chef Murphy put pork chops back on the menu map when he introduced these, cooked in veal stock and red wine and served with a hefty helping of caramelized apples and onions.

¼ cup olive oil
4 center-cut pork chops
Salt and pepper to taste
1 cup red wine
2 cups veal stock
2 medium white onions, roughly chopped
2 Granny Smith apples, roughly chopped
4 sprigs fresh thyme
1 clove garlic, sliced
1 shallot, sliced
2 bunches of spinach, stemmed and washed

Heat a large sauté pan over high heat, and add a thin layer of some of the oil. When the oil is just starting to give off a little haze, season pork chops with salt and pepper and place in pan. Cook for about 5 minutes on each side and set on a plate in a warm oven until ready to serve. Add the wine to the pan and cook until almost dry, then add the veal stock and cook until reduced by half. Strain and reserve.

Heat another large sauté pan on high and add a thin layer of oil. When the oil begins to give off a little haze, add the onions. When the onions start to brown, add the apples and thyme. Season with salt and pepper. Set aside when the apples begin to soften.

Brown garlic and shallot in a hot pan, add spinach and cook briefly until wilted.

TO SERVE

Place a small pile of spinach in the center of the plate, top with apples and onions and then the chop. Spoon some of the reserved sauce over the pork chop; serve immediately. ▧

Mussels Marinière

Cyril Renaud
CHEF AND OWNER, FLEUR DE SEL

The Gallic way

When Cyril Renaud, chef and proprietor of Fleur de Sel, reveals that he knew that he wanted to become a chef from the tender age of 7, you don't doubt him for a moment. For this is a man who is so clearly focused and so sure about following his instincts that he took up paint and paper and fashioned whimsical watercolors to decorate his restaurant—without any previous training. "I just wanted to do it," he states, "so I did." The same might be said of his newest venture, the recently opened brasserie, Bar Breton.

Renaud, who grew up in Brittany, learned the art of Breton cuisine from his mother, and the cooking of that region is still close to his heart. So much so, in fact, that he named his acclaimed restaurant after the sea salt of the region. "It's what I call a feminine salt, very finely grained and refined," says Renaud.

"I use it in most every dish I prepare."

But make no mistake, Renaud's cooking goes far beyond the rustic dishes of his homeland. Before garnering a three-star review from *The New York Times* for his work at La Caravelle in 1998, he worked in restaurants in Paris, Belgium and London. The food at Fleur de Sel reflects this international background. A poussin (baby chicken) from nearby Sullivan County gets a distinctly French touch with a foie gras sauce; New Zealand venison is crusted in pistachio and fennel; diver scallops from Maine are accompanied by curried carrots, fresh grapefruit and honey gastrique. And dishes are constantly evolving because Renaud is always testing and tasting, never content to leave well enough alone.

Indeed, the restaurant itself, which he opened in 2000, put his whole family to the test: his father renovated the space, his mother did the interior, his wife managed the logistics. "There was very little planning, just some ideas," he says. "We wanted to see where the restaurant would lead, and over the years it's almost taken on a life of its own." But what has remained since the opening is the intimate, romantic setting, the friendly service and customer favorites like goat cheese ravioli, parsnip soup and the above-mentioned poussin.

FLEUR DE SEL
5 East 20th Street
New York, NY 10003
212-460-9100
www.fleurdeselnyc.com

On the side...

What do you consider the most overated ingredient?
Nothing. Every ingredient has merit, you just need to know how it use it.

The most underrated ingredient?
The parsnip.

What kitchen gadget is your must-have tool?
A blender.

What is your favorite comfort food?
Something very simple, like a good burger.

If you were not a chef, what would you be?
An artist.

What was the last thing you ate?
Some oranges and rice.

With Fleur de Sel's 10th anniversary in the near future, Renaud is still finessing the concept and looking for inspiration wherever he can find it—in markets, on the streets, through reading. "The important thing is not to fight your soul, but to be happy," he says with a very Gallic shrug. Right now he's fiddling with another endeavor—a small catering operation called Leapfrog. "It's a natural progression from the restaurants, and it's making me adapt to new situations," he states. "I love the adrenaline rush that comes from working under a lot of pressure."

Spoken like someone who's always up for a new challenge. ∎

The recipes

Renaud is (always) looking for inspiration wherever he can find it—in markets, on the streets, through reading. "The important thing is not to fight your soul, but to be happy," he says with a very Gallic shrug.

Butternut Squash Soup with Coconut Foam and Sautéed Scallops

SERVES 4

Diners have come to expect something special from this romantic restaurant, and Chef Renaud knows how to give it to them. Here, he boosts the creaminess of butternut squash soup by stirring in some coconut powder. A dollop of coconut foam on top amplifies the dish even further.

FOR THE SOUP
3 tablespoons olive oil
6 shallots, peeled and sliced into long, thin strips
1 whole butternut squash, peeled, seeded and cut into 1-inch pieces
3 tablespoons coconut powder (see note)
2 tablespoons ground nutmeg
1 tablespoon salt
1 teaspoon white pepper
1 quart whole milk

FOR THE FOAM
1 pint whole milk
3 tablespoons coconut cream

FOR THE SCALLOPS
Olive oil to sear
4 large scallops

TO MAKE THE SOUP
Heat olive oil in a large casserole. Add shallots and sauté until translucent. Add squash and sauté for 10 minutes. Stir in coconut powder, ground nutmeg, salt and pepper. Pour in milk to cover squash. Bring to a light boil and cook until squash is very tender (approximately 12–15 minutes).

Strain the squash and set aside the remaining milk mixture. In a blender, blend the squash to a creamy consistency, adding a small amount of the milk mixture if the squash needs additional moisture in order to become a creamy soup. Set aside the squash soup.

TO MAKE THE FOAM
Bring milk and coconut cream to a boil in a small casserole or saucepot. Remove from heat and set aside.

TO MAKE THE SCALLOPS
Coat sauté pan with olive oil and place on high heat. When oil starts to ripple, add scallops, searing one side for 3 minutes. Turn over scallops. With a spoon, baste each scallop with the oil in the pan and cook about 1 minute longer.

TO SERVE
Place each scallop in the center of 4 individual bowls. Bring the squash soup to a boil. Pour equal portions of the soup into each bowl. Using a hand blender, emulsify the coconut cream until frothy. With a spoon, scrape 2 tablespoons of foam from the surface of the coconut cream and place on top of the soup. ▮

▮ **NOTE** Coconut powder can be found at some gourmet and Indian food stores, or try Baker's Spray Dried Coconut Powder.

■ Fleur de Sel

Halibut with Glazed Endive and Pecan-Bacon Balsamic Reduction

SERVES 4

This is halibut like you've never had it before, served atop slightly bitter endive and drizzled with a sweet-salty sauce that reveals a surprising hint of pecan.

2 teaspoons olive oil
4 (6-ounce) halibut fillets
1 teaspoon butter
½ teaspoon sugar
3 teaspoons smoked bacon, finely chopped
4 teaspoons pecans, finely chopped
1 teaspoon vegetable stock
4 endives
6 teaspoons balsamic vinegar
Salt and pepper to taste
½ bunch fresh chervil, minced

Preheat oven to 200°F.

Over high heat, bring an ovenproof skillet or sauté pan (cast iron works well) to smoking hot and pour in olive oil. Sear halibut until it gets some color on both sides (just a couple minutes on each side). Place the pan in the oven to finish cooking the halibut; this should take about 4 minutes.

In a second skillet, add butter and place over high heat. When butter begins melting, add sugar and let it caramelize until it gets some color. Add bacon and pecans, allowing them to caramelize, and then add vegetable stock and endives. Sauté the mixture for 1 minute or until the stock is reduced and the endives are cooked. Once the endives are tender, add balsamic vinegar and let the mixture reduce by one-third. Add salt and pepper to taste, and the chervil.

TO SERVE

Separate leaves from endives, center and fan out on 4 individual plates. Place 1 halibut fillet on top of the endives and cover with the pecan-bacon sauce. ■

French • Cyril Renaud 123

George Lang
OWNER, CAFE DES ARTISTES

Only in New York

George Lang, a legendary figure in the New York restaurant world, doesn't let his more than five decades in the culinary business dampen his enthusiasm—not about food, not about making customers happy, and certainly not about life in general.

  And what a life it's been. Born in Hungary, he learned to appreciate food by watching his mother and grandmother cook. "They were both very good cooks, but it was how they cooked that was most important. Even if it was scrambled eggs, they did the same thing the same way every time, and so I could learn the dish."

  But his first vocation had nothing to do with food— he became a violinist after attending the prestigious Franz Liszt Academy of Music. But those happy days came to an abrupt end in 1944 when he was sent to a concentration camp. His entire family, save one cousin, was killed.

"Food is dazzling, really... America still is a place where wise experimentation based on knowledge is very accepted."

Using his wits, Lang escaped both the camp and later imprisonment in Communist-controlled Budapest. He found his way to America in 1946, bringing along his beloved violin. In a twist of fate, he was encouraged to play again by an old Russian émigré who lived in none other than the Hotel des Artistes apartment building, above the café he now owns. "I ended up working with the Dallas Symphony and at Tanglewood, but cooked sometimes for friends." Much as he loved to play, a musical career was not in the cards. "One evening, I had the opportunity to hear the great Jascha Heifetz play. The next day I put down the violin. I was not worthy."

His desire for perfection would soon find another outlet. Needing to find work quickly, he landed a job cleaning vegetables in the kitchen of the Plaza Hotel. Recalls Lang, "It was an amazing religion! I learned the simplest things and worked my way up over two or three years." That knowledge came in handy when he took a job downtown at a wedding hall. "I was shocked to see how differently the same dishes could come out for different weddings. I became manager without knowing a damn thing, but I had good taste. I understood what you have to do, the how and when

and—even more important—how to teach other people to do it." That taste level led him to the Waldorf Astoria, the Four Seasons and eventually his own consultancy business.

A few years later Café des Artistes became available for purchase—and partly because his home and office were on the same block, partly because he had his first New York fine-dining experience there, Lang bought the restaurant. In classic bistro style, it had a limited menu of seasonal dishes, and was a gathering place for artists and writers. Under Lang's direction, the menu got updated, but never strayed far from its roots of typical French Sunday-dinner fare, such as pot-au-feu or roasted chicken. But a few outstanding surprises, including sturgeon schnitzel, began to make their appearance.

Musing on the restaurant scene in New York today, Lang states, "It's totally dependent on novelty. I call it 'with' cuisine." What he means is that many dishes are simply lists of ingredients—this with this and that with that. "Almost everything is 'with' so chefs can call it their own, but unless you are a true master, with a real understanding of how to cook with a classical background, this just doesn't work. Sometimes new is just new, not good."

But Lang admits that the restaurant scene is inspiring. "Food is dazzling, really. Americans always want to be first, and America still is a place where wise experimentation based on knowledge is very accepted." Spoken with the knowledge, taste and good humor that are the hallmarks of George Lang. ∎

CAFE DES ARTISTES
1 West 67th Street
New York, NY 10023
212-877-3500
www.cafenyc.com

The recipes

Pot-au-Feu

SERVES 12

Escoffier called this dish the symbol of family life, and Mirabeau, the French revolutionary hero, went out on a metaphoric limb to say: "In the common pot-au-feu lies the foundation of the Empire." Perhaps that's stretching it, but this stew is a cold-weather favorite among nation-builders and common folk alike, and the aromas remind Chef Lang of his childhood.

FOR THE STEW
6 pounds beef short ribs
3 pounds beef brisket
1 (3-pound) veal shank
Coarse salt to taste
1 spice bag (a double thickness of cheesecloth, tied with butcher's twine) containing 6 sprigs of parsley, 1 sprig fresh thyme, 2 teaspoons cracked black peppercorns and 1 bay leaf
1 onion, peeled and halved, each half studded with 2 cloves
3 pounds marrowbones (about 6-inch lengths, individually wrapped in cheesecloth with both ends tied)
1 chicken, about 3 to 4 pounds
10 small carrots, peeled and quartered
1 medium-sized knob of celery, peeled and quartered
5 leeks, washed well to remove sand, trimmed, sliced in half lengthwise, and tied in a bunch
10 small turnips, peeled and trimmed
Freshly ground white pepper to taste

FOR THE HORSERADISH SAUCE
6 tablespoons freshly grated horseradish (or bottled, drained and rinsed)
1½ cups heavy cream
2 teaspoons Dijon mustard
2 tablespoons white-wine vinegar
Pinch of salt

FOR THE TABLE CONDIMENTS
Toast points for marrow
Coarse salt
Cornichons
Dijon mustard
Dark stone-ground mustard

TO MAKE THE STEW
Put ribs, beef brisket and veal shank in a deep soup pot; add salt and enough cold water to cover the meat (about 6 quarts). Bring to a simmer.

Add a few tablespoons of cold water to retard boiling in order to remove foam from the surface. Skim foam, repeating as necessary.

Add spice bag and studded onion halves and simmer, uncovered, for about 2 hours.

Add marrowbones and chicken. Continue to simmer for 1 hour. Skim foam from time to time.

Add vegetables and simmer approximately 45 minutes more, removing each vegetable as it becomes tender (test by pricking with a fork).

Remove string from cooked leeks. Keep all vegetables warm by putting them in a small pot with some of the cooking stock. Do not place over direct heat or vegetables will overcook.

Remove meats from cooking stock and keep warm (as with vegetables).

Strain stock through moistened cheesecloth into another soup pot. Bring to a simmer. Skim off any remaining fat, and season to taste with coarse salt and white pepper.

Discard spice bag and remove cheesecloth from marrowbones.

Remove chicken and reserve for another use (such as the base for chicken salad).

TO MAKE THE HORSERADISH SAUCE
Combine all ingredients in a mixing bowl and blend well. Adjust seasoning to taste with a bit more mustard or another pinch of salt. Serve at room temperature.

TO SERVE
Moisten meat and vegetables with some of the simmering bouillon. Then, ladle remaining hot bouillon in cups as a first course, followed by the hot toasts and marrowbones with marrow spoons for scooping. For the main event, slice the meat and present it on a heated oval platter with a lip. Surround it with vegetables. Offer the horseradish sauce, the coarse salt and other condiments as accompaniments. ■

Café des Artistes

The recipes

Under Lang's direction, the menu got updated, but never strayed far from its roots of typical French Sunday-dinner fare, such as pot-au-feu or roasted chicken.

Bourride with Aioli

SERVES 4–6

Bourride is a second cousin to bouillabaisse, a soup-stew enriched by two important staples of Provence: very fresh garlic and local olive oil. The Café des Artistes' recipe is based on versions Chef Lang has enjoyed in homes and restaurants in and around Marseilles.

FOR THE AIOLI

2 cups cold mayonnaise (preferably homemade)
1 garlic clove, finely minced
1/2 lemon, seeds removed
Coarse salt to taste
Freshly ground black pepper to taste
Cayenne pepper, to taste
2 pinches saffron threads

FOR THE BOURRIDE

1 cup extra-virgin olive oil, divided (French, if possible)
1/4 cup onion, diced
1/4 cup leek, white part only, julienned
1/4 cup fennel, diced
1/4 cup celery, diced
1/4 cup carrot, diced
3 cloves garlic
2 cups white wine
1 cup tomato, diced
Splash of Pernod
1 teaspoon saffron threads
Bouquet garni (bay leaves, fresh thyme, and Italian parsley wrapped in cheesecloth)
2 quarts fish stock (preferably made from bones or head of halibut, grouper, snapper, or a combination of all three)
Coarse salt to taste
Freshly ground black pepper to taste
Zest of 1 orange
2 pounds boneless fish fillet and shellfish (see note)

TO MAKE THE AIOLI

Combine the mayonnaise and garlic. Squeeze the lemon over the mixture, stir, and add salt, pepper and cayenne to taste.

In a small saucepan, simmer the saffron and 1/4 cup water until reduced to 1 teaspoon of liquid.

Whisk mayonnaise mixture into the saffron essence. Chill.

TO MAKE THE BOURRIDE

Put 1/2 cup of the olive oil into a deep, heavy casserole over medium heat. Sauté onion, leek, fennel, celery, carrot and garlic for approximately 10 minutes, stirring, making certain that the vegetables do not change color.

Add white wine, tomato, Pernod, saffron and bouquet garni, and cook for another 10 minutes.

Add fish stock and bring to a boil. Let cook approximately 15 minutes, until vegetables are soft.

Remove bouquet garni and put liquid in blender. Blend until smooth, then add remaining olive oil, salt and pepper to taste.

Return liquid to the pot and bring to boil. Add orange zest. Add fish and simmer until fish is cooked (approximately 5 minutes).

Remove cooked fish from liquid and place in large, rimmed serving dish; keep warm.

TO SERVE

Pour fish stock into a bowl and whisk in 1/2 cup aioli until smooth and creamy. Pour over fish. Place remaining aioli in a small serving dish. Pass both, allowing diners to select fish and top with aioli. ■

■ **NOTE** Choose at least 3 of the following types of seafood for the bourride: halibut, eel, monkfish, grouper, cod, snapper, shrimp, scallops, mussels and clams.

Marco Moreira
CHEF AND OWNER, TOCQUEVILLE

Subway to success

It could only happen in New York City: an 18-year-old from Brazil, homesick for good food and dreaming of opening a restaurant someday, starts talking to a stranger on the subway. The guy hands him a card from a sushi bar, and a short time later, the teenager begins working at that exact venue, learning the art of slicing and dicing. This is the way Marco Moreira, chef/owner of Tocqueville, got his foot in the restaurant door. "This was the early '80s, just when sushi was taking off. I was in the right place at the right time.

I was able to parlay my sushi skills into a catering business (which still exists) and then a consulting job with Dean & Deluca," says Moreira.

"To this day, I'm thankful for the experience because it taught me the importance of quality ingredients, as well as the fact that less really is more."

Many years and many jobs later, including tenures at Bouley, The Quilted Giraffe, and The Mark, Moreira and his wife, Jo-Ann Makovitsky, opened Tocqueville in a narrow, window-lit space on East

Marco Moreira
CHEF AND OWNER, TOCQUEVILLE

15th Street. Almost immediately, the cozy restaurant became the place to go. It was elegant, sophisticated, romantic—and the food was sublime. Patrons came back again and again, especially for the salt-encrusted 60-second steak and angel-hair carbonara with sea urchin.

Sounds like a happy ending, right? Well, yes and no. "The reviews were great, people loved the place, but the dining room was tiny and the kitchen even tinier. I couldn't cook certain dishes because I didn't have the right equipment, and we wanted to serve more people," explains Moreira.

So the couple took a giant gulp and moved. As luck would have it, they're just steps away from their original location, but the increased square footage means they can bake their own bread, cure their own bacon, keep an extensive wine cellar (over 5,000 bottles) and, best of all, offer an expanded menu. The 60-second steak, for instance, has become part of a duo, partnered with luscious braised beef cheeks.

Moreira admits that many people were nervous about the new-and-improved Tocqueville, but he swears the restaurant hasn't lost any of its soul. "I'm still the same kind of cook; I like to take rustic, humble dishes like risotto and grits or braised and roasted meats and turn them into something

> *TOCQUEVILLE*
> *1 East 15th Street*
> *New York, NY 10003*
> *212-647-1515*
> *www.tocquevillerestaurant.com*

On the side...

What do you consider the most overrated ingredient?
Kobe beef.

The most underrated ingredient?
Bananas.

What is your favorite comfort food?
Strawberry Häagen-Dazs, mashed potatoes and hot dogs—not necessarily in that order!

What kitchen gadget is your must-have tool?
My 20-year-old sushi knife. It's 5 inches shorter than when I first bought it!

If you were not a chef, what would you be?
A real-estate developer or a lawyer.

What was the last thing you ate?
Greek yogurt with honey for dinner.

special. From an early age, my grandmother taught me to rely on enhancing the natural flavors of ingredients—and that's what I do to this day."

Another thing Moreira still loves is sushi. So much so that he and Jo-Ann reinvented the old Tocqueville as 15 East, a Japanese restaurant. Although a different chef may be brandishing the sushi knives there, Moreira created the contemporary menu, which features such stellar dishes as tea-smoked duck magret and wild salmon five ways.

All of it just goes to show where a ride on the subway can lead. ∎

The recipes

"From an early age, my grandmother taught me to rely on enhancing the natural flavors of ingredients— and that's what I do to this day."

Brandade-Crusted Cod with Olive Vinaigrette

SERVES 4

Brandade is a classic French puree of salt cod, usually mixed with olive oil, garlic and cream. It's often served as a spread for slices of toasted bread, but Chef Moreira uses it as a coating for cod fillets, jazzing it up with the addition of potatoes, herbs and lemon confit.

FOR THE COD
2 medium Yukon Gold potatoes, with skin on
Salt and pepper
4 (3½ to 4 ounce) cod fillets, plus 5 ounces cod for brandade
2 cups extra-virgin olive oil
6 whole garlic cloves
2 bay leaves
3 sprigs lemon thyme
1 parsley sprig
5 peppercorns
½ cup milk
2 tablespoons butter, cold and cut into pieces
1 tablespoon lemon confit, chopped (if unavailable, use prepared lemon zest; see note)
Cayenne pepper, salt and black pepper to taste

FOR THE VINAIGRETTE
¼ cup niçoise olives, pitted and pureed
Juice of 1 lemon
¼ cup extra-virgin olive oil
Pepper to taste
1 tablespoon pink peppercorns
1 tablespoon chives

In a medium saucepan, cover the potatoes with cold water and a pinch of salt. Bring to a boil over high heat and cook until fork-tender. Meanwhile, season the cod fillets generously with salt and pepper and set aside.

Put olive oil, garlic, herbs and peppercorns into a small saucepan and cook for 20 minutes over medium heat. Add the 5 ounces of cod for the brandade to the pan and cook for 12–15 minutes over 200°F heat.

Drain the cooked potatoes while still hot; scoop out the solids from the olive oil mixture, add to the potatoes and put through a food mill. Heat the milk and add to the cod-potato mixture, then add the butter. Whip all together. Slowly add ½ cup oil that still remains in pan, then add the lemon confit and season with cayenne, salt and pepper to taste. Set aside and chill.

When the brandade is cold, spread it over the cod fillets and set them under a broiler for 8 minutes or until the brandade is a light-golden brown.

Meanwhile, whisk together all the ingredients for the olive vinaigrette.

TO SERVE
Center each cod fillet on individual plates and drizzle vinaigrette around it. ▇

▇ **NOTE** To make prepared lemon zest: In small saucepot, combine 1 tablespoon chopped lemon zest, cold water just to cover (approximately 2 to 3 tablespoons) and ⅛ teaspoon salt. Bring to a rapid boil. Put in a small strainer to drain off the hot water and run under cold water to cool off the lemon zest. Repeat process twice more. Drain and reserve.

The recipes

"I'm still the same kind of cook; I like to take rustic, humble dishes like risotto and grits or braised and roasted meats and turn them into something special."

Oven-Roasted Quail

SERVES 6

Even though this impressive dish uses foie gras and black truffle, there are such tiny amounts that Chef Moriera promises it won't break the bank—but it will send guests into a swoon.

FOR THE STUFFING

1 ounce fresh foie gras
1 ounce smoked bacon, diced
¼ French baguette or two French dinner rolls, crusts removed and diced
1 tablespoon canned, diced black truffle
1 teaspoon truffle juice (from can)
1 teaspoon chopped fresh parsley
1 teaspoon chopped chives
1 teaspoon chopped tarragon
1 egg, beaten
1 ounce quail broth or chicken broth

FOR THE QUAIL

6 semi-boneless quail (with wing and leg bones)

TO MAKE THE STUFFING

In a small sauté pan, heat pan on medium-high heat until smoky. Place foie gras in the pan and turn after it becomes golden brown, about 15 seconds, and repeat on other side. Remove foie gras from pan and place it on a paper towel to drain. Save any fat that is left in pan. Chill foie gras and dice into small pieces.

In small sauté pan over medium-high heat, render bacon until golden brown and reserve fat.

In a large mixing bowl, place the diced bread, foie gras, bacon, truffle, truffle juice and herbs. Add bacon and foie gras fat and mix until combined. Add egg and incorporate. If stuffing is moist and holding together, do not add broth. Add broth only if ingredients have not melded together. (The mixture should have the consistency of a moist stuffing.)

TO MAKE THE QUAIL

Preheat oven to 400°F.

Rinse the quails and pat dry. On a cutting board, lay out quails with the bellies up. Divide stuffing into six parts. Place stuffing in the cavity of each quail. Secure quails underneath legs with a toothpick.

Place quails in a small roasting pan and roast for about 16 minutes, until done.

TO SERVE

Serve each quail breast-side up with a frisée salad tossed with a sherry-oil vinaigrette, parsley and chives. ▪

Oven-Roasted Quail

Terrance Brennan
CHEF AND OWNER, PICHOLINE

Whistle while you work

"When I was 12," recalls Chef Terrance Brennan fondly, "my dad bought a small restaurant. Summers and weekends I worked there, making sandwiches and such. My dad was always singing and whistling in the kitchen." And that pleasant recollection set the course of his life. "By the time I was a sophomore in high school in Virginia, I knew what I wanted to be."

From there, Brennan took a variety of D.C.-area restaurant jobs, but got his real start in the kitchen within the Sheraton chain.

After working his way up in the group, he was offered an executive chef position, but he had other ideas. "I had never worked in a fine-dining establishment and wanted to come to New York and give that a try. I bought some copies of *Bon Appétit* and *Food & Wine* and made a list of the top

Picholine

Terrance Brennan
CHEF AND OWNER, PICHOLINE

restaurants in New York. I received a response from André Soltner at Lutèce, who said, 'I don't have an opening in my brigade, but come in and talk.' When I did, he actually called around and got me a place with Sirio Maccioni at Le Cirque! I slept on the couch of a friend of a friend."

It was hardly a warm, homey, singin'-in-the-kitchen environment, though, laughs Brennan: "At that point, there were 18 cooks—it went up to 36 later. It was crazy. I was responsible for expediting, but this was a true French kitchen—everything in French—and I didn't speak the language! I called it haute-cuisine boot camp. And it was a huge menu, over 30 different sauces alone. But if you could survive there, you could work anywhere." And that's exactly what he did. Several jobs in Europe followed, capped by another New York stint in the wild days of the '80s.

All those varied jobs are how Brennan learned his craft and developed a passion for French food. When it came time to try his hand at his own place in 1993, there was never a question in his mind that Picholine would be anything other than French. "It's a cuisine that lends itself to fine dining," he claims. "It's provocative, but we don't want customers to wonder what they're eating. It's very civilized with really high peaks"—meaning there are no valleys on the menu, just hills and mountains. Those include wild striped

■ Brennan on the line

bass with Basquaise chutney, couscous caviar and romesco mousse; Vermont saddle of rabbit with fresh tagliatelle, ramps and wild snails; or the enormously popular foie gras shabu-shabu.

Says Brennan mournfully of old-style French dining: "It's a dying breed—it's the food, of course, but it's really about the whole experience—the silver, the service, the petits fours at the end. Now you can open up a food counter and get four stars. Fine dining is becoming lost." But Picholine, especially with its 2006 revamp and two Michelin stars, proves that elegant French will always have a place in New York City. ■

PICHOLINE
35 West 64th Street
New York, NY 10023
212-725-8585
www.picholinenyc.com

The recipes

Diver Scallops with Cauliflower and Blood Orange Grenobloise

SERVES 4
Cauliflower may not be the first thing that springs to mind when you hear *scallops*, but don't be dissuaded from trying this recipe. Chef Brennan is known for his unique pairings that result in compelling dishes that are far greater than the sum of their parts.

FOR THE GRENOBLOISE SAUCE
6 tablespoons blood orange juice
1 tablespoon brown butter
1/8 teaspoon lemon juice
Small pinch salt
1 teaspoon parsley, chopped
1 tablespoon capers

FOR THE CROUTONS
1 tablespoon clarified butter
1 1/2 tablespoons 1/4-inch crustless white bread cubes
Salt to taste

FOR THE CAULIFLOWER PUREE
1 cup milk
8 ounces cauliflower, chopped
1 tablespoon mascarpone cheese
1 teaspoon salt

FOR THE ROASTED CAULIFLOWER
6 ounces cauliflower pieces, sliced evenly 1/4-inch thick
1 tablespoon extra-virgin olive oil
Salt to taste

FOR THE SCALLOPS
12 diver sea scallops, jumbo size
Salt and pepper to taste
4 tablespoons olive oil

TO MAKE THE GRENOBLOISE
In a small saucepan, boil the blood orange juice until reduced to 3 tablespoons. Mix with the rest of the ingredients in a small mixing bowl, then whisk until combined. Set aside.

TO MAKE THE CROUTONS
Heat clarified butter in a sauté pan over low-medium heat. Add the bread cubes and cook slowly until the butter begins to bubble around the edges and they turn a nice, even, golden color, approximately 3 minutes. Transfer the croutons to a clean paper towel to drain and season lightly with salt. Set aside.

TO MAKE THE CAULIFLOWER PUREE
Pour the milk plus 1 cup water into a saucepan. Add the cauliflower and cook until tender, approximately 10 minutes. Drain the cauliflower in a colander, place the cauliflower in a blender and puree until smooth. Pour the cauliflower into a mixing bowl and whisk in the mascarpone cheese. Season with salt.

TO MAKE THE ROASTED CAULIFLOWER
Preheat the broiler. Arrange the cauliflower on a baking sheet in a single layer and brush with olive oil. Season with salt and cook under the broiler until golden brown and tender, approximately 5 minutes. Set aside.

TO MAKE THE SCALLOPS
Season the scallops with salt and pepper. Heat a 12-inch sauté pan over medium-high heat. Add the olive oil. Add the scallops to the pan and sear until lightly golden brown on both sides and slightly opaque in the center, approximately 3 minutes on each side. Remove the scallops from the pan and keep warm.

TO SERVE
In a small saucepan over low heat, reheat the cauliflower puree.

Reheat the roasted cauliflower on the original baking sheet under the broiler until warm, approximately 1 minute.

Add the grenobloise sauce, parsley, capers and croutons to the pan and cook for 2 minutes over medium heat.

On 4 warm plates, spread the cauliflower puree evenly in the center of each plate. Place the scallops on top of the puree and spoon the sauce over each of the scallops. Place a piece of roasted cauliflower on top of each scallop. Serve immediately. ▨

Picholine's elegant bar

The recipes

"... It's really about the whole experience—the silver, the service, the petits fours at the end. Now you can open up a food counter and get four stars. Fine dining is becoming lost."

Wild Mushroom and Duck Risotto

SERVES 4

In this earthy fall dish from Picholine, creamy risotto is highlighted with woodsy wild mushrooms, duck confit and truffle oil for a rich and exotic taste sensation.

1 cup fava beans (from about 2 pounds fava beans in the pod)
2 tablespoons olive oil
½ cup wild mushrooms such as chanterelles, oyster or porcini, trimmed and wiped clean with a damp cloth, thinly sliced
6 tablespoons unsalted cold butter, divided
Kosher salt to taste, plus 1 teaspoon, divided
Freshly ground black pepper
¼ cup plus 2 tablespoons diced onion
½ teaspoon minced garlic
2 cups Carnaroli, Arborio or Vialone rice
½ cup dry white wine
4 cups homemade or low-sodium canned chicken stock
½ cup shredded duck confit leg (see note)
1 cup grated Parmigiano-Reggiano cheese (about a 3.75-ounce piece)
1 teaspoon white truffle oil

Fill large bowl half-full of ice water.

Pour 3 cups of water in a 1-quart saucepan and bring it to a boil over high heat. Add the fava beans and blanch for 1 minute. Transfer the beans to the ice water using a slotted spoon, shocking them to stop the cooking. Strain the beans and remove their outer skins. Set aside.

Heat olive oil in an 8-inch sauté pan set over medium heat. Add the mushrooms and cook until they begin to release their juices, about 4 minutes. Add 1 tablespoon of the butter and sauté for 2 more minutes. Season with the salt and 3 grinds of pepper. Remove the pan from the heat and set aside.

Melt 2 tablespoons of the butter in a 4-quart saucepan set over medium-low heat. Add the onions and ¼ teaspoon salt and cook until softened but not browned, approximately 4 minutes. Add the garlic and sauté for 1 minute. Add the rice and stir to coat the rice with the butter. Add the wine and continue to stir. Once the wine has been absorbed into the rice, add 1 cup of the chicken stock, stirring constantly. Once the stock has been absorbed by the rice, add another cup. Repeat the process with remaining stock, adding 1 cup at a time, stirring constantly. When complete, the risotto should be very thick and creamy and should hold its shape when stirred. Fold in the mushrooms, fava beans and duck confit.

Remove the pot from the heat and stir in the remaining 3 tablespoons butter, the Parmigiano-Reggiano, the remaining ¾ teaspoon salt, 6 grinds of pepper and the truffle oil. Mix well.

TO SERVE

Divide risotto among 4 plates or shallow bowls and serve immediately. ▪

▪ **NOTE** Duck confit is available at www.dartagnan.com.

While the term Classic American differs from region to region, certain foods, such as steaks and burgers, chops and chicken, and casseroles of all kinds are very "stars and stripes." Served across the land, from small-town grills and country inns to the great steakhouses of Manhattan, this kind of fare is rooted in the souls of most Americans, and for good reason—versions of these dishes have been around since the 18th century. Even the most adventurous foodie craves such stalwarts every now and then.

What isn't so classic, however, is the way contemporary chefs—both pro and amateur—are amping up this beloved cooking style. Roast chicken, for example, may get a kick from herbed butter under the skin; mashed potatoes might be laced with truffle cream. Part of the explanation lies in the fact that today's Americans have more sophisticated palates. People might want simple, homey food, but they don't want it bland; exposure to ethnic cuisines has increased the demand for more assertive flavors. At Bridge Café, Chef Joseph Kunst isn't content with a plain grilled pork chop; he jazzes it up with Cajun spices and a sweet onion gravy. Beacon, with its open wood-burning oven, couldn't look more American classic, but Chef Waldy Malouf works hard at making the genre hipper. Roasted offerings include surprises like oysters, and his mac 'n' cheese is done with Roquefort.

Indeed, this genre has had a very tasty makeover and is now more appealing than ever.

Classic American

Joseph Kunst, Bridge Café

RECIPES

Sesame-Crusted
Red Snapper with Shrimp
and Pepper Stir-Fry PAGE 144

Crab and Tomato Bisque
with Basil PAGE 146

Crab, Spinach and
Artichoke Fondue PAGE 146

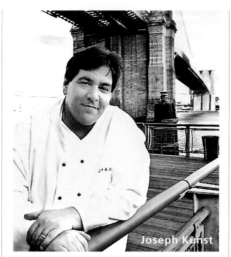

Joseph Kunst

Waldy Malouf

Bill Telepan

Bill Telepan, Telepan

RECIPES

Chickpea Pancakes with Spicy
Carrots and Oregano Oil PAGE 149

Slow-Roasted Shoulder of Veal
with Spring Vegetables PAGE 150

Corn Soup with Scallions
and Roasted Corn Sautéed in
Brown Butter PAGE 150

Telepan's Corn Soup

Waldy Malouf, Beacon

RECIPES

Roasted Oysters with Shallots
and Herbs PAGE 155

Rib Steak
with Citrus Rub PAGE 156

Wood-Roasted Trout with Chervil
Vinaigrette PAGE 156

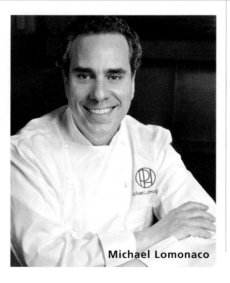

Michael Lomonaco

Michael Lomonaco, Porter House New York

RECIPES

Skillet-Charred Burgers with
Red Onion Jam PAGE 159

Skirt Steak with Chimichurri
Sauce PAGE 159

Philly Cheesesteak
Sandwich PAGE 160

141

Joseph Kunst
CHEF, BRIDGE CAFE

It's never too late

Like many people, Joe Kunst became interested in food at an early age, watching his mother and grandmother cook. Unlike many chefs, however, Chef Kunst was a systems engineer for 18 years before taking the plunge into satisfying his lifelong yearning: cooking professionally for diners who return again and again to sample his tantalizing dishes. So what made him finally follow his heart? A visit to New Orleans back in 1993 and encouragement from two of America's leading chefs, Emeril Lagasse and Paul Prudhomme.

It happened like this: On a business trip to the Crescent City, Kunst was searching for a souvenir for his mother. He bought a cookbook by Lagasse and another by Prudhomme and decided to get them autographed for her. He called Lagasse's restaurant and was told "to come down and see"—maybe the famous chef could find a moment for him. Lagasse ending up talking with Kunst for more than an hour.

When Kunst had a similar experience with Paul Prudhomme, and even ended up as a guest diner on his TV show, the message was clear.

"I had been thinking about culinary school and even though my wife was in favor, I wasn't sure. But," admits Kunst, "both chefs' willingness to share really helped me." Still nervous about forfeiting his financial security, he wrangled a full-time, no-pay kitchen gig at The American Place, in addition to his regular job. He kept up that crazy pace for a year.

Finally, he took the plunge and enrolled in cooking school. After graduation, he became a personal chef and started a consulting business. "Five years ago, I was planning to open a high-end café with 30 or 40 seats for breakfast and lunch." Then his sister-in-law, who was the general manager at Bridge Café, called in a panic. "The chef had just walked out and they needed help right away. He hadn't even written down any recipes, so they had nothing to go on." Kunst promised to pitch in for three weeks to get the kitchen running and to find a new chef. But in that short amount of time he fell in love with the staff and the owners, and they with him.

"I've been here ever since. Diners come in and leave with a good memory and a desire to come back. Bridge gives you a great meal at a good New York price." But Kunst admits it's not just the food that draws diners. "Bridge Café has its own history—the

BRIDGE CAFE
279 Water Street
New York, NY 10038
212-227-3344
www.eatgoodinny.com

building, right under the Brooklyn Bridge on the Manhattan side, has been there since 1794, and the current owners have had it since 1979—pretty long in the restaurant business. I'm just a small part of the restaurant's history, but I fit in here right now."

Befitting its location near New York's historic seaport, Bridge Café takes flavors from all over the world and turns them into out-of-the-ordinary dishes: Cod glazed with Asian spices, corn fritters with jalapeño-cheddar sauce, and Moroccan lamb might all be on the menu. But the food still holds true to its American roots. "I love spice and heat and compound flavors. I cook anything and everything, but it's definitely not froufrou and not chemical cooking. Bridge has nice, simple plating and old-school flavors—nothing too fancy, but it all comes together beautifully." Just as Kunst says, "Things fall in place and happen for a reason." ∎

The recipes

"I love spice and heat [but mostly] I love compound flavors. I cook anything and everything, but it's definitely not froufrou and not chemical cooking."

Sesame-Crusted Red Snapper with Shrimp and Pepper Stir-Fry

SERVES 4

The addition of shrimp turns this snapper dish into something exceptional, but it's still easy enough to put together for a midweek dinner. The Asian-influenced sauce is a snap: Just combine the ingredients, blend and that's that.

FOR THE SAUCE

6 tablespoons oyster sauce
2 tablespoons plum sauce
2 tablespoons sugar
6 tablespoons soy sauce
6 tablespoons hoisin sauce
1 tablespoon sambal chile sauce
2 tablespoons canola oil
1 tablespoon minced garlic
1 tablespoon minced jalapeño pepper
½ tablespoon grated fresh gingerroot
1 cup finely chopped cilantro
¼ cup finely chopped mint
¼ cup vegetable stock (chicken stock may be substituted)
Salt and pepper to taste

FOR THE SNAPPER

2 cups panko (Japanese bread crumbs)
¼ cup white sesame seeds
¼ cup black sesame seeds
1 cup buttermilk
4 (6–8 ounce) red snapper fillets
Salt and pepper to taste
5 tablespoons canola or vegetable oil, divided
1 small onion, finely chopped
1 small red pepper, finely chopped
1 small green pepper, finely chopped
25 rock shrimp or ½ pound (35–40 size) shrimp shelled, deveined
1 pound rice vermicelli (very thin rice noodles), cooked per instructions to al dente
4 scallions, chopped

TO MAKE THE SAUCE

Combine all ingredients in blender and puree. Season to taste with salt and pepper.

TO MAKE THE SNAPPER

In a large, shallow dish, mix together panko, white sesame seeds and black sesame seeds. Set aside.

Place buttermilk in a bowl. Preheat two large sauté pans on medium heat.

Season snapper fillets with salt and black pepper, then dip presentation side of each fillet into buttermilk. Press coated side into bread-crumb mixture and coat well.

Place 3 tablespoons oil in preheated sauté pan and lay fillets in pan, bread-crumb side down. Sauté until golden, then flip and lower heat and cook until moist and flaky.

In the second pan, add the remaining 2 tablespoons of oil, onion, red and green peppers and sauté until tender.

Add the rock shrimp and sauté 1 minute, then add the vermicelli and stir-fry 2 to 3 minutes.

Add most of the sauce to the pan and toss well, then adjust seasoning. The stir-fry should be moist but not overly sauced.

TO SERVE

Lay out 4 warm plates and divide the stir-fry equally in the center of the plates.

Place 1 fillet alongside the stir-fry. Drizzle the extra sauce onto the plate and garnish with scallions, if desired. ∎

Sesame-Crusted Red Snapper with Shrimp and Pepper Stir-Fry

The recipes

Crab and Tomato Bisque with Basil

SERVES 4–6

One of the oldest drinking establishments in New York City, Bridge Café serves hungry downtowners an upscale but accessible seasonal menu that relies heavily on seafood. Chef Kunst's tasty bisque offers lots of fresh basil along with two kinds of crab.

1 pound fresh lump crabmeat
1 pound back fin crabmeat
3 tablespoons unsalted butter
1 large onion, chopped fine
1 tablespoon tomato paste
1 large beefsteak tomato, seeded and finely chopped
1¼ tablespoons garlic, minced
4 tablespoons ketchup
2¼ teaspoons Chesapeake-style seasoning
1¼ teaspoons hot sauce
1 lemon, juiced
2 cups tomato juice
1¼ cups clam juice
1 cup fresh basil, tightly packed, minced
2 cups heavy cream
2 tablespoons chopped chives, for garnish

Carefully pick through the crabmeat for shells/cartilage; set aside.

Melt butter in saucepot over medium heat and sauté onion until tender, then add tomato paste and sauté 1 to 2 minutes longer; be sure not to burn.

Add tomato and garlic and sauté 1 to 2 minutes longer.

Add ketchup, Chesapeake-style seasoning, hot sauce, lemon juice, tomato juice, clam juice and basil, then bring to a boil. Reduce heat and simmer for 10 minutes.

Remove from heat and puree in blender. Return to saucepot, add cream, and then bring to a boil. Reduce heat and simmer for 5 minutes.

Add crabmeat and adjust seasoning.

TO SERVE
Ladle into warm bowls and garnish with chopped chives. ▪

Crab, Spinach and Artichoke Fondue

SERVES 6

Chef Kunst recognizes that not everyone enjoys sharing, so his warm dip, rich with three cheeses and graced with both spinach and artichoke hearts, is broiled in individual ramekins.

1 pound fresh lump crabmeat
2 bags prewashed baby spinach
4 tablespoons unsalted butter
1 large onion, finely chopped
1 tablespoon minced garlic
4 tablespoons all-purpose flour
¼ cup vegetable stock (chicken can be substituted)
1 cup heavy cream
1 teaspoon lemon juice
¼ tablespoon hot sauce
¼ tablespoon coarse salt
4 tablespoons grated Parmesan cheese
4 tablespoons cream cheese
4 tablespoons sour cream
1 cup grated white Cheddar cheese, divided
1 (7-ounce) can artichoke hearts, finely chopped
4 tablespoons chopped chives, for garnish
Assorted crackers and/or toast points

Carefully pick through crabmeat for shells/cartilage and set aside. Preheat broiler. Bring large pot of water to boil over high heat. Trim spinach, then drop in boiling water to blanch. Quickly drain, squeeze dry, and chop spinach fine.

Heat saucepot over medium heat, then add butter. Add onion and sauté until tender, then add garlic and sauté until fragrant. Add flour and sauté 1 to 2 minutes longer. Whisk in stock to avoid lumps, then whisk in cream and bring to a boil. As mixture boils, whisk in lemon juice, hot sauce, salt and Parmesan. Remove from heat and let cool slightly.

Stir in cream cheese, sour cream, ½ cup of the Cheddar, spinach, artichokes and crabmeat.

Divide mixture equally into 6 ramekins and set on a baking dish. Top ramekins with remaining Cheddar and place under broiler until browned and bubbly.

TO SERVE
Garnish with chopped chives and serve with crackers or dry toast points. ▪

Bill Telepan
CHEF AND OWNER, TELEPAN

As you like it

Bill Telepan is a little embarrassed about the name of his restaurant; he never envisioned it being called Telepan, but that's "just the way it turned out. Nothing else sounded good, so we ended up with this," he recalls. Not that the moniker would hurt; he has excellent name recognition thanks to his outstanding work at the three-star JUdson Grill. But Telepan is nothing if not modest. He credits all the chefs he's worked with—Alain Chapel in France; Alfred Portale, Gilbert Le Coze, Daniel Boulud in New York City—for making him the master he is today. And he's just as quick to give kudos to his staff for the success of his eponymous restaurant.

"We take everything we do very seriously and make an enormous effort to get it just right. The French fries are not to your liking? No problem. Back to the kitchen," he says.

And the kitchen at Telepan always seems to be busy. Located near Lincoln Center, it draws tourists, locals from the neighborhood, and New Yorkers from all over

Bill Telepan
CHEF AND OWNER, TELEPAN

the city. Diners are attracted to the homey, sometimes rustic dishes, based on fresh ingredients and simply prepared. (No surprise, considering Telepan's 2004 book is titled *Inspired by Ingredients*.) Favorites, according to Telepan, are the smoked trout blini, the lobster Bolognese, and the pork done four ways. But as he goes over the menu, noticing items like hanger steak with oxtail bone-marrow glaze or roasted leg and 24-hour shoulder of lamb, he realizes "all the entrées really do equally well." And, of course, found throughout the selections are glorious greenmarket sides and garnishes: chickpea pancakes, perhaps (see opposite), or the distinctive corn soup with scallions and roasted corn sautéed in brown butter (see page 150) or, in winter, a root-vegetable ragout.

Certainly, these are the types of food you'd expect from a chef known for unfussy, market-fresh dishes with natural, vibrant flavors. What is unusual on the menu, however, is a category called "mid courses," a designation Telepan compares to the "primi" on an Italian menu. "The idea was to include something bigger than an appetizer, smaller than an entrée, so people would have the ability to mix things up and eat the way they want to eat," he explains. The lobster Bolognese appears here, as do a couple other pastas, a vegetable dish or two, and a spectacular foie gras club. "Many customers order an appetizer, a mid,

TELEPAN
72 West 69th Street
New York, NY 10023
212-580-4300
www.telepan-ny.com

On the side...

What do you consider the most overrated ingredient?
Pepper.

The most underrated ingredient?
Extra-virgin olive oil.

What is your favorite comfort food?
A bacon cheeseburger—made with really good meat, of course—or pizza.

What kitchen gadget is your must-have tool?
An offset spatula.

If you were not a chef, what would you be?
I have no idea.

What was the last thing you ate?
It was weird; I was testing… spaghetti with fresh broccoli, olives, basil and garlic; tomato soup with chile; rice and beans; a salad—and a bottle of nice wine!

some wine and walk out happy."

But the factor that most eloquently distinguishes this restaurant is the personal touch behind the food. The website even begins with a monthly letter from Telepan himself, highlighting what he's cooking at that time of year, based, of course, on the freshness and availability of ingredients.

"I stress seasonality because that's how I learned to cook," he says. "My dishes are based on my life experience; they're what's in my head and my heart, and so that's what ends up on the plate." ■

The recipes

My dishes are based on my life experience;
they're what's in my head and my heart and
so that's what ends up on the plate."

Chickpea Pancakes with Spicy Carrots and Oregano Oil

SERVES 4 AS A LARGE APPETIZER

Nutty chickpea pancakes are perfect vehicles for a mélange of roasted tomatoes, peppers and carrots. One bite and you'll be addicted.

FOR THE PANCAKES

2/3 cup milk
1 tablespoon cream
1 egg
1/2 cup flour
1/4 cup chickpea flour
1/8 to 1/4 teaspoon sugar (more if using frozen chickpeas)
1/4 teaspoon salt
1/2 teaspoon baking powder
3/4 cup crushed cooked chickpeas
1/2 teaspoon butter

FOR THE TOPPING

1 cup sliced onion
6 cloves garlic, thinly sliced
Salt to taste
4 ounces extra-virgin olive oil
1 cup of peeled and bias-cut celery
8 oven-roasted tomatoes, julienned
8 pepperoncini peppers, seeds removed from 2, julienned
2 ounces butter
1 1/2 pounds multicolored carrots, peeled
4 ounces vegetable stock

TO MAKE THE OREGANO OIL

1 tablespoon chopped oregano
1 teaspoon red-wine vinegar
2 tablespoon extra-virgin olive oil
Mix all ingredients together and reserve.

TO MAKE THE PANCAKES

Preheat oven to 450°F.
Mix milk, cream and egg in a bowl. Add flours, sugar, salt and baking powder and combine.

Fold the crushed chickpeas into the batter.

In a medium, ovenproof, nonstick skillet over high heat, melt butter. Swirl butter around pan. Use 2 tablespoons of batter to form a pancake, about 3 inches in diameter. Cook 2 at a time on each side. When the edges start to lightly brown, after about 1 to 2 minutes, place in oven. After 2 minutes, flip the pancakes and return to oven until lightly brown, about 4 minutes longer. Repeat with remaining batter. Keep pancakes warm.

TO MAKE THE TOPPING

Over medium-low heat, cook onion and garlic in olive oil with a pinch of salt in covered pan for 3 minutes. Add celery and another small pinch of salt and cook, covered, for another 5 minutes. Add tomatoes and soften for 2 minutes. Add peppers and cook 3 to 4 minutes, remove from heat and cool.

Cut the carrots into oblique 1-inch segments by cutting on the bias and rotating the carrot 180 degrees before cutting again. In a large sauté pan over medium heat, melt the butter, add carrots, season with salt, and sweat for 6 minutes. Add stock and cook, uncovered, over medium-high heat until carrots are al dente and liquid forms a glaze, about 7 minutes. Remove from heat.

TO SERVE

Add pepperoncini mix to the carrots and warm over medium-high heat. When warmed through, adjust seasoning. Serve on top of pancakes and drizzle with oregano oil. ▪

The recipes

Slow-Roasted Shoulder of Veal with Spring Vegetables

SERVES 4–6

This veal shoulder is typical of Chef Telepan's approach to cooking: fresh, simple, not a bit precious. The meat owes its deep, rich flavor to browned butter and oven roasting.

1 (3-pound) boneless veal shoulder roast, rolled and tied
Salt and pepper to taste
2 tablespoons olive oil
8 tablespoons (1 stick) butter, divided
12 baby spring onions, trimmed to 2 inches
(can substitute scallions)
4 large artichoke hearts, 1 inch of the stem left on, cut into 4 or 5 slices
3/4 cup cooked peas
1/2 cup vegetable or chicken stock
Thyme and parsley for garnish

Preheat oven to 325°F.

Season meat with salt and pepper.

Heat a large sauté pan on high heat, add the olive oil and bring to just about smoking.

Sear all sides of meat in the oil until well browned, about 20 minutes.

After it is seared, add 2 tablespoons of the butter to the pan and brown. Use the browned butter to baste the meat and place in the oven.

Every 15 minutes, turn and baste the meat. After about an hour, drain the cooked butter and oil from the pan, add 2 more tablespoons of the butter and cook until meat reaches an internal temperature of 160°F, about 1 1/2 to 2 hours.

Remove meat from pan and allow to rest at least 15 minutes.

In the meantime, place the pan (do not drain it) on medium heat and add 2 more tablespoons of the butter. Melt the butter, then add the onions and cook until lightly caramelized, about 5–7 minutes.

Add artichokes and cook an additional 3 minutes.

Add peas, stock and remaining 2 tablespoons butter and cook down until glazed, about 5 minutes.

Add thyme and parsley. Adjust seasonings.

TO SERVE
Slice the veal, portion onto individual plates and place vegetables all around. ▧

Corn Soup with Scallions and Roasted Corn Sautéed in Brown Butter

SERVES 4

The rotating seasons are deliciously reflected in Chef Telepan's ever-changing menu, which highlights local produce. Here he pays homage to fresh corn, turning it into a memorable soup topped with grilled corn kernels and scallions.

4 tablespoons butter, divided
1/2 Walla Walla onion plus 5 inches of green
1 clove garlic, sliced
6 ears corn: 4 shucked, kernels cut off the cobs to yield 3 cups; 1 shucked and cut into 2-inch pieces; 1 unshucked
1 1/2 cups water or vegetable stock
Salt and pepper to taste
5 or 6 scallions, sliced thinly up into green part

Heat 2 tablespoons butter in a 2-quart pot over low heat. Add the onion with the green section intact and the garlic; cook until tender, about 7 minutes. Add the 3 cups of corn kernels and the cut-up cob and water (or stock). Bring to a boil and simmer for 15 minutes. Remove cut-up cob and discard. Carefully puree the corn mixture in a blender or food processor. Strain, pressing until solids are dry. Season corn puree with salt and pepper and set aside.

Grill or broil the unshucked ear of corn until husk is charred. Let cool, then cut off kernels. Set aside kernels for garnish.

In a hot pan, add 1 tablespoon butter and heat until brown and bubbly. Add scallions and sauté for 1 minute. Add corn kernels and remaining 1 tablespoon butter and cook additional minute. Season with salt. Set aside.

Put corn puree in saucepot and bring back to a simmer.

TO SERVE
Place soup in bowls and put a dollop of corn kernel–scallion mixture in the center. ▧

Corn Soup with Scallions and Roasted Corn Sautéed in Brown Butter

Waldy Malouf
CHEF AND CO-OWNER, BEACON

Constant evolution

A toque is only one of Chef Waldy Malouf's many hats. "I'm addicted to multitasking," he admits. "I've been accused of being a control freak, but I like to oversee all aspects of the restaurant. I get involved in the bar, the dining room, the kitchen—the whole experience from the phone call to make the reservation to the time the diner walks out the door. At Beacon, we do everything we can to maintain control of the quality, and that includes baking our own bread." Indeed, this kind of quality control may be the key to Malouf's success.

Trained in the European tradition of always cooking with fresh local ingredients, he translated this concept to the aptly named Hudson River Club in the World Financial Center. It emphasized food from the nearby Hudson Valley, so Malouf could have first pick of top-quality seasonal ingredients. "This wasn't what was going on in the early 1990s," remembers Malouf. "People wanted raspberries and asparagus in January. But we wanted to reflect the European style in that what was out the back door was what we would serve. This became the calling card of the restaurant."

From there, Malouf was tapped to reinvent New York's venerable Rainbow Room and earned the restaurant three stars for the first time since 1934. Ready for his next challenge, Malouf decided to open a smaller place, one that still stressed the fresh and the seasonal, but in a whole different atmosphere. The focal point of Beacon, launched in 1999, is an open kitchen with a wood-burning oven, rotisseries and grills. "The original idea was to create a chef-driven steakhouse or bistro—very rustic with smoke and char and no heavy sauces—but some of our customers wanted more than that," says Malouf.

In response, Malouf made some changes. "We decided to grow Beacon into a more sophisticated cuisine. We offer some very unique things you can't find anywhere else, such as wood-roasted oysters, salmon or trout cooked in our ovens. And with the rotisserie, we can roast a suckling pig or a very crisp duck that just can't be done in a gas-fired broiler." Dishes like these may sound simple, but getting everything in working order proved to be anything but. "We had to spend a lot of money, not just on the equipment, but even to clean the air as it's vented to the outside."

BEACON
25 West 56th Street
New York, NY 10019
212-332-0500
www.beaconnyc.com

On the side...

What do you consider the most overrated ingredient?
Pork belly.

What is the most underrated ingredient?
Squab or calf's liver.

What kitchen gadget is your must-have tool?
A wood-burning oven!

What is your favorite comfort food?
A BLT sandwich (preferably made by Mom).

If you were not a chef, what would you be?
A sheep farmer, so I could make cheese.

What was the last thing you ate?
Matzoh-ball soup (it's a long story).

At this point, Malouf says, he's developed such a strong customer base that he'll "be here for a while," but he still wants to move forward. One new direction for him is his upscale pizza shop, Waldy's, based on the flatbread and pita made at Beacon.

"Looking around, it seemed that everything in food had evolved in the last 20 years except the corner pizza place. But one thing I liked is that pizza is so democratic—everyone from businessmen in suits to students and every cultural background likes it. So we make it different by using organic ingredients and our wood-burning ovens." And in reference to the possible revenue that a chain of pizza joints might bring, he laughs. "Maybe when I slow down a little, I can retire with that." ∎

Roasted Oysters with Shallots and Herbs

The recipes

"We offer some very unique things [at Beacon] that you can't find anywhere else, such as wood-roasted oysters, salmon or trout cooked in our ovens."

Roasted Oysters with Shallots and Herbs

SERVES 4

According to Chef Malouf, roasting oysters on the half shell is a little different than cooking other things at high heat. The purpose isn't so much to char as it is to firm them up and get them to release all their flavorful juices. These oysters are topped with little spoonfuls of a shallot-and-white-wine-butter sauce, which mixes with the juices and reduces in the oven so the shallots get crisp. Six oysters make an impressive appetizer, or, follow the chef's suggestion and present all 24 on a baking dish lined with rock salt.

6 tablespoons (3/4 stick) unsalted butter, divided
1 cup thinly sliced shallots
1/4 cup dry white wine or dry vermouth
Coarse sea salt or kosher salt and freshly ground black pepper, to taste
1/4 cup chicken stock, vegetable broth, or water
1 tablespoon chopped fresh chives
1 tablespoon chopped fresh parsley
Rock salt (see note)
3 tablespoons black peppercorns
24 oysters
Lemon wedges, for serving

Preheat the oven to 500°F.

In a heavy saucepan over medium heat, melt 4 tablespoons of the butter. Reduce the heat to low and add the shallots and wine or vermouth. Cover and cook until most of the liquid is absorbed, about 4 to 5 minutes. Season with salt and pepper and add the chicken stock and the remaining 2 tablespoons of butter. Bring to a simmer, then remove from the heat and stir in the herbs.

Cover the bottom of an ovenproof baking dish large enough to hold all the oysters with rock salt. Sprinkle the peppercorns evenly over the salt. Open the oysters by slipping an oyster knife between the shells and prying them open. (Use gloves or a kitchen towel to protect your hands.) Discard the top shell. Loosen the oysters from the bottom shell, being careful not to spill their juices, and lay them in the baking dish. Stir the shallot mixture and spoon some over each oyster. Roast until the edges of the oysters just begin to curl, about 5–8 minutes.

TO SERVE

Keep oysters on the baking dish, add lemon wedges and serve, or portion rock salt and oysters onto 4 serving dishes and add a couple of lemon wedges to each.

■ **NOTE** Rock salt is available at hardware stores. It's very inexpensive and one bag will last forever.

The recipes

Rib Steak with Citrus Rub

SERVES 4

Nothing beats a steak for great taste and ease. Beacon's rib chops, rubbed with a signature powder of baked lemon and orange zest, have a complex flavor that elevates this dish from ordinary to fabulous. Plan this at least a day ahead of serving time.

1 orange
1 lemon
2 tablespoons coarse salt
2 teaspoons freshly ground black pepper
2 double beef rib chops (each with one bone—approximately 2 pounds each)
Extra-virgin olive oil, for brushing

Preheat the oven to 200°F.

Use a vegetable peeler to remove the zest from the orange and lemon. Spread the zest on a baking sheet in a single layer and bake until thoroughly dried, about 2 hours. Let cool before placing in the bowl of a food processor. Process to a powder, then mix with the salt and pepper.

One day before cooking, season the meat all over with 2 tablespoons of the citrus rub and cover with plastic wrap. Refrigerate for 24 hours, turning the meat after 12.

Remove the meat from the refrigerator 2 hours before cooking. Light the grill or preheat the broiler. When the meat reaches room temperature, brush it with olive oil.

Position a broiler pan so that the top of the meat is 3 to 4 inches from the heat source. Broil the steaks for 7 minutes on each side for rare, then remove from the oven, taking great care with the pan, as the fat is extremely hot and will splatter.

For medium to well-done meat, turn the oven to 500°F., and continue to roast the meat for 5–10 minutes longer, until done to taste.

Let the meat rest on a carving board for 5–10 minutes to allow the juices to reabsorb.

TO SERVE

Slice the meat and sprinkle with additional citrus rub. ■

Wood-Roasted Trout with Chervil Vinaigrette

SERVES 4

Beacon is known for offering fresh, simple food that's up to the minute without being too trendy. This trout, marinated in an herb vinaigrette and quickly roasted in the oven, makes an elegant but easy main course.

1 cup chopped fresh chervil or chives
3/4 cup chopped flat-leaf parsley
3 tablespoons roughly chopped shallots (about 1 shallot)
3 tablespoons freshly squeezed lemon juice
2 tablespoons Champagne or white-wine vinegar
1 cup extra-virgin olive oil
2 teaspoons coarse salt, divided
Freshly ground black pepper, to taste
4 skin-on, boned trout, heads removed

Preheat the oven to 500°F.

In a blender, puree the chervil, parsley, shallot, lemon juice, and vinegar with 1/2 cup of the olive oil. Transfer the mixture to a small bowl and stir in the remaining oil, 1 teaspoon of the salt and the pepper, to make a vinaigrette.

Meanwhile, sprinkle the inside of the trout with salt and pepper to taste. Spoon about half the vinaigrette over the trout, both inside and out. Rub the vinaigrette into the fish. Cover the trout and refrigerate for 15–30 minutes.

Lay the fish on a rack in a roasting pan and roast for 15–25 minutes, depending upon the size of the trout, until the flesh is opaque.

TO SERVE

Divide trout among 4 individual plates and serve with the remaining vinaigrette as the sauce. ■

Michael Lomonaco
EXECUTIVE CHEF AND MANAGING PARTNER, PORTER HOUSE NEW YORK

Past forward

Most of us equate the term *porter-house* with a cut of beef—and we're correct, but, according to Michael Lomonaco, there's a much more interesting backstory, one that better explains the name behind his 140-seat restaurant in the famed Time Warner Center. Originally, porter houses were eateries that dotted Manhattan in the 19th century. Similar to English alehouses, they were casual, welcoming restaurants, catering mostly to longshoremen, with a simple menu of big hunks of beef and dark beer (called porter). Eventually, porter houses morphed into steakhouses, but the mission of good food and hospitality remained.

Intrigued by this bit of history, Lomonaco decided he had found the name for his restaurant, but he went a step further, elevating his Porter House to a luxury American grill with an extensive menu that includes seafood as well as other entrées. "I liked the tradition of comfort and hospitality, but wanted to lift it up to a

Michael Lomonaco
EXECUTIVE CHEF AND MANAGING PARTNER, PORTER HOUSE NEW YORK

fine dining experience," says Lomonaco, who trained at Le Cirque, then followed up with executive chef positions at "21" and Windows on the World. "My idea was to create a 'steakhouse plus' with great food, great service and a great atmosphere."

And that's exactly what you find at Porter House. The room is airy and light, with views of Central Park; the wine list is abundant; and most of all, the menu is far more varied than at most steakhouses. Lomonaco is particularly proud of his fish and "other meat" entrées, such as cedar-roasted salmon fillet and a veal chop laced with thyme and Riesling. He's also tickled by his range of sides—16 in all, including toasted polenta with porcini. Even the appetizers aren't typical steakhouse fare; consider big-eye tuna tartare with wasabi caviar and short rib raviolo with truffle cream.

Not surprisingly, the best-sellers are the steaks, specifically the 36-ounce double-cut porterhouse for two and a chili-rubbed ribeye. "The food is very straightforward, not at all precious," explains Lomanaco, which is why his beef is prime, dry-aged, and hand-cut on the premises. But, straightforward cooking aside, the bold, assertive flavors he is famous for show up in the sauces. A skirt steak, for instance, may be topped with chimichurri, while a red onion marmalade partners a burger (see opposite page).

"I'm very involved in the kitchen," says Lomonaco, "but I also like to get out into the dining room and meet

PORTER HOUSE NEW YORK
10 Columbus Circle, 4th Floor
New York, NY 10019
212-823-9500
www.porterhousenewyork.com

On the side...

What do you consider the most overrated ingredient?
Truffle oil.

The most underrated ingredient?
Salt and pepper. Both are the start of good seasoning.

What is your favorite comfort food?
Brick-oven pizza with fresh hand-pulled mozzarella, San Marzano tomatoes, basil and maybe real Italian sausage if I go all out.

What kitchen gadget is your must-have tool?
An 8-inch chef's knife.

If you were not a chef, what would you be?
An architect.

What was the last thing you ate?
Roast chicken. It was the family dinner (staff dinner) at the restaurant.

guests and find out what they're thinking and what they want." This people factor is very significant, because for Lomonaco, the joy of cooking depends on the pleasure of those he feeds. "I come from an Italian family, and the whole cooking thing was about caring for others. It expressed generosity and a desire to please."

It may also explain why he's had TV shows on both the Travel Channel and the Food Network, and why he continues to make television appearances. "I want to show people that if I can do it, they can, too, and encourage them to get creative and have fun. Following a recipe is not the point; you need to get in there and make it your own."

Lomonaco's certainly done that with Porter House. ∎

The recipes

Skillet-Charred Burgers with Red Onion Jam

SERVES 4

Chef Lomonaco refers to this as his "best basic burger" and one bite will tell you why. Mayo, mustard or ketchup could top it off just fine, but why not try the chef's Red Onion Jam for a real standout taste?

FOR THE RED ONION JAM
4 tablespoons olive oil, divided
2 red onions, peeled and thinly sliced
1/2 cup sugar
1/4 cup red-wine vinegar
1/2 cup dry red wine, preferably Syrah or Zinfandel

FOR THE BURGERS
2 pounds ground sirloin and chuck
Kosher salt and freshly ground black pepper
Cheddar cheese
Brioche burger buns
Sliced tomatoes

TO MAKE THE JAM
Pour 2 tablespoons olive oil into a saucepan, add the onions, and sauté until they begin to wilt and sweat, taking care not to burn them. Cook for 8–10 minutes over low heat, add the sugar and sauté for 1 minute. Carefully add the vinegar and wine. Bring to a simmer, cooking until the liquid has evaporated and the onions are caramelized, approximately 3 minutes. Remove from heat and keep warm.

TO MAKE THE BURGERS
Form the meat into 4 burger patties, making them tight, but not overly crushed together. Season each burger with kosher salt and pepper. Set a grill pan, or wide sauté pan, over medium-high heat and let it get nice and hot. Add 2 tablespoons olive oil to grill or pan and heat it for 1 minute. Add the burgers to the pan and char on both sides, approximately 4 minutes per side for medium-rare; 1 or 2 minutes less or longer per side for rare or more well done. Toast buns in grill pan or toaster.

TO SERVE
Top the hot burgers with slices of cheese, allow to melt and serve on buns with sliced tomato and the Red Onion Jam. ▪

Skirt Steak with Chimichurri Sauce

SERVES 4

Chimichurri sauce is a classic Argentinian condiment made with garlic, onion and parsley.

FOR THE CHIMICHURRI SAUCE
1 cup olive oil
1/4 cup white vinegar
1 small bunch flat-leaf parsley, picked over and chopped
1 small white onion, diced (about 1/4 cup)
2 cloves fresh garlic, finely chopped
1 tablespoon smoked Spanish paprika
1 teaspoon dried oregano
Sea salt and black pepper to taste

FOR THE STEAK
2½ pounds skirt steak
3 tablespoons olive oil, divided
Several crushed garlic cloves
Sprigs of parsley
Kosher salt to taste
2 large ripe tomatoes cut into wedges
1 small Bermuda onion, thinly sliced
1 bunch watercress, washed, dried and coarsely chopped

TO MAKE THE CHIMICHURRI SAUCE
Combine all the chimichurri ingredients in the bowl of a food processor, process for 1 minute, and set aside. Season the sauce with sea salt and pepper, and taste. Adjust seasoning if necessary. The chimichurri may be prepared in advance and refrigerated for up to a week.

TO MAKE THE STEAK
Pound the skirt steak flat with a meat tenderizer, marinate with 1 tablespoon of olive oil, some crushed garlic cloves and sprigs of parsley and refrigerate for several hours. Remove steak from refrigerator; preheat a grill pan or cast-iron skillet over medium heat for a minute before adding another tablespoon of olive oil. Season the skirt steak with kosher salt and sear the first side for 2 to 3 minutes before turning to cook the second side, adding remaining olive oil if necessary. Cook to the desired doneness. Remove and allow to rest.

TO SERVE
Slice the skirt steak into thin slices, always cutting the steak across the grain for maximum tenderness. Place the sliced steak on a platter and drizzle chimichurri sauce over the top. Serve with tomato wedges, onion and watercress. ▪

©Michael Lomonaco, 2007

The recipes

*"I want to show people that if I can do it,
they can, too, and encourage them to get creative
and have fun. Following a recipe is not the point;
you need to get in there and make it your own."*

Philly Cheesesteak Sandwich

SERVES 4

According to Chef Lomonaco, the secret of a great cheesesteak, apart from the quality of the meat, is the thinness of the raw beef. Check out his suggestions below for getting the proper cut.

1 (2-pound) ribeye steak, well trimmed and boneless (a single, large steak is best for slicing before cooking)
1 Vidalia or other sweet onion, peeled
4–6 Italian frying peppers
4 tablespoons extra-virgin olive oil, divided, plus extra for bread
Salt and pepper to taste
4 ciabatta, soft hero breads or hoagie rolls
Balsamic vinegar for bread
¼ pound sharp, aged provolone cheese or imported fontina, thinly sliced

Ask your butcher to cut the ribeye into paper-thin slices, following the grain. Or, if that isn't possible, cut the beef using an electric slicer, electric knife or by hand, following the direction of the grain of the steak. Flatten the slices using a meat pounder or mallet. Once all the beef has been cut, refrigerate before cooking until the remaining ingredients are ready.

Cut the onion in half before slicing into half-moon, paper-thin slices. Set aside. Clean the peppers of their seeds by splitting in half and discarding seeds.

Heat half the oil in a skillet, add the onions and cook over a low flame to soften and caramelize the onions, about 10 minutes, being careful not to allow them to brown. Season with salt and pepper. Remove the onions, and in the same pan, fry the pepper halves till soft and tender. Season peppers with salt and pepper. Remove. Keep the onions and peppers covered and warm until ready to assemble sandwich.

In a cast-iron pan, heat the remaining 2 tablespoons olive oil over medium heat. Add the beef in batches and lightly brown, adding salt and pepper as you cook. Cook all the beef, adding olive oil if necessary. Optional: You can flavor the oil with garlic by adding a whole, peeled garlic clove to the oil and browning it for a minute or two while cooking the beef—this will transfer a mild garlic flavor to the oil and season the beef at the same time.

Cut the bread or rolls in half through the middle and pull out a little of the doughy insides before seasoning the bread by drizzling the inside with a little extra-virgin olive oil, a splash of balsamic vinegar and a pinch of salt and pepper.

TO SERVE

Place several slices of cooked beef, up to a 4–6-ounce portion, inside each roll; top with onions and peppers and several slices of cheese. Slice diagonally in half and serve or, for a more authentic touch, wrap in waxed paper before you slice. ■

Philly Cheesesteak Sandwich

6

Not so many years ago, only a limited number of New Yorkers were versed in the art of selecting tapas, and only the well traveled could explain the difference between a buñuelo and a dolma. But these days, people are nearly as familiar with Mediterranean dishes as they are with hot dogs and hamburgers. It's a cuisine that's become a real hit, for reasons that go well beyond the stimulating flavors and exciting food combinations. For one thing, the so-called "Mediterranean diet," based on olive oil and featuring lots of fish and red wine, has been deemed to be very healthy.

For another, the idea of small plates, quite common in Spain, Greece and Portugal, is enormously appealing. Then there are the tastes—redolent of herbs, rich with sun-ripened vegetables and layered with spices like pimentón and saffron.

So it's no wonder that chefs in Manhattan are exploring this cuisine for all it's worth. Some are just using it in bits and pieces, introducing a dish or two or lacing a recipe with ingredients typical of the regions. But many are going all the way, with restaurants that celebrate the cuisine in all its glory. Andy Nusser at Casa Mono, one of the first restaurants to offer Spanish small plates, puts it this way: "There's nothing not to like about this food." And so, diners can pick from his primarily southern Iberian menu or experiment with the food of northern Spain, courtesy of Alex Ureña's Pamplona. A trip to Greece can also be on the itinerary, via Periyali, while Alfama offers yet another choice—the food of Portugal, with such temptations as curried lamb or clams steamed in white wine and garlic.

But best of all, most of this food, reflective of the relaxed lifestyle that led to its rise, is simple to prep at home…just another reason to go Mediterranean.

Mediterranean & Iberian

Andy Nusser, Casa Mono

RECIPES

Andy Nusser

Alfama, Fine Portuguese Cuisine

Alex Ureña

Jim Botsacos, Molyvos

RECIPES

Mark Twersky, Alfama, Fine Portuguese Cuisine

RECIPES

Alex Ureña, Pamplona

RECIPES

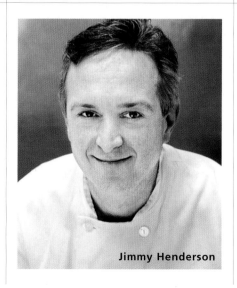

Jimmy Henderson

Jimmy Henderson, Periyali

RECIPES

163

Andy Nusser
CHEF AND OWNER, CASA MONO

A taste of Spain

His restaurant was probably the first in the city to put the word *tapas* on everyone's lips and to make Manchego the cheese to buy. Yet Andy Nusser credits good timing, not any soothsaying abilities, for the incredible success of Casa Mono. "It was 2003, and people were reading about Catalan chef Ferran Adrià and his restaurant El Bulli, judged the best in the world," he says. "Everyone wanted Spanish food." Nusser was there, with a menu that featured 40 different selections ranging from the somewhat familiar (grilled razor clams) to the slightly exotic (piquillo peppers with oxtails) to the way-out-there (duck hearts and cockscombs).

"We might not sell a lot of that last one," he laughs, "but it's fun to include on the menu and it does get people talking." What gets people eating are the always popular pumpkin and goat cheese croquettes and Nusser's pork loin with saffron honey (see page 168).

If these dishes don't sound like tapas to you, you're

right. Technically, tapas are snacks or appetizers served at bars and cafés throughout Spain. But Casa Mono's smaller-than-entrée dishes, meant to be shared, are often called by that name. The distinction doesn't bother Nusser, who's just happy that people are enjoying the food he came to love while living on the Costa Brava as a kid. "The fact that we serve small plates at small prices means less of a commitment on the part of the diner," explains Nusser. "People are more apt to try something different."

Not that Spanish food is as esoteric as many may think. Like other Mediterranean cuisines, it's based on seasonality and fairly simple preparations. Nusser appreciates the emphasis on aggressive seasoning, often a combination of sweet and hot Spanish pimentón (paprika) along with unique ingredients like quince paste, Marcona almonds, sherry and chorizo. "Even though the flavors are bold, they're balanced, so no one taste pops out at you," he says. He points to a grilled skirt steak topped with onion marmalade and served with a romesco sauce of almonds, red-wine vinegar, garlic and piquillo peppers. "It's a simple piece of meat, but the marmalade and sauce give a sweet-tangy-salty flavor—very balanced."

How Nusser comes up with this and other recipes is quite a revelation. He draws the dishes! "I take a blank sheet of paper and make a drawing of how

CASA MONO
52 Irving Place
New York, NY 10003
212-253-2773
www.casamononyc.com

On the side...

What do you consider the most overrated ingredient?
Butter. We use very little and mostly rely on olive oil—Spanish, of course.

The most underrated ingredient?
Salt.

What is your favorite comfort food?
French fries with mayo.

What kitchen gadget is your must-have tool?
Tongs.

If you were not a chef, what would you be?
A gardener. It's following the food source.

What was the last thing you ate?
Orechiette with sausage. I'm lucky. My wife is a private chef and she cooks for me.

something will look on the plate," he explains. Then he figures out the cooking techniques and the other details. This process isn't so startling once you realize that Nusser's first (very short-lived) job was as a designer for General Motors. But he quickly learned that sitting in an office wasn't for him. "My dad was always entertaining, creating very elaborate meals. I realized I loved those times—friends, food, wine—and thought, 'Maybe I could make money at this,'" he recalls. He enrolled in the CIA, then went to work with Mario Batali, first at Po, then at Babbo.

The rest is history. ▧

The recipes

How Nusser comes up with [a recipe] is... a revelation.
"I take a blank sheet of paper and make a drawing
of how something will look on the plate."

Fideos with Cockles and Chorizo

SERVES 4

Fideos is a traditional Spanish or Mexican noodle dish, where thin noodles (similar to capellini or vermicelli) are toasted or sautéed and mixed with all sorts of ingredients, from chiles and tomatoes to present as a side dish, to lobster with vegetables to enjoy as a main course.

FOR THE FIDEOS
1 pound capellini

FOR THE GARLIC AIOLI
10 garlic cloves, peeled
1 cup sweet sherry
1/4 cup sherry vinegar
2 egg yolks
2 cups olive oil
Salt and pepper to taste

FOR THE CHORIZO AND COCKLES
Olive oil (for sautéing)
2 cloves garlic, sliced
1/2 pound chorizo, diced
1 pound cockles or manilla clams, washed
2 cups cava or sparkling wine
2 cups chicken stock
1 pinch saffron threads
1/4 teaspoon salt
1 pinch crushed red pepper flakes
2 scallions, both white and green parts, thinly sliced

TO MAKE THE FIDEOS
Preheat over to 350°F.

Break pasta in a towel into roughly 1-inch pieces.

Toast on a baking sheet for 10 minutes.

TO MAKE THE GARLIC AIOLI
In a small saucepan over low-to-medium heat, cook garlic in the sherry until syrupy and caramelized.

In a food processor, blend garlic-sherry mixture with the vinegar and egg yolks. Slowly add the olive oil to emulsify. Add salt and pepper. Set aside.

TO MAKE THE CHORIZO AND COCKLES
Heat olive oil in a large pan, then add the garlic and chorizo. Cook until fat is rendered from the chorizo and the garlic is golden. Add the fideos and the cockles.

Add the cava, stock, saffron, salt and red pepper flakes. Cover and steam for 4 minutes.

TO SERVE
Fill 4 small bowls with the steamed cockles. Add the fideos over the cockles and top with garlic aioli and sliced scallions. ■

Fideos with Cockles and Chorizo

The recipes

Pork Loin with Saffron Honey

SERVES 4

Chef Nusser's marinated pork loin is tempting enough on its own, but his addition of an orange marmalade and a sherry-infused saffron honey turn it into something memorable and well worth repeating.

FOR THE MARINADE
2 tablespoons olive oil
2 cloves garlic, minced
½ teaspoon ground cumin
½ teaspoon sweet paprika
¼ teaspoon crushed red pepper flakes
¼ teaspoon black pepper
1 teaspoon minced oregano (preferably fresh)
½ teaspoon salt

FOR THE PORK
2 pounds pork loin
Salt and pepper to taste
12 whole sage leaves
1 pound cipollini onions or small Spanish onions, halved

FOR THE ORANGE MARMALADE
4 Seville or navel oranges
1 cup water
1 cup sugar

FOR THE SAFFRON HONEY
½ cup fino sherry
1 pinch saffron threads
1 cup honey

TO MAKE THE MARINADE AND THE PORK
Combine all marinade ingredients in a baking dish or a large zippered bag. Marinate the pork loin in the prepared marinade for at least two hours.

Preheat oven to 350°F.

Season pork to taste, and, in large, ovenproof skillet (cast iron works well) sear the pork on all sides.

Meanwhile, in a medium-sized bowl, toss the sage with the onions, add salt and pepper to taste, and add to skillet with the pork.

Place skillet in oven for 45 minutes.

Remove from oven, cover with foil and let rest for 10 minutes.

TO MAKE THE ORANGE MARMALADE
Quarter the oranges, removing the seeds but leaving skins on.

Cut the quarters into ½-inch dice.

Combine all ingredients in a saucepan and simmer until skin is sweet and tender, about one hour.

Add more water and sugar if necessary to create a marmalade consistency.

Remove from heat; set aside.

TO MAKE THE SAFFRON HONEY
Bring sherry and saffron to a boil until infused. Add honey. Stir and cool. Set aside.

TO SERVE
Combine the onions from the pan with the orange marmalade. Place on platter. Slice the pork and place atop the marmalade mixture. Drizzle saffron honey over the pork. ■

Ensalada Mono

SERVES 4

This salad is Spanish through and through, thanks to slices of full-bodied Manchego cheese, pimentón-toasted almonds and a piquant dressing based on orange juice and quince paste.

FOR THE SPICED ALMONDS
½ pound Marcona almonds
1 tablespoon pimentón dulce (sweet paprika)

FOR THE MEMBRILLO VINAIGRETTE
1 cup orange juice
½ cup membrillo (quince paste), or substitute apple jelly
1 cup olive oil
¼ cup sherry vinegar
Salt and pepper to taste

FOR THE SALAD
2 heads frisée, cleaned, trimmed and cut in 2-inch pieces
¼ pound Manchego cheese, cut into 12 thin slices

TO MAKE THE SPICED ALMONDS
Preheat oven to 350°F.

Toss almonds and pimentón together in a bowl.

Lay on a baking sheet and bake for 5 minutes, watching carefully. Remove from oven and cool.

Pulse in food processor until roughly ground. Set aside.

TO MAKE THE VINAIGRETTE
Heat orange juice and membrillo in a saucepan until quince paste has melted and orange juice is reduced by half. Stir to incorporate. Cool.

Put in food processor. Add sherry vinegar and emulsify with olive oil. Season with salt and pepper. Set aside.

TO SERVE
Dress the frisée with the vinaigrette. Stack the dressed greens on individual plates, as if making snowmen. Support the greens with three slices of Manchego. Dust the top with the spiced almonds. ▪

Jim Botsacos
EXECUTIVE CHEF AND PARTNER, MOLYVOS

It's Greek to him

Holding down executive chef positions at two vastly different restaurants is not an easy task, but the good news is that Jim Botsacos can walk out the door of Molyvos and go right across the street to Abbocatto (see page 44). "It does help," he laughs. And he also brings up the fact that Greek cooking shares much with that of Italy. "The West Coast especially is very influenced by Italian flavors, and since much of Greece was inhabited by the Romans, you see Italian aspects all around. So at least I didn't have to learn an entirely different cuisine."

Botsacos has been on board at Molyvos since it opened in 1997, receiving a three-star rating from *The New York Times*. Over the years, this elegant high-end restaurant has shown New Yorkers that Greek cuisine is much more than souvlaki and baklava. "Sure, we make classics like moussaka, but we add currants to the lamb and beef mixture and use *ras el hanout*, a Middle Eastern spice medley, to give it even more oomph. We also lighten the béchamel with some yogurt so the dish is not as heavy," states Botsacos.

Although he's a master at revamping authentic dishes, Botsacos also has a knack for coming up with very modern, yet very Greek, productions like an ouzo-cured salmon or crab cakes laced with lovage (a green, leafy celerylike plant from which celery seed is derived) and coupled with a horseradish yogurt. To offer an alternative to authentic *arni yuvetsi* (braised marinated lamb shanks), he's introduced a grilled lamb chop with an herb sauce and a potato croquette. "I based the sauce on ingredients from a traditional basting liquid—watercress, oregano, parsley, garlic, lemon—so it has a hint of old-world Greece, but it's lighter and more sophisticated."

Like many people, Botsacos had misconceptions about Greek cooking—and he grew up in a Greek-Italian family! "Before opening Molyvos, a group of us went on an R&D trip to Greece, and I was amazed at the boldness of the flavors, the intensity of the food. In America, the dishes are much more toned down." So part of his goal has been to bring those assertive tastes to the restaurant. One way he does this is by using coriander, fenugreek and turmeric—ingredients most people don't necessarily associate with Greece. Or, to up the flavor quotient of a familiar dish, he

MOLYVOS
871 Seventh Avenue
New York, NY 10019
212-582-7500
www.molyvos.com

Molyvos

might combine it with another beloved item, the way he did by adding pieces of cod to his filling for stuffed grape leaves, or dolmades (see page 172).

"I get inspired by everything," says Botsacos. "An ingredient, another cuisine, a meal eaten someplace else, an idea that comes to me in the night—it's all out there. But," he pauses, "whatever it is, I need to write it down. If I don't, I forget."

Happily for us, he usually has his pencil and paper handy. ■

The recipes

"I was amazed at the boldness of the flavors, the intensity of the food. In America, the dishes are much more toned down."

Bakalaros (Cod) Dolmades

SERVES 8 (AS AN APPETIZER)
Chef Botsacos does the classic stuffed grape leaf appetizer one better by adding bits of flaky cod and fennel to the rice filling.

FOR THE FILLING
1½ cups milk
1 bay leaf
3 garlic cloves, divided
Salt and freshly ground black pepper
2 (7-ounce) fresh codfish steaks, skin on
1 cup short-grain rice (such as Arborio)
1 cup finely diced onion
½ cup finely diced fennel
3 tablespoons chopped fennel fronds,
plus ½ teaspoon for garnish
3 tablespoons chopped fresh dill,
plus 1 tablespoon for garnish
2 tablespoons chopped fresh parsley
Kosher salt
1 tablespoon lemon juice
2 tablespoons extra-virgin olive oil

FOR THE GRAPE LEAVES
34 brine-packed California grape leaves, stems removed, plus 14 to line and cover the baking dish, rinsed and well drained
3 tablespoons lemon juice, divided
4 tablespoons extra-virgin olive oil, divided

FOR THE GARNISH
½ cup herbed olive oil, made with chopped fennel fronds and dill
Sea salt
2 tablespoons chopped chives

TO MAKE THE FILLING
In a large sauté pan, combine the milk, 1 to 1½ cups water, bay leaf, 2 garlic cloves, peeled and crushed, and a heavy pinch of salt and a pinch of freshly ground black pepper.

Whisk to combine.
Place the fish in the liquid, skin-side down.
Place the pan on medium-high heat. As soon as it comes to a simmer, lower to a bare simmer and cover. Cook the fish for about 6–8 minutes, until it just turns opaque. Remove from heat, uncover and allow the fish to cool in the liquid.

Once the fish is cool, transfer to a clean cutting board. Remove the skin and flake the fish into large flakes and place into a mixing bowl. Cover with plastic wrap and reserve in the refrigerator until ready to use.

In the meantime, place the rice in a fine-mesh sieve and run under hot water until the water runs clear. (This will remove the starch.)

Finely chop remaining garlic clove, and in a large, stainless-steel bowl, add the onion, chopped garlic, fennel and fennel fronds, the herbs and 1 teaspoon of kosher salt. Mix with your hands until the mixture becomes moist.

Add the rice and 1 tablespoon of lemon juice and continue to blend the mixture with your hands until the rice becomes incorporated. Transfer to a large baking dish. Cover and refrigerate for 3–6 hours.

Remove from the refrigerator. Fold in the flaked fish, making sure all ingredients are evenly distributed. Add in 2 tablespoons of extra-virgin olive oil.

TO MAKE THE GRAPE LEAVES
Preheat oven to 375°F.
Fill a large pot with cold water. Add a tablespoon of salt along with 2 tablespoons of the lemon juice and place over high heat. Bring to a boil and then add the grape leaves, 3 or 4 at a time, and blanch for 1 minute. Using a slotted spoon, transfer the grape leaves to an ice-water bath to stop the cooking. Then transfer them to a double layer of paper towels to drain.

Line the bottom of a large baking dish with a single layer of grape leaves (about 7). Set aside.

Working with one grape leaf at a time, place the leaf rib-side up on a flat surface. Neatly remove the stem if necessary.

Place 1 teaspoon of the chilled rice mixture near the bottom, widest part of the leaf.

Fold the bottom up over the rice filling and then fold each side in and over to cover. Begin rolling the leaf over the filling to make a tight, neat roll.

Place the finished roll into the grape-leaf-lined dish, seam-side down. Continue making dolmades until you have 34, packing them tightly into the baking dish so that the rolls will stay together.

In a small saucepan over medium heat, combine 2 1/2 cups hot water with 1 tablespoon of the remaining lemon juice, a heavy pinch of salt and 3 tablespoons of extra-virgin olive oil. Bring to a simmer. Remove from the heat and pour the hot liquid over the dolmades in the baking dish.

Cover the dolmades with a single layer of grape leaves (another 7). Then place another, smaller baking pan inside the pan to hold the dolmades firmly in place. Place the pan in the oven and bake for 45–50 minutes or until the leaves are tender and the filling is cooked through. Remove from the oven and immediately drain off all the liquid.

TO SERVE

Place 4 dolmades on an appetizer-size plate and drizzle the dolmades with 1/2 cup herbed olive oil, made by whisking 1/2 teaspoon chopped fennel fronds and 1 tablespoon chopped dill into remaining olive oil. Garnish with a pinch of sea salt and chopped chives. ▒

Roasted Leg of Lamb

SERVES 4

Since lamb is such a staple of Greek cuisine, there are a variety of lamb dishes on the Molyvos menu. This lamb entrée is roasted to perfection and crusted with herbed bread crumbs.

FOR THE LAMB

1 (7- to 8-pound) leg of lamb, main bone removed, shank left in
Salt and freshly ground black pepper to taste
1 garlic clove, quartered
2 tablespoons olive oil, divided
1 1/2 teaspoons dried Greek oregano
1/2 cup dry white wine
2 1/2 cups chicken stock
Herbed bread crumbs (see recipe)

▒ **NOTE** Pan juices can be strained and served with the lamb as a natural sauce.

FOR THE HERBED BREAD CRUMBS

1 cup fresh bread crumbs
1 garlic clove, minced
1 teaspoon dried Greek oregano
Juice of 1 lemon
1/4 cup extra-virgin olive oil
Coarse salt and freshly ground pepper

TO MAKE THE BREAD CRUMBS

Combine the bread crumbs, garlic and oregano in a small mixing bowl.

Squeeze the lemon juice over the mixture, tossing to blend.

Drizzle with the olive oil and season with a pinch of salt and pepper.

The crumbs should stick together when pinched; if they do not, add a bit more olive oil.

TO MAKE THE LAMB

Lay the lamb out on a clean work surface; season the top with salt and pepper.

Starting at the narrow end, roll the lamb up, cigar-fashion.

Using kitchen string, tie the meat in place so that it will hold its shape and cook evenly.

Make 4 slits in the lamb; insert a garlic sliver into each slit.

Using 1 tablespoon of the olive oil, lightly coat the lamb, sprinkle with the oregano and again season with salt and pepper. Wrap in plastic and refrigerate for at least 3 hours, up to 12 hours.

When ready to roast, preheat oven to 450°F.

Remove the lamb from the refrigerator, unwrap and place it in a large roasting pan. Place in the preheated oven and roast for 15 minutes, drizzling with remaining olive oil.

Remove the lamb from the oven and pour the wine into the pan; add the chicken stock. Reduce the oven temperature to 400°F and return the pan to the oven. Roast, basting frequently with the pan juices, for 40–50 minutes. If the pan juices dry up, add more stock or water as needed.

Remove the lamb from the oven. Sprinkle on the herbed bread crumbs and lightly press to make them adhere. Return the lamb to oven and allow to roast an additional 10–15 minutes.

TO SERVE

Remove the lamb from the oven and allow to rest for 15 minutes before cutting the strings and slicing for serving. ▒

The recipes

"I get inspired by everything. An ingredient, another cuisine, a meal eaten someplace else, an idea that comes to me in the night—it's all out there."

Baby Artichoke and Fava Bean Fricassee

SERVES 4

This vegetable side is a bit unexpected: a garlicky mix of leeks, artichokes and fava beans, simmered in wine and broth. Serve it with the lamb recipe on the previous page.

FOR THE ARTICHOKES
12 baby artichokes
Juice of 3 lemons, divided
2 cups chicken stock (or low-sodium broth)
½ cup white wine
2 cloves garlic, peeled and smashed
1 bay leaf
1 sprig thyme
Salt and pepper
2 tablespoons extra-virgin olive oil

FOR THE FRICASSEE
¼ cup extra-virgin olive oil, divided
2 cups finely diced onion
Salt and pepper to taste
1 cup sliced leeks (green and white parts, well washed)
2 cloves garlic, peeled and chopped
1 beefsteak tomato, peeled, seeded and chopped
1 cup chicken stock (or low-sodium broth)
3 scallions, trimmed and sliced
1½ cups cleaned and shelled fava beans
Juice of 1 lemon
1 tablespoon chopped fresh dill
1 tablespoon chopped fresh parsley

TO CLEAN AND COOK THE ARTICHOKES

Begin cleaning the artichokes by removing the dark-green outer leaves until the lighter, more tender leaves are exposed.

Cut about ½ inch of the cone-shaped top off. Peel the stem with a sharp knife, but do not remove stem entirely. Cut artichoke in half and place in a large bowl with the juice of 1 lemon until all artichokes are trimmed. (Storing the artichokes this way will prevent them from turning brown.)

In a small saucepan, combine the remaining lemon juice, stock, white wine, garlic and herbs and bring to a boil over medium heat. Lower the heat to a simmer and season with salt and pepper.

Drain the artichokes and add them to the pot. Add the olive oil and simmer the artichokes until they are tender, about 8 minutes.

Remove the pot from the heat and cool the artichokes in the liquid. Reserve until ready to use.

TO MAKE THE FRICASSEE AND SERVE

Heat 3 tablespoons of olive oil in a medium-sized pot over low heat. When the oil is warm, add the onion with a pinch of salt. Cover and cook 5–8 minutes.

Add the leeks, stir and replace the cover; cook an additional 5 to 6 minutes, until the onions and leeks are soft and sweet. Stir in the garlic and season to taste with salt and pepper.

Add the tomato, stir and cook for 2 to 3 minutes, until the tomato softens slightly.

Add the chicken stock, raise the heat to medium and bring it to a boil. Immediately lower the heat to reduce the stock to a simmer. Fold in the scallions, the prepared artichokes, fava beans and lemon juice.

TO SERVE

Transfer to a large bowl and add the herbs and the remaining tablespoon of olive oil; adjust the seasoning. ■

Mark Twersky
CHEF, ALFAMA, FINE PORTUGUESE CUISINE

A serendipitous chef

Upon Mark Twersky's return from a sojourn in France after college, a sympathetic friend found him a job in the kitchen of a bar and grill in Warminster, Pennsylvania. Somewhat surprisingly, he found he truly enjoyed making the fried foods, pasta and salads that were the core of a bar menu. And thus began Twersky's serendipitous career. As he says, "I became a chef by chance." Knowing he didn't want to stay in a bar forever, he decided to aim for something higher—almost on a whim. "One day I printed out a few résumés and a list of the best restaurants in Philadelphia, and started walking around Center City.

I stopped in restaurants and asked to see the chefs" he recalls.

Believe it or not, this method actually worked. Twersky landed a job on the spot at the original Budakkan in 2002, the trendy spot to eat and be seen in Philly. "Over time, I worked all the stations and learned the hierarchy and flow of how a fine restaurant works," he says. At this point, completely in love with cooking and wanting to know more, Twersky moved to New York to attend the French

Alfama, Fine Portuguese Cuisine

Mark Twersky
CHEF, ALFAMA, FINE PORTUGUESE CUISINE

Culinary Institute. Serendipity again. While still a student, he landed a coveted part-time job at Le Cirque. "It was so amazing. They had state-of-the-art everything—gold on the ceilings and the stoves! I learned so much about high-end food there; types of caviar and truffles I had never seen before. They used the French brigade system [a method developed by culinary master Escoffier to divide the kitchen into specific work areas] and that's really the way a busy top kitchen should run." When the original Le Cirque closed its doors on New Year's Eve of 2005, Twersky spent a while searching for his next position, including trying a stint as a personal chef and a job as a sous chef at Per Se, which he calls "one of the highlights" of his life.

And then, serendipity again—this time in the form of Alfama. "I really wanted to experience Portuguese cuisine. It's generally very simple, but different from what you might expect because of all the foreign influences brought in during Portugal's history of exploration and colonization. There are many one-pot dishes popular in Portugal that incorporate flavors from all around the globe."

Twersky delights in tweaking these one-pot recipes, making them more complex and giving them a beautiful presentation. For example, traditional açorda is a dish based on bread soaked in water, then

ALFAMA, FINE PORTUGUESE CUISINE
551 Hudson Street
New York, NY 10014
212-645-2500
www.alfamarestaurant.com

On the side...
What do you consider the most overrated ingredient?
Chicken.

The most underrated ingredient?
Tomato or pineapple.

What is your favorite comfort food?
Tacos.

What kitchen gadget is your must-have tool?
A small offset spatula.

If you were not a chef, what wouldyou be?
A racecar driver.

What was the last thing you ate?
Meatloaf with mashed potatoes.

drained and combined with savory spices and vegetables or fish. It's always served in a large mound on a plate. Not very pretty, perhaps, but a wonderful mix of flavors. Twerksy's version uses spoonbread infused with fresh corn, cilantro and lobster broth. It's then baked off in round timbales and presented as individual "cakes" with sautéed shrimp and a lobster reduction. "The blending of different cuisines that is so important in traditional Portuguese cooking has made the contemporary dishes we serve possible," explains Twersky. "They already had the range of flavors, but now they're elegant and upscale."

This time it's not serendipity guiding Twersky, it's skill and passion. ▪

The recipes

"The blending of different cuisines that is so important in traditional Portuguese cooking has made the contemporary dishes we serve possible. They already had the range of flavors, but now they're elegant and upscale."

Braised Curried Lamb Shoulder with Coconut Rice

SERVES 6–8

Historians say Portugal had one of the first truly international cuisines because of its colonial possessions in Africa and South America and its position as a seafaring, globetrotting nation. Such a reputation rings true with this recipe, which combines lamb with nuances of curry, orange and, of course, Portugal's beloved mainstay, Madeira.

5 pounds lamb chuck (shoulder), cleaned, fat removed
(or substitute lamb shanks—1 per person)
1 large onion, chopped
2 carrots, chopped
2 parsnips, chopped (optional)
12 cloves garlic, crushed
1/4 cup grated fresh gingerroot
2 tablespoons vegetable oil
1 tablespoon red curry paste
2 cups orange juice
2 cups Madeira wine (or white wine)
2 tablespoons curry powder
Salt and pepper to taste

Preheat oven to 250°F.

Place lamb in a deep, ovenproof casserole dish, just big enough to hold the meat. In a separate pan over medium-high heat, sauté onion, carrots, parsnips, garlic and gingerroot in vegetable oil until soft and slightly colored. Reduce heat to medium, add curry paste and cook for 2 minutes. Add juice, wine and curry powder, and bring to a boil. Pour over lamb and cover. Place in oven and cook 3 to 4 hours until very tender. Cool slightly, then carefully remove lamb and vegetables to a large serving platter, leaving liquid behind. Tent with foil.

Transfer liquid to a saucepan and cook over medium heat until reduced by about half, or until sauce coats the back of a spoon. Season to taste with salt and pepper.

FOR THE COCONUT RICE
3 cups rice
1 (14-ounce) can coconut milk
4 1/4 cups water
2 tablespoons butter

Combine all ingredients in a large, covered saucepan over high heat. Bring to a boil and stir once. Reduce heat to very low and cook, covered, until all liquid is absorbed, about 20–25 minutes. Transfer to a large bowl.

TO SERVE
Remove foil from platter; pour sauce over lamb and serve with Coconut Rice. ◼

Pork, Shrimp and Ginger Meatballs

SERVES 6–8

These delicate little meatballs flaunt Asian flavors, hearkening back to the days when Macao was a territory of Portugal. If you make the sweet and sour sauce, Chef Twersky recommends opening a window and keeping your face away from the pan, since the boiling vinegar can give off irritating fumes.

FOR THE MEATBALLS
2 tablespoons vegetable oil
1 large onion, diced
2 tablespoons grated fresh gingerroot
1 tablespoon chopped garlic
2 tablespoons soy sauce
3/4 pound small shrimp (raw), chopped
1 1/2 pounds ground pork
3/4 cup panko, ground fine
Salt, pepper, ground coriander to taste

FOR THE SWEET AND SOUR SAUCE
1/2 cup white distilled vinegar
1/2 cup sugar
1/2 cup honey
Pinch of crushed red pepper flakes
1 clove garlic, crushed

TO MAKE THE MEATBALLS
Preheat oven to 425°F.

Cover a baking sheet with foil and coat it with nonstick spray; set aside. In a small pan over medium heat, add vegetable oil and sauté onion until golden. Add gingerroot, garlic and soy sauce. Simmer until the liquid evaporates completely. Add shrimp and cook through, about 3–5 minutes. Cool mixture completely. Mix well with pork and panko and season to taste with salt, pepper and ground coriander. To check flavor, tear off a small piece of the shrimp-and-meat mixture and place it on prepared baking sheet in the oven for 5 minutes; let cool and taste. Adjust seasoning if necessary.

Roll meat mixture into 1 1/2-inch balls and lay side by side on prepared baking sheet. Bake until browned and cooked through, 10–15 minutes.

TO MAKE THE SWEET AND SOUR SAUCE
In a saucepan over high heat, combine vinegar and sugar and cook until reduced by half. Add remaining ingredients, bring to a boil and then remove from heat. Allow to cool.

TO SERVE
Place on platter and serve with bowl of sweet and sour dipping sauce. ▨

Clams Steamed in White Wine and Garlic

SERVES 6

This is the ultimate summer party dish that can be doubled or even tripled as needed. Try to use a pan that's wide enough to hold the clams in a single layer. If the clams must be in several layers, watch them carefully and remove each one as it opens.

20–30 littleneck clams, washed thoroughly
1/2 cup minced garlic
1/2 cup extra-virgin olive oil
2 cups dry white wine
1 cup chopped fresh cilantro
1 lemon

In a large saucepan wide enough to hold clams in a single layer, sauté garlic and clams in olive oil over medium heat until garlic begins to color. Add wine and cover. Steam until all clams have opened. Stir in cilantro.

TO SERVE
Squeeze lemon over clams and transfer to a large platter. Pour broth into a large bowl and serve with crusty bread for dipping. ▨

Alex Ureña
CHEF AND OWNER, PAMPLONA

Taking the bull by the horns

Ureña, Alex Ureña's first New York restaurant, generated a lot of buzz in 2006 for its fusion of Spanish flavors and molecular gastronomy. But with its expensive and complicated menu, it was perhaps not the best showcase of this chef's talent and drive. Did Ureña give up? No way. Fast-forward to fall of 2007 and Pamplona is born. Gone are the of-the-moment foams and jellies and in their place is sophisticated fare that elevates the traditional cuisine of Toledo and Valencia to something new, while still staying simple, fresh and accessible.

Star dishes, such as the suckling pig poached in olive oil and served with caramelized apples, share the limelight with an updated paella (see page 182) and sea scallops with truffled Greek yogurt. Homey creations like fried egg with chorizo and white asparagus really "ring the bell for Spain," asserts

Ureña. And the menu has a sense of play, too, with Ureña's enticing Calimocho, a heady cocktail of one part Coca-Cola, two parts rum and two parts Rioja.

So where did a boy from the Dominican Republic learn to cook like this? Not at culinary school. He got his start in the kitchen of River Café, where his father also worked, but his real education came from none other than David Bouley. He worked at the eponymous restaurant for 9 years. "I became a chef because of David Bouley," states Ureña. "I was working in his kitchen and got really inspired and excited by him. He's so good at everything—the food and running the restaurant and all the aspects of the business. I really wanted to be like David."

Three years of travel through France and, most notably, northern Spain convinced him to share Iberian cuisine with New Yorkers. "At that time, there were not a lot of great Spanish restaurants in the city," explains Ureña, who envisioned doing more than serving the usual country-style dishes. "Traditional flavors in Spain can be very strong and I wanted to adapt them to American tastes." And so he keeps the fabulous cheeses, the spicy chorizo, the wonderful shellfish, but combines them in new ways to create something more modern, like a braised rabbit bocadillo, a pressed sandwich that pairs the

PAMPLONA
37 East 28th Street
New York, NY 10016
212-213-2328
www.pamplonanyc.com

On the side...

What do you consider the most overrated ingredient?
Fried milk.

The most underrated ingredient?
Anything classic like a whole, roasted chicken.

What is your favorite comfort food?
Pork.

What kitchen gadget is your must-have tool?
A hand blender.

If you were not a chef, what would you be?
A baseball player.

What was the last thing you ate?
Some roasted pork leg.

tangy rabbit with just-melting goat cheese. Another significant switch involves making the dining experience easier for guests. "I don't want to fight with my food," Ureña says. So he simplifies. "In Spain, the mussels and cockles are still in their shells when the paella is served. Why do that? We just take them out of the shell so the customer doesn't have to deal with it."

As Ureña readily admits, "This is a very risky business, and it's hard to please everyone." But it's personally rewarding, too. "We try to do our best. I don't know how to do anything else, and I don't want to." ■

The recipes

Buñuelos de Queso

These tasty little morsels, typical of Spanish tapas, are ideal fare for any party. Truffle oil and a combination of three cheeses boost the flavor well beyond the ordinary.

3 cups heavy cream
6 egg yolks
1 tablespoon truffle oil
½ bottle of Alhambra beer
1 teaspoon salt
1 teaspoon pepper
3 fresh chorizo links, cooked and finely ground
¼ pound Iberico cheese, grated
¼ pound Manchego cheese, grated
¼ pound Cheddar cheese, grated
2 cups panko bread crumbs
1 quart vegetable oil for deep-frying

In a medium bowl, combine cream, egg yolks, truffle oil, beer, salt and pepper. Fold in ground chorizo and the grated cheeses. Mix until thoroughly blended. Place panko in a shallow bowl or pie plate.

Roll chorizo-egg mixture into 1-inch balls with hands; roll in panko to coat.

In deep fryer or large pot, bring oil to 350°F.

Depending on the size of the pot or fryer, fry in small batches 3 to 4 pieces at a time until golden brown, about 2 to 3 minutes. Remove to paper towels to drain.

TO SERVE
Transfer to a platter and serve immediately—perhaps with Chef Ureña's Calimocho cocktail (page 181). ▪

Paella

SERVES 2

A typical Valencian rice dish, paella is popular throughout Spain. Chef Ureña starts his with a traditional sofrito, or base of peppers, onions and garlic, and gives it a little update with the addition of ribeye steak.

4 tablespoons olive oil, divided
1 chicken leg, cut in small pieces
5 ounces ribeye steak, cut in ½-inch pieces
1 fresh chorizo link, cut in ½-inch pieces
½ small onion, diced
1 small red pepper, diced
3 cloves garlic, finely diced and blanched
1½ tablespoons paprika
Salt and pepper to taste
½ pound rice (Bomba or Gallaparra rice is best)
2 cups chicken stock
10 strands saffron threads
10 mussels
10 cockles
6 large shrimp, cleaned, tails removed

In a very large, wide sauté pan or paella pan, over high heat, add 2 tablespoons of the olive oil and brown chicken, steak and chorizo on all sides. Remove and reserve. Reduce heat to low and, in the same pan, make a sofrito by sautéing the onion, pepper, garlic and paprika in the remaining olive oil until soft. Season with salt and pepper.

Return chicken, steak and chorizo to pan. Add rice and stir to coat. Pour in chicken stock and stir in saffron.

In a separate pot over medium heat, steam mussels and cockles in about 1½ cups water just until they open. Remove mussels and cockles and reserve cooking liquid. Add liquid from mussels and cockles to the paella pan.

When rice is nearly cooked, add shrimp and cook a few minutes until shrimp are pink and rice is cooked through.

TO SERVE
Remove cockles and mussels from shells and mix into rice. Serve immediately on individual warmed plates. ▪

The recipes

"Traditional flavors in Spain can be very
strong, and I wanted to adapt them to American tastes."

Green Gazpacho

SERVES 6–8

This punchy green gazpacho gets its color from
a variety of leafy green herbs and verdant
vegetables and its kick from vodka and two kinds
of vinegar. Save the red gazpacho for the kiddies
and enjoy this one adults-only. (You need to prep
this dish a day ahead, so plan accordingly.)

2½ pounds ripe plum or grape tomatoes,
coarsely chopped

1 stalk lemongrass, peeled and coarsely chopped

¼ cup vodka

2 cucumbers, peeled and chopped

2 green bell peppers, seeded, cored and chopped

4 tomatillos, chopped

2 tablespoons white-wine vinegar

1 tablespoon sherry vinegar

1 tablespoon lemon juice

1 tablespoon sugar

Salt and pepper to taste

½ avocado

Small handful chives

Small handful cilantro

Small handful parsley

1 bunch scallions, trimmed

The day before serving, combine tomatoes, lemongrass
and vodka in a blender and puree until smooth. Line a sieve
with cheesecloth or paper towels, set over a bowl and pour
in tomato mixture. Refrigerate overnight; clear liquid will
slowly drain through. Discard solids.

In a glass or ceramic bowl, combine cucumbers, green
peppers, tomatillos, vinegars, lemon juice, sugar and a
generous sprinkling of salt and pepper. Refrigerate
overnight.

In a blender, blend all marinated vegetables with the
avocado, chives, cilantro, parsley, scallions and tomato
liquid, beginning on low speed and increasing until
mixture is smooth. Taste and adjust the salt, pepper and
vinegar, adding more as needed.

TO SERVE

Refrigerate until ready to serve so soup is very cold.
Ladle into individual chilled bowls. ▪

Jimmy Henderson
EXECUTIVE CHEF, PERIYALI

Chef times two

A native of the city, Chef Jimmy Henderson has been involved in the New York restaurant scene since he was a teenager washing dishes and shucking clams in the joints around his Bronx neighborhood. Although his grandmother was a great cook, some of his earliest recollections about food focus on, of all things, a television show. "I loved watching *The Galloping Gourmet* [Graham Kerr's cooking program]." From that heavy dose of butter and cream, Henderson moved on to a taste for lighter, more uncomplicated dishes "not smothered in sauces and disguised with rubs, but rich in natural flavor."

He was attracted early on to a job at Periyali—the restaurant that made New Yorkers aware there was more to Greek food than meat on a spit—because the food was "so perfect and unaffected, no flavor got lost," he says. "It was just good, fresh food cooked simply and seasoned well with lots of herbs." Indeed,

Jimmy Henderson
EXECUTIVE CHEF, PERIYALI

since it opened in 1987, Periyali has been known for its lively versions of Greek favorites and its incomparable seafood. It's a reputation Henderson maintains today with clean, herb-infused selections like roasted chicken with oregano and lemon potatoes; a smoked trout appetizer, marinated in dill, scallion and lemon; and charcoal-grilled lamb chops alive with the flavor of fresh rosemary.

As Henderson is quick to point out, he so admires the type of food served at Periyali that he's actually worked there twice—the first time around as the head cook when he honed his skills through the restaurant's early years, and now as the executive chef. And he's not alone in loving it. At the start of his most recent stint Henderson was pleased to see waiters he'd known years ago still walking the floor and two of the dishwashers growing into capable sous chefs. Perhaps they, like he, appreciate the satisfaction that comes from working at a restaurant frequented by true food lovers. In fact, customers so appreciate Periyali's food, Henderson was happy to take on the recent challenge of developing a sister restaurant, Persephone.

Two restaurants? Henderson laughs, explaining that the menus for each are very similar, featuring a reliance on quality ingredients and classic preparation. Both include, for instance, his octopus appetizer, served char-grilled and succulently soft and so

> *PERIYALI*
> *35 West 20th Street*
> *New York, NY 10011*
> *212-463-7890*
> *www.periyali.com*

On the side...

What do you consider the most overrated ingredient?
Salmon. Chefs never eat it, so I'm always surprised to see it on so many menus.

The most underrated ingredient?
Mastic, an aromatic spice grown only on the Greek island of Chios.

What is your favorite comfort food?
Risotto.

What kitchen gadget is your must-have tool?
Needle-nose pliers (as a chef in a restaurant that mostly serves fish, it's a tool I have to have).

If you were not a chef, what profession would you be in?
I'd probably be working for immigration or customs because I started studying political science before I went to the Culinary Institute of America.

What was the last thing you ate?
A family meal—barbecued chicken.

renowned that is known as "Periyali octopus" (see page 188) regardless of where it is served. The two venues also spotlight his version of skordalia, a Greek potato spread that's prepared, Henderson-style, with blanched almonds (see page 187). And *kouneli stifado*, braised rabbit with red wine and pearl onions, has proved a hit both downtown and up.

Evidence, we think, that Henderson's return engagement was a wise one for him and for us. ■

The recipes

Henderson has a love of uncomplicated food that's "not smothered in sauces and disguised with rubs, but [is] rich in natural flavor."

Roasted Beets with Almond Skordalia

SERVES 8

Chef Henderson is big fan of skordalia, a garlicky Greek spread that's often served with fish or vegetables or used as a dip with bread. In his twist on the traditional version, he revs up the potato-bread base with blanched almonds for a richer flavor and places red and yellow beets on top.

FOR THE SKORDALIA

5 ounces (about 5 slices) firm, homemade-style bread
1/2 cup whole blanched almonds, coarsely chopped
2 or 3 large garlic cloves, put through a garlic press (about 1 teaspoon garlic puree)
1 small (about 3 ounces) all-purpose potato, peeled, boiled until soft, drained and cooled
3 tablespoons lemon juice
3 tablespoons white-wine vinegar
2 tablespoons extra-virgin olive oil
3/4 teaspoon salt
1/2 teaspoon sugar

FOR THE BEETS

3 red beets
3 yellow beets
1 cup extra-virgin olive oil, divided
1/3 cup red-wine vinegar
Salt and pepper to taste
1/2 bunch parsley, washed and chopped

TO MAKE THE SKORDALIA

Trim the crusts from the bread and spread the slices out on a tray to dry for about 24 hours.

In the bowl of a food processor, place the almonds, garlic and cooled potato. Process until smooth.

Mix the lemon juice, vinegar, olive oil, salt and sugar in a small bowl and set aside.

Fill a large bowl with cool water. Drop the dried bread into the water, 1 slice at a time. When it is soaked, squeeze about half the water from the bread between the palms of your hands. Add the bread to the ingredients in the processor, alternating with the lemon-juice mixture, and process until smooth. Since the skordalia has a tendency to stiffen and become pasty as it chills, the mixture should be quite loose at this point.

Taste and adjust the seasoning. Scrape the mixture into a bowl. Cover and refrigerate for several hours to allow the flavors to mellow and blend. If the mixture seems too stiff, beat in a little water before serving.

TO MAKE THE BEETS

Preheat oven to 350°F.

Wash beets in cold water and toss with 3 tablespoons olive oil, salt and pepper. Spread on a shallow pan and roast until tender. Check for doneness by inserting a large skewer through a beet. (Baby beets take approximately 45 minutes to 1 hour. Large beets could take anywhere from 45 minutes to 2 to 3 hours.)

Cool, then peel and dice into 1-inch cubes.

Place beets in bowl and toss in remaining olive oil, red-wine vinegar and season with salt and pepper.

Sprinkle chopped parsley over beets.

TO SERVE

Spread a large spoonful of skordalia on the center of a plate and add a mound of beets on top. ■

The recipes

Periyali Octopus

SERVES 8

Octopus takes a little planning (you have to work 2 to 3 days in advance), but it's a wonderful dish for a special occasion because it's incredibly tasty and so unusual. Better yet, you'll spend less than 10 minutes grilling it.

FOR THE OCTOPUS

2 onions
1 large carrot
1 celery stalk
1/2 bottle of red wine
4 bay leaves
2 large octopi
1 cup olive oil
3 bay leaves
1 cup chopped oregano leaves (preferably fresh)

FOR THE SAUCE

2 1/2 cups chicken stock
1/2 cup (1 stick) butter
1/2 cup red-wine vinegar
Juice of 1 lemon

TO MAKE THE OCTOPUS

Roughly chop onions, carrot and celery and place in a large stockpot with wine, 3 gallons water and bay leaves. Add octopus and poach over low heat in solution 3 to 4 hours. Allow octopus to cool in solution.

Remove octopus and clean any gelatinous tissue from tentacles. Do not remove ends of tentacles. Remove and discard head. Combine olive oil, bay leaves and chopped oregano in large bowl and add octopus. Marinate in refrigerator for 2 to 3 days. Octopus can be eaten cold at this point or grilled. If grilling, preheat grill to hot. Gently shake off marinade. Grill octopus 7 to 8 minutes.

TO MAKE THE SAUCE

Combine all ingredients in a saucepan over medium heat and reduce by two-thirds.

TO SERVE

Transfer octopus to platter, cover with sauce and serve. ▪

Lamb Tenderloin with Roca Salad

SERVES 8

Nothing is more classically Greek than a simple dish of lamb, cooked to a turn and served over a bed of peppery roca, a cousin of arugula. Add some feta and a few kalamata olives and dinner is on the table in minutes.

2 pounds lamb tenderloin, trimmed
1/2 cup extra-virgin olive oil, plus more for rubbing
Salt and pepper to taste
4 tablespoons red-wine vinegar
1/2 cup black olive puree
8 cups roca, washed, with any long stems removed
1 pound feta cheese
Pitted kalamata olives for garnish

Preheat oven to 475°F.

Rub tenderloin lightly with olive oil and season with salt and pepper.

In a heatproof pan (cast iron works well) over very high heat, sear tenderloin on all sides. Place pan in oven and finish to desired temperature:

Rare: 4 minutes

Medium: 6 to 7 minutes

Well-done: 10 or more minutes

Remove from oven; let rest for 5 minutes and slice.

While lamb is resting, in small a bowl, combine vinegar, 1/2 cup olive oil and olive puree; whisk gently.

TO SERVE

Dress the roca with vinaigrette. Divide among 8 individual plates, crumble feta cheese over each and place slices of lamb on top. Garnish with olives. ▪

Lamb Tenderloin with Roca Salad

7

New York, where the term *melting pot* was first used to describe the immigrant neighborhoods of the Lower East Side, is still a city of newcomers. Of the more than 8 million people who live here, a whopping 35 percent or more are foreign-born. Over 150 different languages can be heard on the city's streets. Which isn't to imply that the natives lack their own singular viewpoints. So what's this got to do with food?

It's a rare week in New York that at least one or two intriguing new restaurants don't open their doors. And more and more often, these establishments are featuring cuisines from all over the globe or one-of-a kind formats that could thrive only in such a diverse urban setting. Whether they're run by people who grew up with the food they're serving, or whether they're opportunities for chefs to share a cuisine they've grown to love, they provide a memorable experience for diners. New Yorkers, tourists, and yes, the homesick can enjoy a meal they couldn't get just anywhere.

But for New York chefs, it's not enough to simply copy a national dish or duplicate a regional specialty. What's exciting for them is to create food that's totally their own. From a Mexican Salmon Ceviche with Watermelon at Crema, to ilili's Lebanese Lamb Pizza or the Avocado-Coriander Soup from raw-food master Neal Harden, each dish is something you'll find only in New York.

Specialty Cuisines

Julieta Ballesteros, Crema Restaurante

RECIPES

Salmon Ceviche with Watermelon and Mint   PAGE 194
Tinga Poblana   PAGE 194
Roasted Chilean Sea Bass, Yucatán-Style   PAGE 196

Julieta Ballesteros

Neal Harden, Pure Food and Wine

RECIPES

Avocado-Coriander Soup with Watermelon, Passion-fruit and Watercress   PAGE 199
Cremini Mushroom Skewers with Pistachio Curry Sauce, Tamarind Chutney and Saffron Radish "Rice"   PAGE 200

ilili

Jose Salgado, Nomad Restaurant

RECIPES

Chicken and Olive Tajine   PAGE 204
Fooul   PAGE 204
Spinach Briwats   PAGE 205

Ben Pollinger, Oceana

RECIPES

Steamed Grouper with Lotus Root, Yu Choy and Wood-Ear Black Bean Sauce   PAGE 208
Sautéed Nantucket Bay Scallops with Citrus Salad and Mamey   PAGE 210
Pan-Roasted Lobster with Chestnut Polenta, Brussels Sprouts and Spiced Maple Sauce   PAGE 211

Philippe Massoud, ilili

RECIPES

Brussels Sprouts with Fig Sauce   PAGE 214
Black Cod with Pomegranate Molasses and Zaatar   PAGE 214
Lahmajeen (Lebanese Lamb Pizza)   PAGE 214

Sam Hazen, Tao New York

RECIPES

Crab Cakes with Thai Chile-Mango Sauce   PAGE 218
Tataki Beef with Asparagus and Shitake   PAGE 218
Lobster Wonton in Ginger Shitake Broth   PAGE 220

Neal Harden

191

Julieta Ballesteros
EXECUTIVE CHEF AND OWNER, CREMA RESTAURANTE

Artful ways

In the tiny open kitchen at Crema, the cooks are prepping tostadas. No surprise, given that this is a Mexican restaurant. But what they put onto the fried tortilla shells is a revelation: ostrich. "There are many ostrich farms in Mexico these days, and I thought it would be a great idea to try the meat back here," says chef/owner Julieta Ballesteros. She pauses and begins to laugh. "At first I wasn't very successful. Diners weren't interested, so I started sending the tostadas out as freebies and they finally caught on." Now the pan-seared ostrich, served with goat cheese, fresh avocado and a guava-chipotle glaze, makes a regular appearance as a popular appetizer.

Such a story gives a small glimpse into this chef's creativity and passion. Growing up in Monterrey, Mexico, Ballesteros was always cooking—if she wasn't painting. "I was torn between the two arts, but decided on the culinary one because you get quicker gratification. Working on a painting takes months and months, and I realized I didn't have the patience for that," she states. But her painterly side can certainly be seen in her dishes: Critics have praised the beauty of her food, pointing to the way she layers ingredients to contrast their colors, how she swirls escabeche into imaginative flourishes, or her use of a whimsical giant spoon to serve guacamole. "I care very much about how something looks on the plate," she says. "To me, every dish is a piece of art."

But Ballesteros's reason for opening Crema wasn't to show off her artistic talent: "I wanted people to know that Mexican food goes beyond tacos and enchiladas, that even though it has intense flavors, the dishes can be delicate and sophisticated." At the restaurant, she infuses the techniques she learned at the French Culinary Institute to give her creations a more refined touch (she calls it "la cucina Mexicana refinida"). She also makes an effort to highlight regional dishes, such as a pork-filled tamale wrapped in a banana leaf from Oaxaca to a silky sea bass coated with achiote paste from the Yucatán (see page 196). Even familiar items like empañadas benefit from a Ballesteros touch; hers might be filled with shrimp and sea bass and sautéed in a squash-blossom puree with portobellos and goat cheese.

"What I love about cooking is that it involves all the senses, so it's extremely creative," she says. "I get

CREMA RESTAURANTE
111 West 17th Street
New York, NY 10011
212-691-4477
www.cremarestaurante.com

On the side...

What do you consider the most overrated ingredient?
Mushrooms.

The most underrated ingredient?
The mamey fruit (a tropical fruit native to the Caribbean and Central America).

What kitchen gadget is your must-have tool?
A knife. I wear mine out.

What is your favorite comfort food?
Pecan pie and French fries.

If you were not a chef, what would you be?
An artist, of course!

What was the last thing you ate?
Some taquitos and guacamole.

inspired by what I see in the market and what I see in other places." She feels a real kinship with the cooking of India. "It shares similarities with Mexican food. Both have a real explosion in the mouth."

In fact, prompted by the vegetarian offerings on Indian menus, Ballesteros now serves a vegetarian plate that may include an enchilada, two different moles, a vegetable skewer and a stuffed poblano. "It's been a big success," she asserts.

But when all's said and done, this is just another example of Ballesteros's willingness to try something new. "I express myself through food," she states. "It's my way of translating my feelings. Every dish that goes out there is me." ∎

The recipes

Salmon Ceviche with Watermelon and Mint

SERVES 6–8

A watermelon pico de gallo gives this quick-to-make Mexican ceviche a bracing coolness. The chef serves it with fried tortillas.

FOR THE SALMON

2 cups finely cut fresh salmon (preferably organic)
1 tablespoon soybean, corn or vegetable oil

FOR THE WATERMELON PICO DE GALLO

1 tomato, chopped
2 to 3 cups watermelon, cut into small pieces
1/4 red onion, finely minced
1 clove garlic, finely minced
6 or 7 sprigs cilantro, finely minced
6 spears mint, finely cut
1/2 cup lime juice
Pinch sugar and salt

FOR THE CHILE DE ARBOL OIL

1 cup soy oil
5 chiles de arbol, seeded
1/2 white onion, peeled
3 cloves garlic, peeled
Pinch sugar and salt and pepper to taste

FOR THE GARNISH

Fried tortillas, flour or corn
Chile de arbol oil (see below)
Toasted sesame seeds

Place the cut salmon in a bowl and stir in the oil to coat. Refrigerate for 1 hour.

In the meantime, in a bowl, combine all the ingredients for the watermelon pico de gallo. Refrigerate for 1 hour, covered, then mix with the pieces of salmon.

Just before serving, make the chile de arbol oil. In skillet over medium-high, heat oil and sauté the chiles, onion and garlic until golden brown. Season with a pinch of sugar and salt and pepper to taste. Blend until mixture is very smooth.

TO SERVE

Drizzle chile de arbol oil over the salmon mixture, sprinkle on sesame seeds and serve with fried tortillas. ▓

Tinga Poblana

SERVES 6–8

Tinga poblana is basically a slow-cooked meat dish flavored with tomatoes and chiles and served on tortillas. Chef Ballesteros composes hers with chorizo, chicken, pork and adds corn for crunch.

1 pound chorizo
1 teaspoon soybean or vegetable oil
1 pound chicken breasts, or chicken legs
1 pound pork shank, cut up
10 fresh tomatoes
3 cloves garlic, peeled
2 onions, peeled
1 (8-ounce) can chipotle peppers
1/2 cup jalapeño vinegar
Salt and pepper to taste
Pinch sugar
4 ears corn, shucked
10 ounces Chihuahua cheese
1 cup Mexican cream (see note)
2 chile poblanos, roasted, peeled, seeded and cut into strips
Warm tortillas and refried beans for serving

In a large pot on medium heat, sauté the chorizo in the teaspoon of oil. Add the chicken and pork and sauté until brown. Turn heat down to low.

In the meantime, in a food processor or blender, blend the tomatoes, garlic, onions, chipotles and jalapeño vinegar until chunky. Add a little water if necessary and season with salt and pepper. Stir this salsa mixture into the pot of meats, cover and let sit over low heat.

In another pot, boil the corn for 10 minutes; add salt and pepper to taste, plus a pinch of sugar. Cut corn kernels from cobs and add to pot of meats. Continue cooking until the meat is tender, 35–45 minutes. Remove from the heat and let cool. Shred the meat before adding the cheese, cream and poblano strips.

TO SERVE

Ladle on plate and serve with warm flour tortillas and refried beans. ▓

▓ **NOTE** Mexican cream is available at Mexican grocery stores and some specialty food shops, or substitute sour cream.

Salmon Ceviche with Watermelon and Mint

The recipes

Roasted Chilean Sea Bass, Yucatán-Style

SERVES 6–8
Crema features dishes from all over Mexico, and this one, from the Yucatán, highlights the achiote and bananas traditionally used in that region. The fish itself is simply sautéed, then spread with achiote paste and roasted. But it becomes sea bass with sass when placed over banana puree and topped with spicy pineapple.

FOR THE BANANA PUREE
2 Idaho potatoes
Salt and pepper to taste
4 bananas, peeled
½ cup butter
2 chipotle chiles in adobo
½ cup (4 ounces) cream cheese, softened
Pinch of sugar

FOR THE ACHIOTE
8 ounces achiote paste
1½ cups orange juice
½ cup jalapeño vinegar
1 red onion, chopped
2 cloves garlic, peeled
1 habanero chile, chopped
1 tablespoon cumin
1 tablespoon oregano
½ cup honey
½ cup cilantro
½ cup soybean or vegetable oil

FOR THE ESCABECHE
1 cup diced pineapple
4 garlic cloves, minced
½ cup carrots, julienned and blanched
1 red onion, sliced and blanched
1 small bunch cilantro, finely chopped
2 habanero chiles, minced
Salt, pepper, sugar to taste
Juice of 1 lime
½ cup orange juice

FOR THE FISH
3 tablespoons butter
6 (8-ounce) pieces Chilean sea bass
Frizzled tortillas and toasted sesame seeds, for garnish (see note)

TO MAKE THE BANANA PUREE
Cut potatoes and boil them in water with salt and pepper until soft. When they are ready, in another pan, combine potatoes, bananas, butter and chipotle chiles with a little bit of water, simmer for 5 minutes and then puree in a blender with cream cheese until smooth. Season with salt and pepper and a pinch of sugar. Set aside.

TO MAKE THE ACHIOTE
Blend all the ingredients except the soybean oil, until almost smooth. Add soybean oil to emulsify. Set aside.

TO MAKE THE ESCABECHE
In a bowl, combine pineapple, garlic, carrots, red onion, cilantro and minced habaneros, salt, pepper and sugar (to taste) along with the juice of one lime and the orange juice. Strain, taste and adjust seasoning if necessary. Set aside.

TO MAKE THE FISH
Preheat oven to 400°F.

Heat the butter in a sauté pan over medium heat, add the fish and cook for 1 minute, then turn over and cook other side. Transfer the fish to an ovenproof pan and spread about 3 tablespoons of the achiote over each piece. Bake until done (approximately 10–12 minutes).

TO SERVE
On a plate, spread approximately 3 tablespoons of the banana puree and place a piece of the sea bass on top. Garnish with frizzled tortillas and 1 tablespoon pineapple escabeche and top with sesame seeds. ▣

▣ **NOTE** To make frizzled tortillas, cut tortilla into thin strips (about ⅛-inch wide and 2 inches long) and lightly fry in oil until slightly curled.

Neal Harden
CHEF, PURE FOOD AND WINE

Raw talent

Neal Harden is one of the city's most innovative chefs, and yet he never cooks a thing. Never. The reason? He's the chef at Pure Food and Wine, New York's premier vegan, organic, raw-food-only restaurant. And if you think that means he serves wilted lettuce and sprouts eaten by antimeat protestors, think again.

"Surprisingly," asserts Harden, "most of our customers are not vegetarians. They're just people who are simply interested in food." While it may be health or novelty that lures people to the restaurant the first time around, what keeps them coming back is the truly delicious food.

"The biggest fear people have walking in is that they won't be satisfied, but they're always surprised and pleased once they taste the dishes," says Harden. "I think people expect just veggies on a plate or endless courses of salads, but what we offer is not like that at all."

Neal Harden
CHEF, PURE FOOD AND WINE

Although the key feature of the restaurant is that no food is heated to more than 118°F (to preserve natural enzymes, vitamins and minerals), Harden says the food tastes so good because it's rooted in traditional flavors. Take the well-loved zucchini and Roma tomato lasagna, for example. It has all the intensity of the traditional version of lasagna, but since Harden couldn't boil the pasta or bake the casserole, he had to craft the dish a special way. "For the noodles, we had to come up with a completely different kind of dough, and we dehydrate it for over six hours." And, of course, the classic milk ricotta had to be replaced with something else—in this case, a version made from pignoli.

Even after an item such as the first-course creamy cauliflower samosas with banana-tamarind sauce, mango chutney, garam masala and mint gets onto the menu, it's still extremely complicated to make for each diner. Explains Harden, "It takes us much longer to prepare a dish. We can't just put something in the oven and walk away and do five other things. It's extremely labor-intensive. We have a very large staff of about 40 people altogether.

"As a chef, you always run into things that don't work," continues Harden. "There are limitations, but we also do stuff other restaurants don't. One I'm most proud of is our technique for making crackers or

> *PURE FOOD AND WINE*
> *54 Irving Place*
> *New York, NY 10003*
> *212-477-1010*
> *www.purefoodandwine.com*

On the side...

What do you consider the most overrated ingredient?
Foie gras.

The most underrated ingredient?
Kale.

What kitchen gadget is your must-have tool?
A suribachi, a Japanese mortar and pestle.

What is your favorite comfort food?
Indian food, especially dosa.

If you were not a chef, what would you be?
A musician.

What was the last thing you ate?
Falafel.

bread. Instead of using white flour, we grind up pistachios, fresh basil, flaxseed and red pepper, then spread the mixture very thinly and dehydrate it. We get an extremely delicious and crisp cracker without baking. It's not what you'd expect from those items, but we get to show a side of an ingredient you otherwise wouldn't see."

But for Harden the best thing is diner satisfaction. "The main comment people make when exiting is that they feel different—satisfied and elated, but not bogged down," he says proudly. "They didn't sacrifice their well-being to have a good time and a great meal." ■

The recipes

"The biggest fear people have walking in is that they won't be satisfied, but people are always surprised and pleased once they taste the dishes."

Avocado-Coriander Soup with Watermelon, Passionfruit and Watercress

SERVES 4–6

A bright starter or a tempting main dish, this unique soup gains creaminess from avocado and tang from lemon juice, orange zest and coriander.

1 cup chopped cucumber, skin on and seeds included
1½ medium avocados
1 tablespoon shallot, roughly chopped
1 large celery stalk, roughly chopped
2 tablespoons lemon juice
¼ teaspoon coriander
¼ teaspoon cumin
2 pinches orange zest
1½ cups water
½ cup drinkable sake
1½ teaspoons salt, plus more to taste
½ bunch cilantro, leaves only
2 cups watermelon, cut into 1-inch cubes
1 fresh ripe passionfruit
1 cup watercress leaves, picked from the stem

Blend all ingredients except watermelon, passionfruit and watercress in a high-speed blender until very smooth. Add more water if needed to thin out; if too thin, add more avocado. Taste and add salt if necessary. Soup should thickly coat a spoon, but it should not hold its shape in a bowl.

TO SERVE

Evenly divide the soup between 4–6 bowls. Top the soup with watermelon cubes and spoon the inside pulp of the passionfruit over the top. Garnish with the watercress leaves. ◼

The recipes

Cremini Mushroom Skewers with Pistachio Curry Sauce, Tamarind Chutney and Saffron Radish "Rice"

SERVES 4
If you don't own a dehydrator, Chef Harden suggests turning the oven to the lowest heat setting possible, about 112°F, and drying the vegetables in the oven for about 2 hours.

FOR THE SAFFRON RADISH "RICE"
2 cups of jicama, pulsed in a food processor to the size of rice and squeezed dry in a clean towel (measurement is after processing)
¼ teaspoon saffron threads
2 scallions, white parts only, finely minced
½ jalapeño pepper, seeds removed, finely minced
½ cup Easter egg radish, cut into small wedges
1 tablespoon virgin coconut oil (or virgin olive oil if coconut oil is unavailable)
½ teaspoon salt
Mix all ingredients together and set aside.

FOR THE CURRY SAUCE
2 teaspoons curry powder
½ teaspoon ground cumin
¼ teaspoon garam masala
¼ teaspoon turmeric
⅛ teaspoon cinnamon
1 Thai chile, seeds included
½ small shallot, roughly chopped
1-inch piece of gingerroot, peeled
¼ cup pistachios, shelled
Scant ½ teaspoon salt
½ Roma tomato
½ cup coconut water (from Thai coconuts; available at natural food stores)
½ teaspoon lime juice
1 teaspoon brown mustard seeds

Blend all ingredients except mustard seeds in a high-speed blender. When mixture is as smooth as possible, transfer to a bowl and whisk in mustard seeds. Let sit for at least 30 minutes in order for the mustard seeds to soften in the liquid.

FOR THE TAMARIND CHUTNEY
½ cup tamarind paste
3 tablespoons agave nectar
Pinch of salt
Blend all ingredients in a high-speed blender until very smooth. Set aside.

FOR THE BREADING
¼ cup pistachio flour (available at natural food stores)
½ teaspoon turmeric
1 teaspoon curry powder
1 teaspoon nutritional yeast
½ teaspoon salt
Whisk together all ingredients. Makes about ½ cup.

FOR THE SKEWERS
2 teaspoons lime juice
2 tablespoons olive oil
3 cups cremini mushrooms, stems removed
1 cup zucchini, sliced into rounds
1 cup cherry tomatoes, halved
Bamboo skewers

Whisk together lime juice and olive oil. Toss the vegetables in the mixture and let marinate for 10 minutes. Strain the vegetables and toss them in the breading until well coated. Divide the vegetables equally among 8 bamboo skewers. Place the skewers in a dehydrator for 1–2 hours until vegetables are broken down and chewy.

TO SERVE
Place an equal amount of the saffron radish rice onto 4 plates, and place 2 skewers on top of each portion of rice. Serve with curry sauce and tamarind chutney on the side. ■

Cremini Mushroom Skewers with Pistachio Curry Sauce, Tamarind Chutney and Saffron Radish "Rice"

Jose Salgado

CHEF, NOMAD RESTAURANT

Out of Africa

North Africa was the crossroads of the ancient world. Middle Easterners fleeing Baghdad, Moors returning from Spain, restless Turks, roving Berbers, Arabs and Jews, as well as the empire-building French and English—all brought their culinary influences to this area. And what a rich cuisine they created, drawing from the seafood of the Mediterranean; the sheep and cattle of the plains; and the citrus fruits, olives and figs of the Atlas Mountain valleys. But just as important were the native and imported spices brought in through ancient trade routes—these are what most influence Jose Salgado's food.

"I love spicy food," enthuses Nomad's chef. "And I don't mean hot, which is what many people mean by spicy, but the combined flavors of items such as cumin, coriander and tumeric." They're the heart of the cuisine and a big part of the culture, too. Something of a nomad himself, Salgado was born in Portugal but was raised in France, where he went to culinary school. He honed his skills in Paris and on the Riviera before taking the leap to New York eight years ago. What keeps him in his new city is the variety of the flavor combinations and the conviviality of the kitchen. Explains Salgado, "Cooking in New York is very different from cooking in France. There, the cuisine is very much centered on the classics, but here it is more eclectic. There are influences from everywhere, which makes the food very exciting." A fan of all types of food, he almost makes a science of eclecticism by taking ingredients from all over and remaking them into North African–style dishes.

Salgado has two approaches to this. He may start with a traditional European dish, such as escargot cooked in butter and garlic. He then completely re-creates it by combining the snails with cumin and cilantro and cooking them in olive oil. Or he might begin with a typical North African ingredient, such as the Mediterranean crabs that are a seaside staple, and create something unique by forming them into cakes with unconventional spices. "We can be very creative here," Salgado points out. "It's not just about serving dishes that are traditionally North African or Moroccan—it's also about presenting new concepts with the flavors that identify the cuisine."

But it is often the age-old recipes that are his inspiration. "I love the boureks, the tajines and, of course, couscous. That's something North Africans practically can't live without—I think it's older than

NOMAD RESTAURANT
78 Second Avenue
New York, NY 10003
212-253-5410
www.nomadny.com

On the side...

What do you consider the most overrated ingredient?
Sugar—too many chefs make things too sweet.

The most underrated ingredient?
Any kind of organic greens, really.

What kitchen gadget is your must-have tool?
A paring knife.

What is your favorite comfort food?
Chocolate.

If you were not a chef, what would you be?
A tour guide.

What was the last thing you ate?
Cauliflower.

bread!" And he prepares several different couscous dishes, including the popular couscous royale, served steamed under a mixture of three different meats and a variety of vegetables. Salgado, like a true nomad, is intent on moving forward, but he cherishes and maintains links with the past. And so his merguez, a lamb sausage, may be paired with roasted peppers and caramelized onions. "I think it's important to adapt from different influences," asserts Salgado. This allows him to create something fresh and new that's still rooted in the culture.

And that's a sentiment that's as classically North African as the restaurant itself. ■

The recipes

"It's not just about serving dishes that are traditionally North African or Moroccan—it's also about presenting new concepts with the flavors that identify the cuisine."

Chicken and Olive Tajine

SERVES 10

Chef Salgado's tajine is made in a modern skillet instead of the traditional conical clay pot.

4½ ounces green cracked olives
1½ preserved lemons
3 pounds chicken pieces (thighs, breasts, wings)
2 tablespoons oil
1 onion, finely chopped
¼ cup butter
3 garlic cloves
1 teaspoon ground gingerroot
Pinch saffron
1 teaspoon salt
1 teaspoon ground white pepper
3 tablespoons chopped fresh parsley

In a medium saucepan over low heat, simmer olives in water for 30 minutes. Drain olives. Remove peel from lemons and slice; set aside.

In a large skillet over medium heat, brown chicken in oil. Remove chicken and set aside. In the same pan, fry onion in butter until softened. Add garlic, gingerroot, saffron, salt, pepper and 2½ cups water and stir well to mix spices. Return the chicken pieces to skillet and turn to coat. Bring liquid to boil, cover and reduce heat to simmer for 1 hour, stirring occasionally. Add the cooked olives, preserved lemon and parsley and cook an additional 15 minutes. If sauce is too thin, remove chicken to platter and reduce to desired consistency.

TO SERVE

Pour sauce over chicken. Serve with couscous, if desired. ▪

Fooul

SERVES 4

Fooul is a flavorful North African bean stew that incorporates an ingredient nearly unique to that region's cooking—the preserved lemon.

3 cloves garlic, diced
3 tablespoons olive oil
2 cups fava beans
1 tablespoon paprika
1 teaspoon cumin
Salt and pepper to taste
½ cup olives, green or kalamata
1 preserved lemon, chopped
2 tablespoons fresh cilantro, chopped

In a large pan over medium heat, sauté garlic in olive oil until soft, 3 to 4 minutes. Add fava beans, paprika, cumin, salt and pepper, olives and preserved lemon and cook, stirring occasionally until beans are tender, about 30 minutes.

TO SERVE

Transfer to a serving bowl and garnish with cilantro. ▪

Spinach Briwats

SERVES 4

North African briwats—pastry pockets—can be packed with almost anything from chicken to lamb to cheese, but Chef Salgado goes light with a garlicky mix of spinach and onion.

1 pound fresh spinach
3 tablespoons olive oil
1 medium onion, chopped (about ½ cup)
4 cloves garlic, crushed
½ teaspoon salt (or to taste)
¼ teaspoon ground white pepper
¾ cup melted butter
1 box phyllo pastry sheets (#10)
1 egg, beaten
Oil for frying

Wash spinach, pull off tough stems and discard. Place spinach in a large pan with ¼ cup water. Cover and cook over medium heat for 3 minutes. Drain spinach and let cool.

Press out liquid. Set spinach aside.

Heat the olive oil in a skillet over low heat. Add onion and garlic and sauté 1 minute. Add salt and pepper. Cover and cook 5 minutes. Add spinach and stir to combine. Cover pan and simmer 15 minutes. Remove from heat and allow to cool.

To assemble, brush a large baking sheet with melted butter. Place 1 phyllo sheet on the baking sheet and cut lengthwise into four (3-inch-wide) strips. Brush with butter. Place 1 tablespoon spinach mixture at 1 end of 1 strip. Fold 1 corner of phyllo over filling. Repeat folding of dough down strip, forming a triangle. Brush end of dough with egg and smooth to close. Repeat with remaining 3 strips and then with 3 more sheets of phyllo to form 16 briwats.

In a deep fryer or large pot of hot oil, gently drop in briwats in batches and cook until golden. Remove to paper towels to drain.

TO SERVE

Place 4 briwats on small plates and serve hot. ■

■ Nomad

Ports of call

The menu at Oceana reads like a cruise ship's ports of call, with dishes hearkening back to places all over the world. Hungry for French? Try a rockfish bouillabaisse. Craving Caribbean? Sample sautéed sea scallops with mamey and citrus salad. Curious about Spanish? Taste almond and garlic soup with fresh sea urchin. It's global seafood—a foodie tour of the oceans—and it's the brainchild of Executive Chef Ben Pollinger, who's earned a three-star review from the *New York Times* critic Frank Bruni. "I wanted to give people a sense of adventure by experimenting with different cuisines," he says.

"I've been to some of these places, and those I haven't visited, I research until I'm comfortable with the stories and techniques behind the food." In cases like that, Pollinger cooks a dish the authentic way, then gives it his own delicious touches. Certainly the process is working: Since Pollinger launched his new menu in

2007, Oceana has been on everyone's radar. One reason may be its ever-evolving menu. "I'm always working on something and probably introduce a new dish or change an existing one every week or so," states Pollinger. "I enjoy experimenting with things I haven't used before: abalone, whelks, sea robin or even a type of seaweed I found on a recent trip to Iceland." It's all part of his around-the-world cooking trip.

Closer to home is yet another source of inspiration: Pollinger's own organic garden. "Being out in the garden is very peaceful. It's a place and time to think about food, to imagine what I might do. I play around with the herbs and various greens, figuring out how I can use them in recipes," he states.

But as often as menu changes occur, certain favorites do remain. One in particular is Florida pompano wrapped in taro, served with a basmati rice cake and baby bok choy. "I also always do something with salmon and Arctic char, since they're so popular, and I use black sea bass and cod, but I'll vary the preparation," says Pollinger. A more recent addition is red ocean perch: "I went Southern with this one, crusting it with cornmeal and creating a side of hominy, black-eyed peas and bacon."

All this from a guy who went off to college planning on a career in finance. But while interning with a stockbroker, he realized "this wasn't my

OCEANA
55 East 54th Street
New York, NY 10022
212-759-5941
www.oceanarestaurant.com

On the side...

What do you consider the most overrated ingredient?
Truffle oil.

The most underrated ingredient?
Acidic items like vinegars and citrus juice—you need these to heighten flavors.

What is your favorite comfort food?
Taylor ham, egg and cheese sandwich. I'm a Jersey boy.

What kitchen gadget is your must-have tool?
A large spoon for stirring and mixing.

If you were not a chef, what would you be?
A lawyer. I like to argue.

What was the last thing you ate?
I'm embarrassed, but I can't remember. Probably something here at Oceana.

thing" and changed course. "I remembered I liked working in the dorm cafeteria, but before making any decisions, I took a job in a restaurant as a test," he explains. Obviously, the test was a success.

Pollinger worked in more restaurants, then enrolled in the CIA. As for his global style, he credits that to positions with Alain Ducasse at Monaco, Michael Romano at Union Square Cafe and Floyd Cardoz at Tabla. "These experiences gave me an understanding of different flavors and techniques—American, Italian, French, Indian. And I try to incorporate all of them into the dishes here." ■

The recipes

Steamed Grouper with Lotus Root, Yu Choy and Wood-Ear Black Bean Sauce

SERVES 4

East meets West in this seafood delight in which grouper fillets team up with crunchy Asian vegetables and a black bean sauce injected with cardamom and ginger.

FOR THE SAUCE
1 tablespoon canola oil
2 shallots, sliced
1 clove garlic, sliced
1/2-inch piece gingerroot, peeled and sliced
1/4 pound wood-ear mushrooms, trimmed and diced
Salt and pepper to taste
1 teaspoon spice mix (recipe below)
1/4 cup cooked black beans (cooked in water with mirepoix, which is equal parts minced carrot and celery)
1 cup bean cooking liquid
3 cups fish fumet

FOR THE SPICE MIX
1 piece black cardamom
2 pieces green cardamom
1-inch piece Indian cinnamon
2 cloves
1 tablespoon cumin
1 tablespoon coriander
1 dried chile

Grind ingredients finely and mix together.

FOR THE GROUPER
4 (6-ounce) grouper fillets
2 tablespoons butter, softened
Salt and pepper to taste
2 tablespoons each: minced shallot, gingerroot, chiles, chives
1 tablespoon cilantro, chiffonade

FOR THE VEGETABLES
1 tablespoon canola oil
1 piece lotus root, peeled and sliced, slices halved or quartered if necessary
1 bunch yu choy, stems and leaves separated; stems blanched and sliced
Salt and pepper
1 teaspoon butter
1 teaspoon minced shallot
1 teaspoon minced gingerroot
1 teaspoon minced finger chiles
1/4 cup green mango, julienned
1/4 cup young coconut meat
1 tablespoon each cilantro and chives, chopped, plus some longer pieces of chive

TO MAKE THE SAUCE
Sweat the shallot, garlic and gingerroot in canola oil over low heat in a covered skillet. Add mushrooms, season with salt and pepper and sweat again. Add the spice mix and cook until aromatic. Add beans, cooking liquid and fish fumet; simmer for 20 minutes. Puree and strain through a fine strainer. Reserve. (This can be made in advance and reheated quickly.)

TO MAKE THE GROUPER
Brush the grouper fillets with butter and season with salt and pepper. Mix shallot, chiles, chives and herbs together and dot approximately 2 tablespoons of the herb mixture on top of each fillet. Place 1 to 2 inches of water in the bottom of a steamer pot and place fillets in the steaming bowl. Steam grouper about 6 minutes, until cooked through.

TO MAKE THE VEGETABLES
Sauté lotus root and yu choy stems in canola oil for 1 minute. Season with salt and pepper.

Add butter, shallot, gingerroot and chiles and sweat by placing a lid on the pan. Cook over low heat until tender, just about 1 minute.

Stir in yu choy leaves, mango and coconut.

Add in a little of the pan juices from the steamed fish. Cook 1 minute longer.

Add cilantro and chives.

TO SERVE
Place vegetables in middle of plate; place fish atop vegetables. Serve the sauce on the side and garnish with long pieces of chive. ◼

Steamed Grouper with Lotus Root, Yu Choy and Wood-Ear Black Bean Sauce

The recipes

"I'm always working on something... I enjoy experimenting with things I haven't used before: abalone, whelks, sea robin or even a type of seaweed I found on a recent trip to Iceland."

Sautéed Nantucket Bay Scallops with Citrus Salad and Mamey

SERVES 4 (AS AN APPETIZER)

In this spectacular salad, golden-brown bay scallops celebrate a perfect marriage with herb-studded citrus segments. The surprise in the relationship is sliced chiles and a puree of mamey, an exotic fruit with a berrylike taste. If mamey is not to be found, Chef Pollinger suggests substituting avocado.

One of each of the following fresh citrus fruits: orange, grapefruit, mandarin orange, plus reserved zest from all
Salt and fresh ground pepper to taste
1 tablespoon minced fresh gingerroot
1 tablespoon sliced red and green finger chiles
1/2 cup extra-virgin olive oil
1 mamey (or substitute 1 avocado)
1 teaspoon fresh lime juice
1/2 pound Nantucket Bay scallops
2 tablespoons canola oil
2 tablespoons butter
8 leaves Thai basil, chiffonade
8 leaves mint, chiffonade
8 leaves cilantro, chiffonade
1/4 cup toasted cashews
1/2 cup baby greens

Peel fruits and divide into segments, removing all pith and membranes. Cut the citrus segments into small pieces. Season with salt and pepper. Sprinkle zest, gingerroot and chiles around all the citrus pieces.

Drizzle with olive oil. Set aside.

Scoop out enough flesh from the mamey to make 1 cup. Puree in a blender with 1 teaspoon lime juice until smooth. Set aside.

Season scallops with salt and pepper. In a skillet over medium heat, sauté the scallops in the canola oil and butter. Swirl around so butter browns and scallops cook to an even golden brown, but remain medium-rare inside.

TO SERVE

Place a few dollops of mamey puree on the side of each plate. Evenly distribute the citrus salad and sprinkle with the basil, mint and cilantro chiffonade. Toss on toasted cashews. Garnish with a few sprigs of spicy baby greens. Distribute the scallops evenly onto the salads. ▦

▦ **NOTE** To toast cashews: Preheat oven to 350°F. Place cashews on ungreased baking sheet and toast until they turn golden brown, about 5–10 minutes. Shake baking sheet occasionally to prevent sticking or burning.

Pan-Roasted Lobster with Chestnut Polenta, Brussels Sprouts and Spiced Maple Sauce

SERVES 4

Chef Pollinger's adventurous approach to seafood is clearly seen in this lobster entrée, partnered with polenta and Brussels sprouts.

FOR THE LOBSTER
4 (1¼-pound) lobsters
2 tablespoons extra-virgin olive oil
Salt and pepper to taste

FOR THE SAUCE
1 tablespoon canola oil
1 tablespoon minced shallot
½ clove garlic, minced
1 teaspoon spice mix (recipe below), mixed with water to form a medium-thick paste
2 tablespoons maple syrup
1 cup lobster stock reduction, from 1 quart stock
1 tablespoon lime juice reduction (reduce 1 cup juice to 4 tablespoons; reserve remainder)
Salt to taste

SPICE MIX
1 teaspoon Szechuan peppercorns
2 pieces star anise
¼ teaspoon fenugreek seed
1 teaspoon pepper
1 teaspoon coriander
¼ teaspoon turmeric
Grind ingredients finely and mix together.

FOR THE VEGETABLES
1 tablespoon canola oil
2 cups Brussels sprouts, blanched for one minute, shocked, drained and cut into wedges
1 cup white honshimeji mushrooms
1 teaspoon butter
1 teaspoon minced shallot
1 teaspoon minced gingerroot
1 teaspoon minced red or green chile
1 tablespoon cilantro, chiffonade
1 tablespoon minced chives

FOR THE CHESTNUT POLENTA
¼ pound chestnut flour
1½ cups cold milk
Salt and pepper to taste

TO MAKE THE LOBSTER
Preheat oven to "Warming" setting or 200°F.

Fill a large stockpot with salted water. Bring to a rolling boil. Boil lobsters for 5 minutes. Remove and chill in ice water.

Remove claw and tail meat from shell, making sure to keep pieces intact for presentation. Remove vein from back of lobster tail by pulling out with a toothpick. Discard shells and body or reserve for making stock.

Just before serving, drizzle lobster meat with the olive oil, season with salt and pepper and place in an ovenproof glass dish. Cover with aluminum foil and place in oven until warmed through, about 7 or 8 minutes.

TO MAKE THE SAUCE
Sweat shallot and garlic in canola oil over low heat in a covered skillet. Add spice paste and cook until aromatic. Add maple syrup and lobster-stock reduction. Reduce until mixture is syrupy enough to coat the back of a spoon. Add lime-juice reduction. Season with salt. Adjust as needed with more maple syrup or lime reduction.

TO MAKE THE VEGETABLES
Sauté the Brussels sprouts and mushrooms in canola oil over medium heat for 1 or 2 minutes. Add butter and sweat the shallot, gingerroot and chile by lowering the heat and covering the pan. Cook until tender. Stir in cilantro and chives at the very end.

TO MAKE THE CHESTNUT POLENTA
Whisk chestnut flour together with half the cold milk in a bowl until smooth. Heat the remaining milk in a pot. Whisk in flour-milk mixture. Season with salt and pepper. Cook a few minutes, adjusting as needed with milk to achieve a creamy consistency.

TO SERVE
Place polenta in the center of plate, top with vegetables on the left. Stand the lobster tail up on the right side and place claws over vegetables. Drizzle sauce around the edges of the plate. ■

Philippe Massoud
CHEF AND OWNER, ILILI

A bite of Beirut

Manhattan is known as a place where you can find any and all kinds of food, and thanks to Philippe Massoud, this is truer than ever. A year and a half ago he opened ilili, a dramatic Fifth Avenue venue offering authentic Lebanese dishes. "Even though Middle Eastern restaurants existed, I couldn't find the traditional Lebanese I grew up with in Beirut," says Massoud. "My dream was to bring the food of my homeland here, but offer it in a chic, modern setting." Massoud goes on to explain that Lebanese food differs from that of other Middle Eastern countries because the land is blessed with water.

"Our dishes are lighter, with more vegetables, herbs and citrus. Our tabbouleh, for instance, is greener; it contains less bulgur, more parsley and mint," he says. "We also use lots of sumac in our recipes, along with the typical cinnamon, allspice, coriander and black pepper." He points out, too, that Lebanese cuisine reflects a wealth of European influences.

And he should know. Massoud literally grew up in the kitchen of his family's hotel, where they moved when their home was destroyed by war. "Our block was there one minute, gone the next," he recalls. "But we were lucky and had a place to go. I especially loved hanging out in the kitchen and started cooking around the age of 8. Back then it was sweets, especially chocolate cake, but I did move on to other things," he laughs. He fondly reminisces about "Sunday lunches at Grandma's" where his favorite meal was *kibbe bi laban*—beef or lamb meatballs with a knob of butter in the middle, baked and served with a yogurt/stock mixture. While this particular version of kibbe is not on the ilili menu, other traditional specialties like fried red mullet with lemon and tahini, succulent lamb sausage (called *mekanek*) and a variety of grilled kebabs offer a taste of well-loved Lebanese classics. But Massoud also delivers some new food for thought. "Since I spent a lot of time in southern Spain, an area that shares some flavors with the food of Lebanon, I've introduced some Mediterranean-influenced dishes like black iron shrimp with cilantro, jalapeño and garlic."

> *ILILI*
> *236 Fifth Avenue*
> *New York, NY 10001*
> *212-683-2929*
> *www.ililinyc.com*

On the side...

What do you consider the most overrated ingredient?
Butter. Olive oil has much more to offer.

The most underrated ingredient?
Sumac.

What is your favorite comfort food?
Roast chicken with garlic whip (garlic mayonnaise).

What kitchen gadget is your must-have tool?
A very sharp knife. It makes all the difference in the world.

If you were not a chef, what would you be?
A food-industry techie. We need better software to keep track of recipes, inventories, and so on. Most of the people doing this stuff now are not part of the industry, and therefore the material falls short.

What was the last thing you ate?
Amberjack with wasabi, the red mullet and lamb chops—all at my restaurant.

Originally, the menu centered on small plates that guests could mix and share. But some items proved so popular, they're now offered in larger versions. "Like any restaurant, we went through a learning experience and we're still evolving. We rotate dishes based on availability and introduce new ones every so often. Sometimes I get inspired by a new ingredient or a conversation with my sous chef. But in the end it's all about creating food that celebrates life." ■

The recipes

Brussels Sprouts with Fig Sauce

SERVES 4

Transform this oft-denigrated vegetable by first frying it, then tossing in a warm fig sauce, enlivened with roasted walnuts and grapes.

½ cup dried figs, chopped
½ cup fig jam
¾ cup sherry vinegar, divided
½ cup yogurt
1 teaspoon fresh mint, chiffonade
½ cup walnuts
4 cups fresh Brussels sprouts, cut in half
Cooking oil (for frying)
½ cup seedless red and white grapes, cut in half
Salt and pepper to taste

Preheat oven to 400°F. In a small saucepan over medium-high heat, cook the dried figs, fig jam and ½ cup of the sherry vinegar until thick and syrupy. Put in a blender and blend until smooth. Pass through a strainer to remove any seeds.

Mix the yogurt and mint and reserve. Roast walnuts in oven until brown (about 5 minutes, but watch carefully); reserve. Deep-fry the sprouts in cooking oil until golden brown.

TO SERVE

Place sprouts in a bowl, toss with the fig sauce and add walnuts, grapes and remaining sherry vinegar. Drizzle the minted yogurt over the top. Salt and pepper to taste. ▓

Black Cod with Pomegranate Molasses and Zaatar

SERVES 4

Chef Massoud employs pomegranate molasses and zaatar for this sweet-tart spin on cod.

4 (4-ounce) black cod fillets
2 tablespoons pomegranate molasses, plus more for garnish
1 cup white wine
1 fennel bulb, cut into ¼-inch slices
2 tablespoons extra-virgin olive oil, plus more for sautéing fish
Salt and pepper to taste
1½ teaspoons Lebanese green zaatar (see note)
1 cup frisée salad with lemon vinaigrette

Marinate the fish with the pomegranate molasses and wine for at least 8 hours, covered, in the refrigerator.

Brush the fennel with olive oil and bake in oven on low heat (275°F) for approximately 1½ hours. Set aside.

Salt and pepper fish to taste, coat with green zaatar on both sides; sauté in pan with a little olive oil until cooked through. Warm the cooked fennel.

TO SERVE

Drizzle pomegranate molasses onto plates, then place the fennel on top, followed by a fish fillet. Serve alongside a small helping of frisée with a simple lemon vinaigrette.

▓ **NOTE** Zaatar is a spice mixture, a staple in Middle Eastern cooking, usually made of thyme, sumac and sesame seeds. It's available at specialty and Middle Eastern food stores.

Lahmajeen

SERVES 4–6

This traditional Lebanese dish is usually made with pita dough, but Chef Massoud prefers thin-crust pizza for the base.

¼ cup ground lamb (80/20)
¼ cup chopped tomatoes
¼ cup chopped onions
1 jalapeño pepper, chopped
¼ teaspoon allspice
¼ teaspoon cinnamon
⅛–¼ teaspoon cayenne pepper (optional)
Salt and pepper to taste
1 round thin-crust pizza dough
Squeeze of fresh lemon juice

Preheat oven to 450°F.

Combine the lamb, tomatoes, onions, jalapeño and spices until thoroughly mixed. Season to taste. Spread the meat mixture evenly over the pizza dough, leaving about ¼ inch uncovered all around the edge. Bake for 8–10 minutes or until crispy. (This is enough time for the lamb to be thoroughly cooked.)

TO SERVE

Squeeze a little fresh lemon juice on top. Serve with a side of yogurt infused with fresh mint. ▓

Sam Hazen
EXECUTIVE CHEF, TAO NEW YORK

The man behind the Buddha

One of the most memorable things about Tao is the dramatic 16-foot Buddha that sits behind a reflecting pool on the ground floor of the restaurant. But it isn't Buddha who's responsible for the phenomenal success of this pan-Asian venue; it's Chef Sam Hazen. "People are always surprised that an Asian chef isn't running the kitchen," says Hazen. "I tell them that cooking is a universal thing, and if you know the techniques and you know the ingredients, you can manage any kind of cuisine."

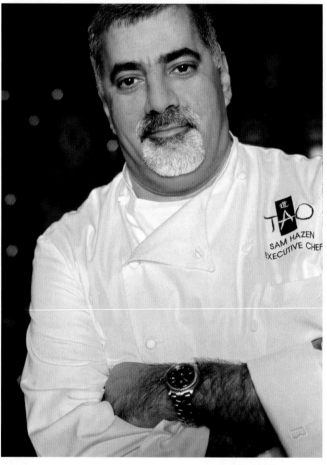

The fact that Tao is one of the highest-grossing restaurants in the city (Tao Las Vegas, where Hazen also heads up the kitchen, is the highest in the country) proves his point. The inventive menu melds Thai, Chinese and Japanese cuisine with a distinct French flair. "I've come up with dishes that use Asian ingredients—and there are always lots of those—but prepare them with the discipline I learned during my years working in French restaurants, notably La Côte Basque in New York," explains Hazen. "That means I plot everything out, down to exact number of scallion curls. It's different from the way many chefs in the Far East build the flavors in the ladle with a slightly different result every time, but it guarantees consistency. And when you're responsible for turning out 7,000 meals a week, you need to be spot-on every time."

Such a precise approach also applies to Tao's menu. It's sensual and theatrical, but it's calculated so that one dish complements another and there's something for everyone. "I've included a couple of wow dishes like the Peking duck and the wasabi-crusted filet mignon, but they don't overpower the other choices," Hazen says. The same approach should be applied to home menus, he continues. Everything needs to work together, and no one dish should outshine the others.

When it comes to developing new dishes, Hazen imagines himself "as a bank robber planning a heist, figuring out what could go wrong before coming up with the final plan." In recipe terms, that means envisioning a dish, then working backwards, taking it apart to discover any possible glitch. He'll tweak it until he gets what he wants, maybe substituting one ingredient for another or trying a different cooking technique—sautéing, perhaps, instead of wok-frying. "I need to do what it takes to get the taste right, the look

TAO NEW YORK
42 East 58th Street
New York, NY, 10022
212-888-2288
www.taorestaurant.com

On the side...

What do you consider the most overrated ingredient?
Kobe beef.

The most underrated ingredient?
Yuzu, in all its forms—whole, freeze-dried, juiced.

What kitchen gadget is your must-have tool?
A Korin chef's knife.

What is your favorite comfort food?
Ribeye steak with a baked potato topped with butter and sour cream.

If you were not a chef, what would you be?
A basketball player. I'm a great sports fan.

What was the last thing you ate?
A bowl of cut-up fresh fruit: pineapple, blackberries, mango and strawberries.

right and to make the prep go smoothly." Not surprisingly, Hazen's advice to the home cook is "Get organized. You need to have everything out of the fridge and the cupboard, all the utensils set to go. And, just as important, you need to be mentally ready—familiar with the recipe and the necessary techniques. It's my elaboration on what the French call *mise en place*—having all the ingredients necessary for a dish prepared and ready to combine—and it's absolutely essential to good cooking."

Buddha, we think, would agree. ■

The recipes

Crab Cakes with Thai Chile-Mango Sauce

SERVES 4

At Tao, you're surrounded by artifacts from China, Japan and Thailand, along with a towering Buddha that reigns over the restaurant. What a space to nibble on these sublime crab cakes that Chef Hazen presents with a triple dose of mango: in the cakes, in the sauce and in a powerful chutney.

FOR THE MANGO SAUCE

1 cup Thai chile sauce
1/2 cup mango puree
Combine and mix well.

FOR THE CHUTNEY

1/4 cup diced mango
3/4 teaspoon chopped bird chiles
1/2 cup Thai chile sauce
Mix together ingredients gently.

FOR THE CRAB CAKES

1 1/2 pounds crabmeat, jumbo lump, picked clean
1/2 cup mango, diced
1 1/2 tablespoons kaffir lime leaf, chiffonade
1 1/2 tablespoons chopped cilantro
1 1/2 tablespoons Thai chile sauce
6 tablespoons mayonnaise
2 tablespoons diced shallots, sautéed
Salt and pepper to taste
Very fine panko for dredging
Grapeseed or canola oil for frying

To prepare the crab cakes, mix first nine ingredients together and shape in 4 ring molds. Dredge in panko. Pan-fry at medium heat in a little canola or grapeseed oil until golden. Remove to paper towels to drain.

TO SERVE

Pour a pool of sauce on each of 4 plates.
Place a crab cake on each plate and garnish with Asian greens or maché if desired. ■

Tataki Beef with Asparagus and Shitake

SERVES 1–2

Rubbing the steak with a compelling combination of spices gives it a mellow smokiness that Chef Hazen's easy but exotic sauce sets off to a "T."

1 (12 ounce) boneless sirloin steak
Spice rub made by mixing together:
4 tablespoons each cumin, chile powder, cayenne pepper, paprika and 2 tablespoons each ground black pepper and kosher salt
2 tablespoons sliced garlic
2 tablespoons sliced shallot
1 tablespoon vegetable or olive oil
3 stalks asparagus, woody parts removed
3 shitake mushrooms, sliced
Salt and pepper to taste
4 tablespoons kabayaki sauce (see note)
2 tablespoons yuzu juice
1 tablespoon butter
Scallion for garnish, julienned

Season the beef well with the spices, rubbing into the meat. Place meat in a smoking-hot skillet (cast iron works well) and brown slightly on all sides. Keep warm while making sauce.

In a nonstick skillet over medium heat, sauté garlic and shallot in the oil. Add asparagus and mushrooms and sweat, covered, over low heat until tender. Season with salt and pepper. Add kabayaki and yuzu juice and stir in butter.

TO SERVE

Sear steak quickly and slice on the bias; top with sauce and garnish with julienned scallion. ■

■ **NOTE** Kabayaki is a Japanese sauce. If you cannot find it, combine 1/2 cup soy sauce, 1/2 cup mirin and 1/2 cup sugar. Stir well. Cook over low heat and simmer for a couple of minutes. Remove from heat and cool. This mixture can be refrigerated.

Crab Cakes with Thai Chile-Mango Sauce

The recipes

"I've come up with dishes that use Asian ingredients…
but I prepare them with the discipline I learned
during my years working in French restaurants."

Lobster Wonton in Ginger Shitake Broth

SERVES 10 AS AN APPETIZER

This lovely appetizer is an Asian-style delight:
shrimp and lobster-filled wontons swimming in a
gingery shitake broth. And it's much easier to
make than you might expect—more
a matter of assembly than cooking.

FOR WONTONS
1 pound shrimp, cooked
1 pound lobster meat, cooked
½ head of napa cabbage
2 tablespoons cornstarch
1 tablespoon lobster glacé
1 teaspoon salt
1 tablespoon sesame oil, plus more for
oiling wontons
50 wonton wrappers

FOR BROTH
1 pint miso broth
1 pint chicken stock
1 pint veal jus
1 pint teriyaki sauce
1 knob fresh gingerroot, peeled, chopped and crushed
6 cloves garlic
8–10 shiitake stems, julienned
Salt and pepper to taste
¼ bunch fresh thyme (about 6–8 sprigs)
1 tablespoon butter
Chopped chives, chopped scallions and
julienned gingerroot for garnish

TO MAKE WONTONS
In a food processor, puree the shrimp.

Chop up lobster meat into small pieces.

Finely dice the cabbage, blanch, and dry well.

Place shrimp, lobster and cabbage in a bowl. Fold in
cornstarch, lobster glacé, salt and 1 tablespoon sesame oil.

Place 1½ to 2 teaspoons of the filling onto center of each
wonton wrapper. Fold up sides of wonton into a triangle
shape, pressing edges tightly together with fingers to close.
(If wonton edges are not sticking together, simply dab
finger in water and crimp together again.)

In large pot of boiling water, blanch wontons for
6 to 7 minutes.

Drain, cool and lightly oil with more sesame oil. Set aside.

TO MAKE BROTH
As wontons are blanching, make broth. Place miso, chicken
stock, veal jus, teriyaki sauce, crushed gingerroot, garlic,
shitake stems, and salt and pepper in a large saucepan.

Bring to a boil. Reduce heat to simmer and cook 10–15
minutes, adding the thyme for the last 5 minutes.
Strain and cool.

TO FINISH AND SERVE
Place broth in a large pot over medium-high heat;
add wontons. Reduce broth by half. Finish by stirring in
1 tablespoon butter. Season with salt and pepper.

Place 5 wontons in 10 individual bowls with broth.

Garnish with chopped chives and scallions, and
julienned gingerroot. ▪

Index

PHOTOGRAPHY CREDITS

COVER PHOTO: Ben Fink/FoodPix

FOOD PHOTOGRAPHY: Mark Thomas, Photographer; Michael Pederson, Food Stylist; Tracy Keshani, Assistant Food Stylist; Nancy Micklin, Prop Stylist

P. 9, 19, 28, 31, 50, 53, 73, 87, 105, 123, 127, 135, 171, 176, 183, 205, 215 by Jared Flood

P. 4 Image Source
P. 7 Mark Thomas
P. 10 Bill Bettencourt
P. 15 Michael Smith
P. 20, 25 Courtesy of Town at the Chambers Hotel
P. 27 Alan Batt of Battman Studios
P. 32 Courtesy of Union Square Cafe
P. 38 Courtesy of Annisa
P. 44, 170 Paul Johnson Photography
P. 49 Courtesy of Patrick Nuti
P. 54 Graham Lott
P. 60 Jocelyn Fillet
P. 66 Daniel Krieger
P. 71 Gregory Goode and courtesy of The Bowery Hotel
P.78 Courtesy of John Schaefer

P. 83 Courtesy of Neil Ferguson
P. 88 Courtesy of Market Table
P. 92 Courtesy of The Little Owl
P. 97 Quentin Bacon
P. 102 Courtesy of Melissa O'Donnell
P. 110, 115, 134, 136, 138 Courtesy of Picholine
P. 116 Courtesy of Landmarc
P. 120 Courtesy of Fleur de Sel
P. 124 Courtesy of Café des Artistes
P. 129 Jim Salzano
P.142 Christopher Vilano of Vilano Photography
P. 147 Alan Batt of Battman Studio

P. 152 Courtesy of Beacon Restaurant
P. 157 Francis Janisch
P. 164, 169 Courtesy of Casa Mono
P. 175 Paul Amato for LVARepresents.com
P. 180 Zandy Mangold
P. 185 Daphne Borowski Photography
P. 192 Courtesy of Crema Restaurante
P. 197 Ryu Kodama
P. 202 Courtesy of NYCrestaurants.com
P. 206 Courtesy of Paul Johnson Photography
P. 212 Courtesy of Adla Massoud
P. 216 David Lazarus

METRIC CONVERSION TABLE
1 teaspoon = 5 milliliters
1 tablespoon = 15 milliliters
1 ounce = 30 milliliters
1 cup = 240 milliliters
2 cups (1 pint) = 470 milliliters
4 cups (1 quart) = .95 liter
4 quarts (1 gallon) = 3.8 liters

WEIGHT CONVERSIONS
1 ounce = 28 grams
1 pound = 454 grams
1 gram = .035 ounce
100 grams = 3.5 ounces
1 kilogram = 2.20 pounds
1 kilogram = 35 ounces

EQUIVALENT MEASUREMENTS
3 teaspoons = 1 tablespoon
16 tablespoons = 1 cup (8 ounces)
2 cups = 1 pint (16 ounces)
4 cups (2 pints) = 1 quart (32 ounces)
8 cups (4 pints) = ½ gallon (64 ounces)
4 quarts = 1 gallon (128 ounces)